CULTURE
RE-BOOT

CULTURE
RE-BOOT

Reinvigorating School Culture
to Improve Student Outcomes

Leslie S. Kaplan
William A. Owings

CORWIN
A SAGE Company

CORWIN
A SAGE Company

FOR INFORMATION:

Corwin
A SAGE Company
2455 Teller Road
Thousand Oaks, California 91320
(800) 233-9936
www.corwin.com

SAGE Publications Ltd.
1 Oliver's Yard
55 City Road
London EC1Y 1SP
United Kingdom

SAGE Publications India Pvt. Ltd.
B 1/I 1 Mohan Cooperative Industrial Area
Mathura Road, New Delhi 110 044
India

SAGE Publications Asia-Pacific Pte. Ltd.
3 Church Street
#10-04 Samsung Hub
Singapore 049483

Printed in the United States of America

A catalog record of this book is available from the Library of Congress.

ISBN 9781452217321

Acquisitions Editor: Dan Alpert
Associate Editor: Megan Bedell
Editorial Assistant: Heidi Arndt
Production Editor: Amy Schroller
Copy Editor: Pam Schroeder
Typesetter: C&M Digitals (P) Ltd.
Proofreader: Theresa Kay
Indexer: Maria Sosnowski
Cover Designer: Anupama Krishnan
Permissions Editor: Karen Ehrmann

This book is printed on acid-free paper.

Certified Chain of Custody
SUSTAINABLE Promoting Sustainable Forestry
FORESTRY
INITIATIVE www.sfiprogram.org
SFI-01268
SFI label applies to text stock

13 14 15 16 17 10 9 8 7 6 5 4 3 2 1

Contents

Additional materials and resources related to *Culture Re-Boot* can be found at http://www.corwin.com/culturereboot.

Preface

The lack of serious attention to school culture has stymied efforts to improve schools. While the past 40 years of research have prompted a huge shift in what we know about successful teaching and learning and despite decades of school reform to advance all students' achievement, little improvement is evident. Many reform efforts fail because they do not consider school culture or respect its capacity to derail even well-intentioned efforts. Until teachers and principals can recognize and modify those aspects of their school's culture that inhibit positive change, all their good intentions and innovations will be no more than seasonal window dressing.

The good news is that purposeful educators can shape their school's culture. "Culture is organic to its community; if the culture changes, everything changes."[1] School culture is not static. Rather, it is constantly being assembled and shaped through interactions with others and by reflections on life and the world in general.

In order to reinvigorate their school cultures in ways that better support teaching and learning, school leaders must re-boot. Similar to restarting a computer or other electronic device because the applications are not responding, school leaders must consciously design ways to assess current practices and start over, that is, *re-boot,* with new ideas and approaches that promise to deliver better results.

WHAT IS SCHOOL CULTURE RE-BOOT?

Typically implicit and operating outside conscious awareness, school culture is the general feel people get when they walk through a school's halls. It is the unwritten rules that guide how people think, feel, and act in the organization. Culture influences every aspect of schools, including staff

---

[1]Donahoe, T. (1993). Finding the way: Structure, time, and culture in school improvement. *Phi Delta Kappan, 75*(4), 298–305 (p. 302).

wardrobe, what staff discuss in the teachers' lounge, how teachers decorate their classrooms, their emphasis on certain curricular topics, their willingness to change, and their confidence in their collective abilities to achieve their goals. School culture determines how principals and teachers relate to each other and how educators relate to students and their parents. Their interactions shape and reinforce the culture in a self-perpetuating cycle. By influencing attitudes and behaviors, school culture influences how well teachers teach and how much students learn. Because all school cultures are highly resistant to change, they may present either barriers or bridges to long-lasting school improvement.

Why *culture re-boot*? To *re-boot* is to restart a computer or other electronic device because the applications are not responding. *Re-boot* has the connotation of starting over.

While school cultures are not computers, they do have unwritten norms and ways of behaving that resemble computer software. Sophisticated software makes the computer operate as we expect, although we do not see the actual lines of code that direct its behavior.

Applied to media dealing with serial fiction, such as comic book or TV series, *re-boot* means to step aside from the previous series and start anew with fresh ideas. In film, *re-boot* means to revamp and reinvigorate an existing franchise.

Just as *re-boot* suggests a restart or reset to improve performance outcomes, to *re-boot schools* means rethinking, redesigning, and enacting new practices in leadership, teaching, ethics, and relationships. It means readjusting the student learning environment, working with parents and community in ways that reshape the school culture, and restarting a cycle of positive dynamics that result in improved student outcomes.

Re-boot—with the hyphen—is emphatic. The more uncommonly spelled *re-boot* graphically stresses the deliberate growing together that comes not only from linking the prefix *re-* to the noun *boot* but also from refocusing a school's leadership and staff on challenging and replacing their familiar cultural assumptions and ways of doing business with those more conducive to student achievement and teacher satisfaction.

Culture Re-Boot: Reinvigorating School Culture to Improve Student Outcomes is written to help principals and teachers understand their school's culture and enact specific strategies to shape it in ways that promote greater teacher efficacy and student learning. Using a practitioner-friendly and constructivist approach, this book presents best practices in school improvement supported by professional literature while focusing readers on generating personal meaning, shared reflection, and deliberate applications of content to their own work settings. Meant to be read, discussed, and applied individually or in small groups, *Culture Re-Boot* builds what Michael Fullan and Andy Hargreaves call "the professional capital"[2]—human, social, and decisional—to make meaningful and sustainable school improvements.

The authors and intended readers share many common goals that this book can promote:

- A user-friendly resource that educators will find readable, interesting, practical, relevant, and scholarly
- A way to work smarter, not harder
- Insight into how school culture impacts school norms, expectations, and behaviors
- Helping school leaders drive cultural change
- Knowing how schools can learn and the varied ways school leaders and teachers can shape school culture to enhance student learning and teacher satisfaction
- Developing professional capacity for shared influence and teachers' instructional and leadership growth
- Ways to establish a student-centered learning culture throughout the school and in every classroom
- Strategies for promoting strong parent–community ties to improve teaching and learning
- A practitioner's orientation from authors with 50 years of combined, successful K–12 school improvement leadership
- Best practices for school improvement supported by professional literature
- Ongoing opportunities for readers to make the content relevant and personally meaningful as they generate shared beliefs with colleagues to improve teaching and learning in their schools
- Many occasions to apply theory to practice, generating deeper understanding, and developing plans for shaping school culture for sustainable school improvement

FEATURES OF *CULTURE RE-BOOT: REINVIGORATING SCHOOL CULTURE TO IMPROVE STUDENT OUTCOMES*

This book offers special features to help principals and teachers learn and apply the content of each chapter.

- *Anchored in reality.* Each chapter's content and activities are written in keep-it-real language, a practical tone, and a pragmatic grounding of theory, leading to doable practice, by two former K–12 school improvement leaders.

---

[2]Fullan, M., & Hargreaves, A. (2012). *Professional capital: Transforming teaching in every school.* New York: Teachers College Press.

- *Focused, readable, practitioner-oriented chapters.* The content emphasizes key aspects of school culture that impact leading, teaching, and learning and incorporates the best scholarship on these topics into clear and useful tools for school leaders.

- *Re-boot activities.* Located immediately following major concepts in each chapter, these reflective and practical exercises help you make relevant connections between the content and your own school, build personal meaning from the ideas just discussed, strengthen collegiality, and begin applying re-boot ideas to your own setting.

- *Questions and surveys.* Use these to identify and assess school culture and plan for improvement.

- *A road map and planning calendar.* The final chapter includes a detailed road map of how to pull all the chapters together to implement culture re-boot into your school with a planning calendar for Years 1 through 5.

- *Optional activities.* The book includes suggestions for additional activities to improve school culture by working with teachers, students, and parents and suggests possible no-cost, highly valid, and reliable resources to use for conducting teacher surveys.

WORKING WITHIN A SCHOOL DISTRICT

Although we focus on re-booting the individual school, we recognize that schools are not orphans. Rather, they are part of a system. Schools are organized into school districts headed by superintendents and school boards. Typically, principals need their superintendent's awareness and prior approval before initiating any substantial changes in their schools. And, successful re-boot leads to substantial changes.

Superintendents who are aware that the school's improvement process will include a re-boot and who buy into this approach can offer the moral, material, and political support essential to helping the re-boot succeed. Onboard superintendents may want to view the re-booting school as a pilot site that offers local leadership and a model for innovative school improvement. Or, they may want to invite all schools at that level (elementary, middle, or high) to participate voluntarily in a common *Culture Re-Boot* training linked with individual school implementation and professional development. In this way, each principal and his or her leadership team would learn and experience the re-boot process together along with their district peers, but they would conduct all the re-boot activities as a school team and lead the professional development activities within their individual schools.

In a winning scenario, the superintendent actively supports the culture re-boot process and the changes it brings, and school leaders construct their own support networks among district peer re-boot leaders who can understand their work and help them resolve issues that may arise during re-boot implementation. The result is positive, systemic, and sustainable change that leads to improved student outcomes.

Principals and school leaders who wish to re-boot their schools know best which approach will work in their particular settings. We encourage them to think through the organizational and system implications of re-boot as they begin planning.

A WORD ABOUT FACILITATING
RE-BOOT ACTIVITIES

Rather than use case studies, vignettes, or stories to demonstrate our points, we make frequent use of re-boot activities to apply the learning to your own school and students. In this way, we help teachers and principals generate personal meaning, relevance, and critical conversations by investing the concepts into their own work settings. "We, here, and now" creates much more powerful learning than does "Them, there, and then."

Because re-boot activities address educators' own beliefs, assumptions, and practices, they invite cognitive and emotional responses. These may generate strong affect among the leadership team members. Finding personal meaning often prompts an emotional connection; this is a good thing. Such powerful activities, however, require a greater expertise in group facilitation—skill and comfort working with colleagues' thoughts and feelings—than most principals have trained for.

To this end, it might be advisable to invite the school district's staff development expert, the school district's director of counseling and guidance, or the school counselor to lead—or colead—the school's re-boot leadership activities. A skilled facilitator who can help members accurately reflect and express their thoughts and feelings and keep the group working constructively brings several benefits. First, using the principal as a team member rather than as its leader in re-boot activities may reduce teachers' fears about speaking their minds. Likewise, a skilled facilitator engages teachers' thoughts and feelings more directly in effective clarification, problem identification, and problem solving rather than allow partially formed ideas and unclear feelings to remain volatile, unanchored, and open to possibly undermining group progress and collegiality.

CHAPTER ORGANIZATION

The book is organized into the following parts. Each chapter contains a discussion of the chapter's topic and several re-boot activities that principals can use with their leadership teams, teachers, students, and parents to better understand—and begin re-booting—their own school settings.

Chapter 1: School Culture and Change as Learning defines *school culture* and *school culture re-boot* and describes how they affect leading, teaching, and learning. We explain how school culture re-boot is able to do what 40 years of externally imposed school reforms could not: allow school leaders to deliberately shape school culture for improved student outcomes. We identify ways that school cultures shape organizations, how school cultures develop, the levels of school culture, the components of positive school cultures, change as organizational learning, and the characteristics of organizations that can learn. The chapter also discusses three mental models (the three-step change model, single- and double-loop learning, and multiple frames model) that boost organizational learning. Re-boot activities help school leaders develop their school's cultural profile and assess themselves as a learning organization, so they can determine what is working well and what needs to be rethought and re-booted. We also cite research supporting the impacts of school culture on improved teaching, learning, and student outcomes.

Chapter 2: School Leadership as Culture Building discusses the principal's role in shaping school culture. Main topics include leadership as culture building; how principals can transform their schools; understanding the dynamics, resources, and obstacles for culture re-boot; and how principals can prepare cognitively and emotionally for the re-boot process. We highlight the overlaps between leadership and management, evidence on the principal's role in increasing student achievement, and principal's five key leadership responsibilities that lead to improved student learning. And, we discuss how a principal can establish a schoolwide vision for the success of all students, create a safe environment for learning, and build a school leadership team for the re-boot process in how-to-do-it detail. The chapter also depicts the school culture re-boot concept and process graphically and verbally. Re-boot activities include developing symbols, images, and key words that can support a school vision and creating a school touchstone that links the school's core values to its daily practices and goals.

Chapter 3: School Culture, Ethical Behavior, and Relational Trust describes education as an ethical endeavor that depends on relationships. Topics include the importance of relational trust, cooperation, and responsibility in a positive school culture and supporting research linking relational trust and school performance. Principals and teacher leaders consider the ways and extent to which their schools are fulfilling their moral dimensions, consider examples of behaviors that build—or discourage—relational trust, and assess their schools' cultures on trust-promoting behaviors. Team members also generate feedback for each other on how well each individual is communicating the varied aspects of trust and reflect on incidents of insensitivity and broken trust in their schools and how they were repaired.

Chapter 4: Developing Professional Capacity for Shared Influence looks at capacity building for teaching effectiveness and teacher leadership. The chapter discusses instructional capacity and the contemporary factors that increase expectations for effective teaching (such as 21st-century skills, the Common Core State Standards, and the New Teacher Assessment and Support Consortium Standards) and identifies and describes the school culture factors that affect the development of professional capacity. We also note professional learning communities' (PLCs) features and practices—and the school culture elements that support them. Re-boot activities include assessing the school's capacity for 21st-century teaching, identifying areas for instructional improvement, and identifying potential teacher leaders.

Chapter 5: Establishing a Student-Centered Learning Culture describes a student-centered learning environment and the factors that create and sustain it. The chapter discusses how the following topics—holding high teacher expectations for each student's learning, creating a safe and orderly learning environment, providing academic press and academic and social supports, fostering caring and respectful relationships, and providing supportive peer norms—can promote student attendance, learning, achievement, and positive behaviors. We also address ways to build student resilience. Re-boot activities ask teachers and principals to describe what each of these factors looks like if practiced effectively in a school and has them assess the extent to which their school currently supports each factor.

Chapter 6: Promoting and Creating Strong Parent–Community Ties discusses the challenges and benefits of educators working effectively with parents and communities to promote student learning. Chapter topics include the importance of mutual respect and engagement among schools, families, and communities if students are to learn and achieve well; the concept of *cultural competence* and how it can improve teachers' relations with diverse students and parents; the varied roles available for parents to engage with schools; strategies for increasing and strengthening parent–community involvement; the importance of resilience and social capital on student learning; and the research on family involvement and student achievement. Re-boot activities ask team members to identify and discuss varied barriers to school and family involvement and to assess their school—and themselves—on the degree to which they are overcoming these obstacles.

Chapter 7: Developing a Plan for Action brings all the chapters together with a realistic road map of what school leaders should consider as they plan for school culture re-boot and presents a 5-year, month-by-month timetable for shaping school culture. It ends with conclusions about educators shaping school culture.

Acknowledgments

Thank you, Dan Alpert, our acquisitions editor across educational topics and publishers, for your enthusiasm, keen vision and insight, and timely guidance in shepherding our books from brainstorming through publication. We deeply value your friendship.

Thank you, Elliott Merenbloom, a school improvement consultant with hundreds of school districts, and our valued mentor, for provoking our thinking about the superintendent's role in school culture re-boot.

Finally, working with the Corwin team has been a pleasure. We deeply appreciate Heidi Arndt, our editorial assistant; Megan Bedell, our associate editor; Pam Schroeder, our copy editor; and Amy Schroller, our production editor, who always gave thoughtful attention to our manuscript and promptly responded to all our questions. And a special shout-out to Anupama Krishnan, who integrated our ideas into a compelling and attractive cover.

Publisher's Acknowledgments

Corwin gratefully acknowledges the contributions of the following reviewers:

Cynthia Church
Principal
G. Stanley Hall Elementary
   School
Glendale Heights, IL

Margarete Couture
Elementary Principal
South Seneca Central School
   District
Interlaken, NY

Karen Kemp
Senior Coordinator, Professional
   Development Support and
   Evaluation
Polk County School District
Lakeland, FL

Steve Knobl
Principal
Gulf High School
New Port Richey, FL

Brian Matney
Principal
Landstown High School
Virginia Beach, VA

William Richard Hall, Jr.
Principal
R. C. Longan Elementary School
Henrico, VA

Joanne Rooney
Codirector
Midwest Principal's Center
Wheaton, IL

Linda Shifflette
Superintendent
Hampton City Schools
Hampton, VA

About the Authors

With more than 50 years of combined experiences as on-the-ground education practitioners at the school building and central office levels, Leslie S. Kaplan and William A. Owings are widely recognized as a writing team who know first-hand how to apply theory to practice.

Leslie S. Kaplan, EdD, is a retired school administrator in Newport News, Virginia, and is currently a full-time education writer. She has provided middle and high school instructional and school improvement leadership as an assistant principal for instruction as well as central office leadership as a director of program development. Before becoming a school administrator, she worked as a middle and high school counselor, and these insights continue to infuse her leadership behaviors. Her professional interests focus on teacher quality, principal quality, and school finance and their relationship to school improvement and increasing student achievement. She has coauthored several books and monographs with William Owings, including *American Public School Finance* (2nd edition); *Educational Foundations* (2nd edition); *Leadership and Organizational Behavior in Education: Theory into Practice; The Effective Schools Movement: History, Analysis, and Application; Teacher Quality, Teaching Quality, and School Improvement; Best Practices, Best Thinking, and Emerging Issue in School Leadership;* and *Enhancing Teacher and Teaching Quality.* Kaplan's scholarly publications, coauthored with Owings, appear in numerous peer-reviewed professional journals. Kaplan is coeditor of the *Journal for Effective Schools* and also serves on the *National Association of Secondary School Principals (NASSP) Bulletin* editorial board. She is a past president of the Virginia Counselors' Association and the Virginia Association for Supervision and Curriculum Development and presently sits on the board of Voices for Virginia's Children.

William A. Owings, EdD, is currently a professor of educational leadership at Old Dominion University in Norfolk, Virginia. Owings has worked as a public school teacher, an elementary and high school principal, assistant superintendent, and superintendent of schools. His professional interests are in school finance, principal quality, and teacher quality as they relate to school improvement and student achievement. In addition, his scholarly publications coauthored with Leslie Kaplan include articles in the *NASSP Bulletin, Journal of School Leadership, Journal of Education Finance, Journal of Effective Schools, Phi Delta Kappan, Eurasian Journal of Business and Economics,* and the *Teachers College Record.* Owings has served on the state and international board of the Association for Supervision and Curriculum Development (ASCD), is currently the editor of the *Journal for Effective Schools,* and is on the *Journal of Education Finance* editorial advisory board. He is a frequent presenter at state and national conferences and a consultant on educational leadership, school finance, and instructional improvement. Owings and Kaplan share the 2008 Virginia Educational Research Association Charles Edgar Clear Research Award for Consistent and Substantial Contributions to Educational Research and Scholarship.

School Culture and Change as Learning

FOCUS QUESTIONS

- What is school culture, and how does it affect leading, teaching, and learning?
- How can culture re-boot succeed in improving school performance when school reform has not?
- In what visible and implicit ways does a school's culture express itself to teachers, administrators, students, and parents?
- Which aspects of school culture support hard work and high achievement?
- In what ways is change organizational learning?
- What are the characteristics of organizations that can learn?
- Which conceptual models can help educators make sense of, plan for, and facilitate change?

WHY 40 YEARS OF SCHOOL REFORM HAS NOT WORKED (AND WHY CULTURE RE-BOOT WILL)

Anthropologists have an old saying: Fish would be the last creatures to discover water, even though water is the most ever-present and influential aspect of a fish's existence. The same might be said of those working within a school's culture. Just as water surrounds fish, shaping their world view and influencing where they swim, culture surrounds and envelopes principals, teachers, students, and parents, shaping their perspectives and influencing their beliefs, assumptions, decisions, and actions.

The lack of serious attention to school culture has stymied efforts to improve schools. While the past 40 years of research have prompted huge shifts in what we know about successful teaching and learning—and despite decades of school reform to advance all students' achievement—little progress is evident. Research strongly suggests that school improvement occurs when multiple elements are in place, including strong school leadership, a safe and stimulating learning climate, strong ethical and trusting relationships, increased teachers' professional capacity for instruction and leadership, student-centered instruction, and links to parents and the community. These features cannot occur without supportive, shared school culture norms.

Although school district superintendents and principals feel relentless pressure to raise student achievement, many reform endeavors fail because educators do not understand the complexity of change, consider a school's culture, or respect its capacity to derail even well-intentioned efforts. A continuous stream of seemingly superficial, unconnected "reforms" has convinced teachers that the system does not know what it is doing. Many teachers feel defensive from external attacks. Others, often the most eager and idealistic, become burned-out reformers.

Attempts to improve schools have largely focused on imposing new rules and practices—restructuring them—rather than reculturing them by making schools the kind of places that stimulate and support teachers to make meaningful changes from the inside.

School cultures are the shared orientations, values, norms, and practices that hold an educational unit together, give it a distinctive identity, and vigorously resist change from the outside. Unless teachers and administrators act intentionally to re-boot the culture of their school, all innovations, collegiality, shared decision making, high standards, and high-stakes tests will have to fit in and around existing cultural elements. Although any type of change presented to schools often meets resistance, implementing new approaches without considering school culture will remain no more than crepe and tinsel, incapable of making much of a difference.

WHAT IS CULTURE RE-BOOT?

Re-booting school culture is more subtle and complex than simply pressing Start or Ctrl+Alt+Del to re-boot a personal computer. One cannot simply discard a shared and habitual way of understanding and acting upon the world. At one time, these shared assumptions and actions worked well and consistently enough to solve school problems. Today, many of them are no longer effective. But although the assumptions have faded from conscious awareness, the practices they drive remain.

Rather, re-booting school culture requires, in its most basic form, the following:

1. Consciously identifying the school's influences—the basic underlying assumptions, norms, values, and organizational rules that teachers and administrators have been practicing and that students and parents have been following.

2. Examining publicly how well the underlying norms, assumptions, and practices support—or hinder—the faculty and administrators' (and parents') goals for student learning.

3. Challenging those outdated or incompatible assumptions and practices and replacing them with beliefs and actions that directly or indirectly help improve all students' achievement.

4. Monitoring, assessing, and adjusting the outcomes of these changed behaviors where and when needed to create a school where all students can achieve academically and where teachers feel professionally satisfied that they are doing important and high-quality work.

School culture re-boot is a process that makes the implicit explicit. Within a climate of mutual respect, trust, honest self-awareness, and openness to new ideas, teachers and administrators look closely at their own beliefs and behaviors and identify the ways they inadvertently add to the school's and students' difficulties. Then instead of the faculty adapting their behaviors in accord with no-longer helpful assumptions and norms, the re-boot provides a space for teachers to rethink, revise, and refine what they value and believe, what they want to accomplish, and how they think and act. Culture re-boot occurs in a continuous cycle of critical reflection and conversation, action, feedback, reflection, and upgraded action. Culture re-booting is a cognitive, emotional, and behavioral process. The dynamic activity of culture creating and aligning followers' efforts is the essence of leadership.

Re-booting a school culture works because—unlike *knowledge*, which is external—self-reflection, action, and feedback create *knowing*, which is internal. Even valuable information has little meaning to individuals unless it is connected to their personal experiences and gains personal meaning. The re-boot process also builds the school's professional capital: well-qualified, thoughtful individuals working together in focused and committed ways to do better and achieve real improvements.

The good news is that school culture is not static. It is constantly being assembled and shaped through interactions with others and by reflections on life and the world in general. And, purposeful educators can re-boot and reshape it in ways that make schools into effective leading, teaching, and learning environments.

WHAT IS SCHOOL CULTURE?

School culture may be understood as a historically transmitted cognitive framework of shared but taken-for-granted assumptions, values, norms, and actions—stable, long-term beliefs and practices about what organization members think is important. School culture defines a school's persona. These assumptions, unwritten rules, and unspoken beliefs shape how its members think and do their jobs. They affect relationships, expectations, and behaviors among teachers, administrators, students, and parents. They give meaning to what people say and mold their interpretations of even the most minor daily events. Everything in the organization is affected by its culture and its particular forms and features. Generated, deeply ingrained, and strengthened over the years, these patterns of meaning generally resist change.

Importantly, culture is what the organization's members perceive it to be—not whether the members like or agree with it. In addition, one organization's culture differs from another organization's culture: No two schools have the same culture.

The terms *school culture* and *school climate* are often used interchangeably. Developed as a concept in the late 1950s, "organizational climate" was used to describe what is now defined as "culture"—an enduring quality of organizational life.[1] Currently, *organizational culture* is the more popular term for studying effective schools, largely because many 1980s books on successful business corporations made the word part of our daily language.

Schools as Complex Organizations

Schools are complicated places—multifaceted organisms as well as part of larger systems. Some avow that, as institutions, schools are far more socially and politically complex than businesses.

To begin, students bring numerous ethnic cultures, languages, and habits of mind to the classroom, each associated with varying child-rearing approaches, communication styles, and cultural and educational customs.

---

[1]For a discussion of the history and development of organizational culture and climate concepts, see: Hoy, W. K. (1990). Organizational climate and culture: A conceptual analysis of the school workplace. *Journal of Educational and Psychological Consultation, 1*(2), 149–168.

Next, the formal education system in itself embodies middle-class assumptions and traditions, several of which—democratic community, individualism, and corporate capitalism, for example—hold inconsistent values, norms, myths, and cardinal virtues. For instance, as "the great equalizers," American public schools are supposed to give diverse students, through their hard work and merit, opportunities to reach any station in life. At the same time, schools vigorously sort and select students for qualitatively different education programs and, ultimately, diverging future economic, social, and life roles.

Meanwhile, the culture of bureaucracy provides another layer, enforcing its own values, beliefs, assumptions, and communication methods as well as prescribed processes for decision making, prioritizing issues, and allocating resources. Finally, the essentially political nature of educational governance and bureaucracy interacts with all the other variables in ways that affect the intellectual, material, moral, and fiscal resources available to students in any particular school at any given time.

Clearly, schools are not simply buildings with people inside. They are systems. Each part is dependent upon the other parts, and changes in one part cause cascading reactions in all parts. To transform schools, therefore, it is necessary to consider the effects of change on all the parts of the enterprise.

As a result, all educators work within a cultural context that impacts every facet of their work but that is pervasive, elusive, and difficult to define. Culture is the general feel people get when they walk into a school and through its halls. A school's culture—"the way we do things around here"—influences every aspect of school life, including how teachers feel about their students, how administrators relate to teachers, what teachers consider as professional attire, what staff do and don't discuss in the teachers' lounge, whether teachers work in isolation or with colleagues, how teachers decorate their classrooms, their emphasis on certain curricular topics, their willingness to change, and their confidence in their collective abilities to achieve their ambitions. These culturally determined attitudes and behaviors are interrelated and interact.

Specifically, school culture appears in many aspects of school life:

- **Social climate**—including a safe and caring environment in which all students feel welcomed and valued and have a sense of ownership of their school.
- **Intellectual climate**—in which every classroom supports and challenges all students to do their very best and achieve work of quality; this includes a strong, rigorous, and engaging curriculum and a powerful pedagogy for teaching it.

- **Rules and policies**—in which all school members are accountable to high standards of learning and behavior.
- **Traditions and routines**—established from shared values and that honor and reinforce the school's academic, ethical, and social standards.
- **Structures**—for giving teachers, staff, and students a voice in, and shared responsibility for, making decisions and solving problems that affect the school environment and their lives in it.
- **Partnerships**—ways of effectively joining with parents, businesses, and community organizations to support students' learning and character growth.
- **Norms for relationships and behavior**—expectations and actions that create a professional culture of excellence and ethics.

All these aspects must be addressed in the culture re-boot process.

How School Culture Shapes the Organization

School culture creates a psychosocial environment that profoundly impacts teachers, administrators, and students. A school's culture shapes its organization. By strengthening shared meaning among employees, culture serves a variety of functions inside the school:

- **Identity**—culture's clearly defined and shared perceptions and values give organization members a sense of who they are and their distinctiveness as a group.
- **Commitment**—culture facilitates the growth of commitment to something larger than individual self-interest.
- **Behavior standards**—culture guides employees' words and actions, providing a behavioral consistency by specifying appropriate norms and unwritten rules for what employees should say and do in given situations.
- **Social control**—shared cultural values, beliefs, and practices direct behavior through informal rules (institutionalized norms) that members generally follow, enhance the social system's stability, and reinforce and shape the culture in a self-repeating cycle.

Aspects of school culture can either benefit or harm the organization. On the positive, strong culture can reduce ambiguity, increase faculty and staff members' commitment and consistency, and direct all efforts toward a desired common goal. A strong and positive culture can increase the scope, depth, complexity, and success of what teachers teach and what students learn and achieve. In contrast, culture is a liability when the shared values are not in agreement with those that will advance the school's goals and effectiveness. This is most likely to occur when the organization's environment is undergoing rapid change. While employee consistency is an advantage in a stable environment, during times of fast-paced social or technological transformation—such as we are presently experiencing in our interconnected, information-rich world—the attitudes and behaviors valued by the established culture may no longer be appropriate or useful.

How School Cultures Develop

A school's current customs, traditions, and general way of doing things largely reflect what has been done before with some success. Schools develop their organizational cultures through three different but closely linked concepts:

- A body of solutions to external and internal problems that has worked consistently for a group is taught to new members as the correct way to perceive, think about, feel, and act in relation to those problems.
- These eventually come to be assumptions about the nature of reality, truth, time, space, human nature, human activity, and human relationships in that setting.
- Over time, these assumptions, crystalized by repetition and reinforcement, come to be presumed, unchallenged, and finally drop out of awareness. A culture's power lies in the fact that it operates as a set of unconscious, unexamined assumptions that are taken for granted. They are strictly enforced through social sanction.

School cultures develop in their unique ways because they once solved problems and continue to serve a useful purpose. Because society, people, objectives, and resources change over time, however, once useful solutions may no longer function in the organization's best interests. School leaders can nurture the formation of new norms—and re-boot their culture—when they facilitate a shared set of values, goals, and behaviors along with continuous individual and collective efforts to enact them, creating the new "way we do things around here." If sustained collegial activities centered on improving individual and collective practice and increasing student learning are not part of the school culture, then developing these norms and capacities becomes an important objective. Culture re-boot is essential to ensure that the schools' orientation, assumptions, norms, and practices are still—or become—effective means to pursue the current vision, values, and goals.

Why the Traditional Public School Culture
No Longer Works

Public school culture is shaped and maintained by experiences with the larger environment, historical eras, and contact with others. Historically, American public school cultures and programs developed for an industrial age. In the 19th and much of the 20th centuries, the booming industrial economy welcomed low-skill, low-information workers for factory assembly lines and a few college-educated professionals. Rigid divisions of responsibilities and social status separated management and workers. Preparing future employees for industrial jobs, schools were designed to run like factories, sorting, selecting, and preparing labor for assembly lines or professions, using bell schedules to organize learning time and academic and vocational departments to guide instruction. Principals were expected to be efficient managers of people, time, space, and funds.

With the traditional public school culture reflecting a bureaucratic, top-down authority, teachers could choose to ignore imposed decisions and directions by closing their classroom doors. In contrast,

Figure 1.1 The factory model school no longer works in today's world.

Source: Art by Jem Sullivan.

today's successful schools require a culture in which spheres of influence operate by consensus around mutual goals and assume the function that authority played in a traditional organization. Today's information-rich, hyper-connected, society requires every high school graduate to have high levels of reading and mathematical literacy, written and oral communication skills, and competence in problem solving and teamwork, regardless of the student's ethnic, racial, or economic background.

Yesterday's economic realities did not require every student to learn at high levels. Today's realities for students are different. School assumptions and practices that worked well enough then do not work well enough now. Systemic changes are needed. While decision-making power that resides in one person or group may change other people's public actions, it may not change their preferences or behind-closed-door behaviors. In schools with shared influence, positive collegial pressure sways teachers to enact their roles differently than they may have done before. What teachers give up in individual autonomy, they make up in their collective ability to do things to enhance student learning that the teacher was not able to do while working alone. And when all teachers are working collaboratively to ensure every student is learning and achieving, all students benefit.

Three Levels of School Culture

Despite the generalities needed to describe it, school culture is not merely an abstraction. People can see, hear, touch, and feel an organization's culture in its facilities, art, technology, and human behaviors.

Edgar Schein, an expert in organizational culture, asserts that a school's culture can exist on three levels, ranging across a continuum from concrete to abstract (Figure 1.2). At the first level, artifacts—such as school colors, mascots, or slogans—can be seen and touched. But, these signs are only cultural symbols usually below most people's awareness. Next, less visibly, the school's cultural values lie it is written mission statement (such as "Relationships, Relevance, and Rigor"), philosophy, or motto (e.g., "Children First"). These documents or slogans help express the school's basic assumptions and goals. Finally, the assumptions taken for granted, those that are invisible and outside consciousness—the culture's essence—deal with individuals' relationships to the environment and other people. Although outside awareness, they form implicit, unconscious patterns that members uncritically accept unless some questioning process—such as school culture re-booting—calls them to the surface.

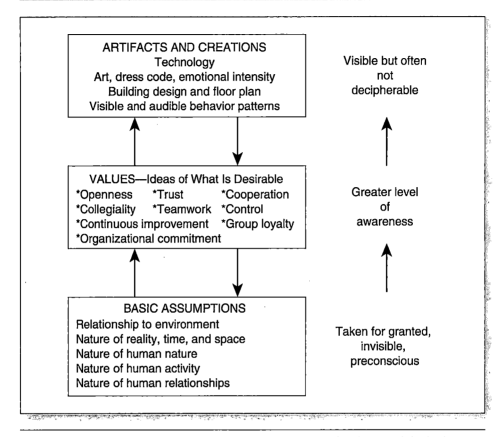

Figure 1.2 Three Levels of School Culture

ARTIFACTS AND CREATIONS
Technology
Art, dress code, emotional intensity
Building design and floor plan
Visible and audible behavior patterns

Visible but often
not
decipherable

VALUES—Ideas of What Is Desirable
*Openness   *Trust   *Cooperation
*Collegiality   *Teamwork   *Control
*Continuous improvement   *Group loyalty
*Organizational commitment

Greater level
of
awareness

BASIC ASSUMPTIONS
Relationship to environment
Nature of reality, time, and space
Nature of human nature
Nature of human activity
Nature of human relationships

Taken for granted,
invisible,
preconscious

Sources: Adapted from Schein, E. H. (1985). *Organizational culture and leadership.* San Francisco: Jossey-Bass, p. 14, Figure 1; Schein, E. H. (1990). Organizational culture. *American Psychologist, 4*(2), 109–119, p. 114, Table 2; Hoy, W. K., & Miskel, C. G. (2008). *Educational administration. Theory, research, and practice* (8th ed.). Boston: McGraw Hill, p. 178, Figure 5.1

SCHOOL CULTURE RE-BOOT 1.1
Using Levels of Culture to Understand Your School Culture

Teachers and administrators can begin to know their school culture better by considering the three levels of culture and noticing how they appear in their school. As with all activities in this book, you may use an outside facilitator or have a school leader serve in this role.

1. Separate into three groups. Assign a group to each of the following culture levels: artifacts, values, or basic assumptions.

2. Ask each group to take 10 minutes to brainstorm all the school culture items or beliefs they can identify for their level that convey what their school values.

3. Then, conduct a 15-minute walkabout with your group to observe and identify school culture elements in your main entry, main office, halls, classrooms, cafeteria, teachers' lounge, gymnasium, and teacher and student restrooms. When teachers spot a cultural element, they should point it out to colleagues and see if they agree that it does reflect the school's culture and whether they think it effectively or indifferently motivates teachers' and students' best efforts.

4. Groups return to meeting room and report findings back to the larger group.

5. Discuss:

- Which group had the most difficult time identifying elements in the school's culture level? Why do you think this is so?
- Identify some of the school culture elements you observed and where you observed them.
- What do these cultural elements express about what the faculty and administration value?
- Which of these cultural elements express what your students and parents value?
- Which cultural elements are the most effective in conveying these messages? Which are the least effective? Which give the wrong message?
- What else do the faculty and administrators value that are not clearly expressed by these varied cultural elements?
- What else do students and parents value that are not clearly expressed by these cultural elements?
- How can thinking about school culture and how you express what you believe are your most important goals help you do your jobs better?
- What is the worth in having teacher leaders or faculty spend more time (on another occasion or occasions) thinking about values and assumptions in order to make work more meaningful, satisfying, and productive for yourselves and your students?

6. On a different day, conduct this same activity with teachers in each department, the student council, and the parent teacher student association members for their experience, identification of the school's cultural elements, and feedback from these essential school community members.

Learning an organization's culture is at once a behavioral, cognitive, and emotional process. The unique culture is taught to new members as the correct way to perceive, think, and feel in relation to organizational problems—"the way we do things around here." Once the group has learned these common assumptions, the resulting automatic patterns of perceiving, thinking, feeling, and behaving provide meaning, stability, and comfort. The shared learning helps reduce group anxiety that results from the inability to understand or predict events. In part, reducing this anxiety strengthens the culture.

As a result, challenging school culture elements and practices can be emotionally upsetting to those who follow these unwritten rules. To question their beliefs and practices may seem as an assault on their identities. It is important to recognize that discussions of school culture need to deal not only with people's ideas but also with their feelings about these ideas. Change facilitators are advised to be people sensitive and to listen and watch team members carefully, so they can fully understand what each member means and respond respectfully to their views—which may be expressed verbally and nonverbally.

COMPONENTS OF POSITIVE SCHOOL CULTURES

Considering the levels of school culture and the ways people identify and understand their own schools' artifacts, values, and assumptions begins to sensitize them to these influential aspects of their work environments. A more comprehensive frame of reference about school culture can show how it may enhance their professional effectiveness.

Positive School Culture Characteristics

Research suggests that school cultures that support hard work and high achievement contain the following 10 characteristics:

- **An inspiring vision**—the extent to which a school has a clear and motivating purpose, expressed by a charismatic leader, focused on all students meeting challenging academic goals and backed by a well-defined, limited, and stimulating mission. The widely shared perception of these school goals as important supports this factor.
- **Leadership**—the people and process that help others define and invest in the inspiring vision and that encourage teachers, staff, students, and parents to fully endorse the other characteristics on this list as they adapt to change.
- **Innovation and risk taking**—the degree to which principal, faculty, and staff are encouraged to be innovative, experiment, and take thoughtful risks rather than work to maintain the status quo. This includes flexibility and backing from the school district.
- **High expectations**—the extent to which the school members hold a pervasive focus on student and teacher learning along with a continual conversation about the quality of everyone's work.

- **Trust and confidence**—the extent to which those in the organization can depend on close, supportive teacher–student, teacher–teacher, teacher–administrator, student–student, and parent–school relationships. A sense of community aids this factor.
- **Referring to the knowledge base**—the extent to which administrators and faculty use timely and accurate quantitative and qualitative information to continuously improve their processes, performances, and outcomes. This includes curriculum, modes of instruction, assessment, and learning opportunities clearly linked to the vision and mission and tailored to the students' needs and interests.
- **Involvement in decision making**—the degree of participation granted by administrators to teachers, staff, students, and parents to receive relevant and timely information, discuss its meaning in terms of school values and goals, and share in making decisions that affect the school.
- **Honest, open communication**—the degree to which the school provides many opportunities and venues for sharing information in clear and unambiguous ways among organization members. This includes creating culture, discussing fundamental values, taking responsibility, coming together as a community, and celebrating individual and group successes.
- **Tangible support**—the degree to which faculty and staff receive sufficient encouragement, resources (including teamwork and time), and opportunities to effectively meet their professional responsibilities as well as contribute to their organization's well-being.
- **Appreciation and recognition**—the degree to which the school community shows its gratitude and esteem for those members who are making meaningful contributions to the organization or to its members. A school's customs, traditions, and general ways of doing things illustrate the extent of this characteristic in action.

Each of these characteristics exists on a continuum from low to high. Assessing the school as an organization on these 10 characteristics can provide a composite profile of the organization's culture. Does the organization respect people? Does it encourage collaboration and teamwork? Does it reward innovation? Does it encourage or discourage initiative? Does it value differing viewpoints? Does it welcome individuals from differing ages, backgrounds, genders, races, ethnicities, languages, or abilities? Does it value continuous improvement? In turn, this profile becomes the foundation for the members' shared understanding about the organization, how it accomplishes its purposes, the way members are expected to act—and helps identify areas ripe for re-booting.

School cultures may be weak or strong. In a strong culture, the organization's core values are both intensely held and widely shared. The more members agree on what the organization stands for, the greater their commitment to those core values and the stronger the culture. A strong culture will have a powerful influence on its members' behaviors because the high degree of common ideals and intensity create an internal climate of high behavioral control. This unity of purpose builds group cohesiveness, loyalty, and organizational commitment, while it lowers employee turnover. In weak cultures, the opposite occurs.

Likewise, school cultures may be healthy or toxic. As described in Table 1.1, healthy organizational cultures are organizations that treat their people well. Toxic organizational cultures are organizations in which people do not feel valued and are considered only as valuable as their production, much as cogs in machinery. In healthy school cultures, members share a consistent sense of purpose and values. Administrators, teachers, students, and parents enact norms of continuous learning and school improvement. All feel a sense of responsibility for student learning. Staff members have collaborative and collegial relationships in which they can exchange ideas, identify problems, and determine workable solutions. Everyone prizes professional development, staff reflection, and sharing of professional practice, so members can interact around their craft to improve teaching and leading. In toxic cultures, the opposite occurs.

Table 1.1 Characteristics of Healthy and Toxic School Cultures

Healthy School Culture Characteristics	Toxic School Culture Characteristics
Faculty and staff feel valued and esteemed by the principal, students, parents, and central office administrators.	Staff feel as if they are treated poorly, disrespected, and as if they were part of the furniture.
Faculty and staff have a shared sense of meaningful purpose, what is important, an ethos of caring and concern, and a genuine commitment to helping students learn.	Faculty and staff lack a shared sense of meaningful purpose; norms reinforce inertia. Employees want to do their jobs and leave. Faculty believe that it is their job to teach and the students' job to learn.
Underlying norms are collegiality, collaboration, continuous learning, openness to new ideas, problem solving, improvement, and hard work.	Administrators and faculty are unwilling to change. Interpersonal tone is oppositional and prickly. Collaboration is discouraged.
Every faculty and staff member feels responsible for every student's learning to high levels.	Faculty and staff blame students for their lack of progress and achievement.

Healthy School Culture Characteristics	Toxic School Culture Characteristics
Everyone values professional development and reflection, sharing professional practice, so all can improve their skills in teaching and leading.	Professional development and staff reflection viewed as a waste of time: "If it ain't broke, don't fix it" and "this too shall pass" are the ethos.
Data, problem solving, and decision making are shared with faculty, staff, students, and parents.	Principals see all data and make all decisions.
Faculty and staff feel motivated, productive, successful, and mutually supportive.	Faculty and staff feel exhausted, unproductive, frustrated, and unhappy, unsupportive of colleagues with occasional hostility among staff.
Rituals and traditions celebrate student accomplishment, teacher innovation, and parental commitment.	Individual and group innovations and achievements go unnoticed.
Informal network of storytellers, heroes, and heroines provide a social web of information, support, and history.	No school traditions or heroes exemplify the school's purpose or values.

In addition, most large schools have several cultures operating within them.

While most organizations have a *dominant culture*—a distinctive, over-arching personality that reflects its strongest perceptions and core values—people tend to have more attitudes and values in common with others working close to them than with those working elsewhere in the organization. These various groups have several different *subcultures*—cultures existing within defined parts of the organization rather than throughout it. These subcultures may be noted by their work functions or geographic distances.

For instance, a high school's English department teachers may have a different culture that the English supervisor and curriculum specialists at the central office. Math department members may have very different ways of seeing and organizing their responsibilities than do social studies department members. The counseling department may see the school in still another way. Similarly, younger teachers may hold different expectations for their careers and how they conduct their work lives than do veteran educators in their own departments.

CHANGE AS ORGANIZATIONAL LEARNING

Learning involves *change*, an alteration in the individual as a result of interaction with the environment. Because learning is inherent in the concept of change, any change in behavior implies that learning is occurring or has occurred. Change in organizations, therefore, is organizational learning. But, only people—not facilities—can learn. And, one of the first things that educators need to understand if they are to re-boot and refine their school culture in fruitful ways—and create organizational learning—is the nature of change and the change process. This knowledge supports the perspective, persistence, and patience they will need to successfully re-boot.

In his book, *The Challenge of School Change* (1997),[2] Michael Fullan observes that the change process is uncontrollably complex, dynamic, and often unpredictable. Productive change rests on a constant search for comprehension and seeking better ways of thinking about and managing a naturally erratic process. Understanding interrelationships rather than cause-and-effect links and recognizing processes of change rather than one-point-in-time snapshots provide real leverage for organizational learning.

Just as travelers use up-to-date road maps to help them visualize and plan journeys, educators can use a set of conceptual maps—or models—to help them anticipate, plan for, and conduct a successful culture re-boot. Change is nonlinear, full of uncertainty. Difficulties are assured—early and often—even when doing the right things and doing things right. Change, therefore, is best understood as a journey, not as a static blueprint. Having the best maps and reading them correctly will help us choose the most efficient routes to our destination. It will also help us avoid selecting roads that would move us in the wrong direction. At the same time, we must keep the flexibility to assess daily the road conditions, the resources, and the weather and make necessary adjustments en route.

Conceptual Models That Boost Organizational Learning

Conceptual models help us predict, understand, and respond more effectively to complex interactions. If, as Fullan observes, change is an uncontrollable, complex, dynamic, and often unpredictable process, having clear ways of understanding and thinking about the change process and its interrelationships can help us manage it. Such models also provide increased leverage for organizational learning.

We will consider four archetypes: characteristics of a learning organization that support continuous improvement; a three-step model for understanding change; a double-loop learning model that improves outcomes by addressing causes rather than symptoms; and a model of the multiple frames that sustain a school's culture. These conceptual maps help mark the psychosocial contours of school change and culture re-boot. They are

---

[2]Fullan, M. (1997). *The challenge of school change.* Thousand Oaks, CA: Sage, pp. 33–56.

also practical tools for school leadership teams to use during culture re-boot to make sure they consider all relevant dimensions that impact their work.

Characteristics of a Learning Organization

A learning organization is one that culls past and present experiences for important lessons and principles, uncovering yesterday's important ideas and meanings to help clarify purpose and energize employees for tomorrow. Experimentation and learning from mistakes help people discover what works and what doesn't. Without shared values, norms, and goals, an organization drifts from one new idea to the next, often repeating past mistakes and failing to learn from either successes or disappointments.

Viewing organizational learning from a systems' perspective, Peter Senge, a management expert, believes that organizations—like schools—that excel will be those that discover how to develop people's commitment and capacity to learn at all organizational levels. Learning organizations are those where people continually expand their capacity to create their desired results. Schools can only improve through individuals who learn. While individual learning does not guarantee organizational learning, no organizational learning occurs without it.

To Senge, most organizations learn poorly. The way they are designed and managed, the way people's job descriptions are defined, the way individuals have been taught to think and interact create fundamental "learning disabilities."[3] In his book *The Fifth Discipline*, Senge identies five factors that together enhance an organization's—in our case, a school's—ability to learn. Briefly, these include the following:

- **Personal mastery**—a lifelong process of continually clarifying and deepening individual understanding of reality and what is important to us, integrating reason with intuition, and perceiving and working with forces of change. Personal mastery fosters individuals' motivation to keep learning how their actions affect the world.
- **Mental models**—deeply ingrained assumptions, generalizations, or images—frequently operating unconsciously—that influence how we understand and act, including what can and cannot be done in life or in organizations. Opening our thinking to more accurate models, rigorous scrutiny, and challenge allows us to identify shortcomings in our present ways of seeing the world and become open to change.
- **Building a shared vision**—a critical leadership role that motivates people in organizations to a common identity, the desire to excel and

---

[3]Senge, P. M. (1990).*The fifth discipline. The art & practice of the learning organization.* New York: Doubleday.

learn, and collective advancement of their agenda because they *want* to rather than because they are *told* to.

- **Team learning**—developed through shared focus, openness, and interactions (especially using reflection, inquiry, and thinking together without defensiveness). The intelligence of the team exceeds the intelligence of the team's members, and the team develops extraordinary capacities for coordinated reflection and action.
- **Systems thinking**—a holistic conceptual framework by which understanding the whole depends on recognizing the contributions of its individual parts. All parts of the school organization are connected to all other interrelated parts, which must be considered in any organizational change.

For a school to successfully re-boot its culture, all aspects listed above must be considered, assessed, and put into play. Making these characteristics essential parts of your school culture will ensure a healthy and productive environment for leading, teaching, and learning.

SCHOOL CULTURE RE-BOOT 1.2
Making Our School a Learning Organization

Effective schools are learning organizations that have certain qualities that make them capable of positive change and meaningful outcomes. See if you think you and your school have these essential features, and decide what it would take to re-boot your school as a learning organization.

1. As a large group, using Senge's idea of personal mastery, identify the types of personal mastery that you and your colleagues need in order to help each student be academically successful in your classes. Also, define what mental models, shared vision, team learning, and systems thinking look like, sound like, or feel like if functioning well in your school.

2. Consider the definitions above and your discussion of what learning organization characteristics look, sound, and feel like, and complete the brief table below individually. Then, compare answers in groups of four. Finally, compare answers with the large group.

3. Discuss your findings as a small and large group:

   - Which of these five characteristics seems most alive and well in your school? What do they look, sound, or feel like in your school?
   - Which of these characteristics seems most missing in action in your school? What does their absence look, sound, or feel like in your school?

- What learning organization characteristics does this group need to strengthen before it can help the rest of the faculty build its capacity as a learning organization?
- What could your school's leadership team, or you, do to help build these capacities among yourself and your colleagues? In what realistic time frame? What resources would be needed? What would be the indicators of growth in any of these areas?

Learning Organization Characteristic	This Characteristic in Me: Yes/Not sure/No	This Characteristic in Our Leadership Team: Yes/Not sure/No	This Characteristic in Our Faculty: Yes/Not sure/No
Personal Mastery Examples:			
Mental Models Examples:			
Building a Shared Vision Examples:			
Team Learning Examples:			
Systems Thinking Examples:			

4. As an informal assessment of your school's growth as a learning organization, have your leadership team redo this activity after your group has completed each chapter and again after completing this book.

The Three-Step Change Model

Kurt Lewin, a pioneer of modern social and organizational psychology, gives us a useful template for understanding change. Reducing complex change dynamics to its essence, his model's simplicity helps us identify the key factors in the change process. Lewin sees fundamental organizational change as having several distinct phases: initiating, moving, and sustaining. Figure 1.3 illustrates these as Unfreeze, Movement, and Refreeze. Follow-through is as essential as starting. We will describe what the stages entail with familiar school language and examples.

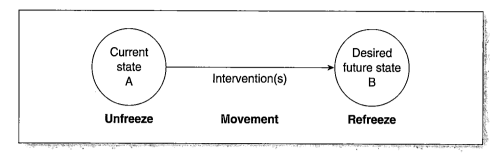

Figure 1.3 Kurt Lewin's Three-Step Change Model

Source: Marshak, R. J. (1993). Lewin meets Confucius: A review of the organizational development model of change. *Journal of Applied Behavioral Science, 29*(4), 397.

Stage 1—Unfreeze: Motivate teachers to change. This can be done by upsetting one's sense of safety and control. Faculty and staff tend to seek settings that give them an identity and comfortable stability. If they become uncomfortable—perhaps by receiving information that makes them dissatisfied with the current conditions—they become more willing to let go of (unfreeze) old ways of thinking and behaving in favor of more effective ones and those more in line with their goals.

For instance, a high school faculty says they believe in educational equity—giving each student what he or she needs to be academically successful in class. They take pride in their social justice bent. When looking at student achievement data, however, teachers discover that their affluent high achievers tend to be in classes with 1:15 teacher–student ratios (largely in advanced placement, or AP, and international baccalaureate, or IB, classes), while low-achieving and free- and reduced-price lunch students tend to be in classes with 1:33 teacher–student ratios (mainly in the general "college prep" curriculum). These data disrupt teachers' beliefs about their fairness to their neediest students. The facts and their experiences show that the students who require the most individual teacher–student time in order to learn actually receive the least. This uncomfortable reality may provoke teachers to rethink how they organize students for instruction, how they staff certain courses, how they deliver instruction, and how they assess students' progress to advance their learning.

Stage 2—Movement: Change what needs to be changed. Once teachers are sufficiently unhappy with the current conditions and ready to make a positive change, it is necessary to specify exactly what needs to be altered. Teachers need a clear and concise view of the new desired state, so they can plainly see the gap between the present situation and the proposed one.

For example, when teachers who say they value educational equity view disconcerting school data that show they are doing the opposite, they may gradually recognize that they have much to learn if they are to make their espoused views a reality. Teachers, counselors, and administrators may decide they want two semesters of job-embedded professional development from a well-respected expert on each of two related topics: how to make educational equity a reality in their school and combining engaging instruction with formative assessments to help all students, especially those who need additional teacher help (through feedback and reteaching) to master challenging content.

Stage 3—Refreeze: Make the change permanent. Refreezing seeks to stabilize and maintain the teachers in the new condition to ensure that the unfamiliar behaviors are relatively safe from backsliding. Here, the new practices become a habit (refreeze), and the teachers develop expanded skills, an enhanced self-concept, and more supportive personal relationships.

Providing professional development in the equity scenario above is a start, but it is not enough to ensure actual teacher behavior changes or improved student outcomes. Administrators and counselors also will have to change the staffing for certain courses to improve the teacher–student ratios and place appropriate (able and willing) teachers into these classes. In addition, scheduling bimonthly peer and administrator observations, enabling peer coaching (if desired), team planning with other teachers of the same subject, and using frequent assessment results to revise instruction and promote learning are strategies that can reinforce and refine teachers' new behaviors. In this way, new behaviors become regular practices. And, equity in action becomes part of the school culture.

Of course, the new practices must be congruent to some degree with the rest of the teachers' behavior, personality, and environment, or they will simply lead to a fresh round of unfreezing, moving, and refreezing. Because teachers want to help each student be academically successful, conducting change as a group activity creates a positive peer pressure that makes it more likely that the organizational culture, group norms, policies, and practices will sustain the new behaviors. Likewise, educating parents about the "whys" for this change can garner wider support.

SCHOOL CULTURE RE-BOOT 1.3
Using the Three-Step Change Model

The three-step change model provides a straightforward paradigm for understanding the essence of change. Discuss as a group:

- Which of the three steps in the change model do you tend to see most often in school improvement? Which steps do you see less often? Explain why this may be so.
- Describe a time when you experienced personal or professional change. Did you initiate the change, or was it forced on you? How well did the three-step change model fit your experiences? Which steps were present? Which steps were lacking? What was the result of the change for you? What role does your desire for the change play in the decision to include all three steps?
- Identify and describe a major attempt at change that you have observed in our society. How successful was the change attempt? Which steps were present? Which steps were lacking? How might the change have been different had all steps been part of the process?
- Discuss the factors that make it difficult for the three-step change model to work in schools.
- Discuss the personal, social, cognitive, and institutional factors that would help the three-step change model work effectively in schools. Which of these are available in your own school? If any are missing or insufficient, how do you make them available in your school?

The Single- and Double-Loop Learning Model

Fixing school problems by treating their symptoms rather than their causes is a recipe for frustration and failure. Management professors Chris Argyris and his colleague, Donald Schön, believe that learning involves detecting and correcting a problem by addressing its underlying causes rather than treating its surface indicators. Their model explains why solutions that address an organization's governing variables—its underlying values and assumptions, such as those in school culture—can meaningfully change the organization. Simply adding new programs and practices (without challenging the underlying assumptions and behaviors) cannot.

They consider three elements (Figure 1.4).

- **Governing variables**—dynamics that keep the status quo, such as underlying values, assumptions, and organizational rules that people are trying to keep within acceptable limits. In a school context, governing variables are the school culture.

- **Action strategies**—the plans and moves people use to keep their governing variables within the acceptable range. In schools, these might include school improvement strategies and their implementation.
- **Consequences**—what happens as a result of an action—both intended and unintended—which may affect both an individual and others. In schools, these may include a range of student, teacher, and parent outcomes, including achievement test results and survey findings.

In single-loop learning, when something is not working well, many look for a practice that will solve the problem within the same set of assumptions and norms (governing variables or school culture). They tweak the symptoms instead of challenging the underlying norms upon which their actions rest. As in Figure 1.4, feedback from consequences returns to the action strategies and not to the governing variables. As a result, typically, the problem will continue or reappear in another form.

Double-loop learning, in contrast, involves questioning the organization's norms, values, and assumptions (the governing variables or school culture) that support the problematic or ineffective practice. With double-loop learning, principals and teachers first challenge and change the underlying governing values and norms and then fix the action. As seen in Figure 1.4, the outcome's feedback goes to the governing variables and assumptions, which then influence the action strategies and affect the resulting consequences. Ideally, constructive change occurs and stays.

Here's an educational parallel: The school norm is for teachers to teach and students to learn. Teachers believe that the responsibility for mastery and achievement rests with the student. In single-loop learning, algebra teachers require failing students to spend more time practicing homework problems before taking the unit's test. For double-loop learning, algebra teachers diagnose the nature of the students' mistakes on homework, classwork, and quizzes and reteach the relevant math skills to the students

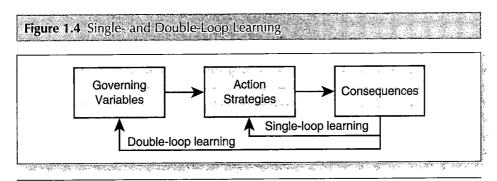

Figure 1.4 Single- and Double-Loop Learning

Source: Adapted from Argyris, C. (1993). *Knowledge for action: A guide to overcoming barriers to organizational change.* Jossey Bass, p. 51. Copyright © 1993 John Wiley & Sons.

at the apppropriate level of difficulty—regardless of the grade-level curriculum at which the weak skills typically belong. The teachers might also provide tutoring after school, rejecting the notion that all teaching and learning must occur during classroom time. In double-loop learning, teachers challenge the school's core beliefs and norms (governing variables) that students are fully responsible for their own achievement and then act in ways to change the teachers' expectations and behaviors by sharing the accountability for student success.

Argyris has compared single-loop learning to a thermostat that "learns" to turn on the heat if the room temperature drops below 68 degrees. Double-loop learning happens when an error is detected and corrected in ways that involve modifying the organization's underlying norms, values, assumptions, policies, and objectives. Imagine an "intelligent" thermostat that can evaluate whether 68 degrees is the right temperature for optimum efficiency for the purposes and activities expected to occur in that room.

SCHOOL CULTURE RE-BOOT 1.4
Using Single- and Double-Loop Learning

Understanding how single- and double-loop learning operates and helps explain why many school improvement innovations fail—and what it takes to make school improvements succeed.

1. In groups of four, identify several school improvement innovations either in your own school or in other schools that reflected single-loop learning. What was the problem or problems the innovation was intended to solve? How effective were these strategies in accomplishing their goals? What is your evidence for this conclusion?

2. In the same groups, identify a school improvement innovation either in your own school or in other schools that reflected double-loop learning. What was the problem the innovation was intended to solve? How effective were these strategies in accomplishing their goals? What is your evidence for this conclusion?

3. Come together as one large group. Discuss:
   • What makes this small group discussion activity difficult to do?
   • Give an example of a decision your school made that involved single-loop learning and its outcomes.
   • Give an example of a decision your school made that involved double-loop learning and its outcomes.
   • Why do you think educators rely on single-loop learning strategies rather than double-loop learning strategies for school improvement?
   • What do you think makes designing and implementing double-loop strategies so difficult for teachers and administrators?

- How can educators overcome these difficulties?
- What do you see as possible gains from designing and implementing double-loop learning strategies?
- How would you know if you had designed a single- or double-loop learning strategy? What would you look for in order to find out?
- How can understanding the differences between the two approaches be helpful in making positive changes in your school?

The Multiple Frames Model

In *Reframing Organizations: Artistry, Choice, and Leadership* (2008), educational leadership professors Lee G. Bolman and Terrence E. Deal observe that individuals tend to examine issues and organizations through one predominant mental model or lens (like a school culture)—restricting their ability to see the whole picture and consider the issues' actual complexity.[4] These lenses are preconditioned filters that often resist questioning their view of how an organization works—or how it might work better. When their frames of reference accurately fit the circumstances, they can understand and shape human experience. In contrast, when their frames of reference do not correctly define the situation, misconceptions can result. Then, faulty diagnosis leads to faulty action.

In an increasingly multifaceted and ambiguous world, they argue, the best leaders use multiple frames or lenses to consider common challenges, pinpoint what is really happening, and influence outcomes.

Bolman and Deal also believe that leadership is contextual; different situations require different patterns of thinking. Framing, and then *reframing*—consciously sizing up a situation from multiple perspectives and then finding a new way to address it—helps leaders (or anyone) clarify, anticipate, and comprehensively resolve dilemmas. Additionally, having more than one option generates reasonable alternatives that lead to effective solutions.

Accordingly, Bolman and Deal suggest four categories by which we can accurately frame our experiences:

- **Structural frame**—emphasizes clear organizational standards and goals, rationality, coordination, efficiency, structure, and policies. Structural leaders value analysis and data, keep their eye on budgeting, set clear direction and measurable standards, hold people accountable for results, and try to solve organizational problems with new policies and rules.

---

[4]Bolman, L. G., & Deal, T. E. (2008). *Reframing organizations: Artistry, choice, and leadership* (4th ed.). Thousand Oaks, CA: Corwin.

- **Human resource frame**—stresses interaction between individual (relationships, feelings, needs, preferences, or abilities) and organizational needs. Showing concern for others, providing sufficient opportunities for participation and shared decision making, and seeking win-win collaborations are among the ways to nurture a sense of commitment and involvement with the organization.
- **Political frame**—focuses on conflict or tension among different groups and agendas competing for scarce resources. Political leaders are advocates and negotiators who invest much of their time and energy networking, creating coalitions, building power bases, resolving disputes over resource allocations, and finding compromise and renewal.
- **Symbolic frame**—emphasizes the socially constructed meaning and predictability in organizational culture, rituals, beliefs, and symbols—including myth, ritual, ceremony, stories, and other figurative forms—that govern behavior through shared values, informal agreements, and implicit understanding.

Each frame offers new possibilities for generating positive outcomes. In addressing school situations, most educators rely on the structural or human resource lenses. Is the proposed solution acceptable within the district's or school's policy handbook and guidelines? Is the proposed solution acceptable within the limits of teachers' contracts? Yet, many school situations are politically charged and emotionally symbolic. Will changing the school's mascot or motto upset veteran teachers, parents, alumni, or the community? Reframing helps individuals see what they had once overlooked, gaining a more meaningful and holistic appreciation for what is happening, so they can respond with more versatility and effectiveness.

SCHOOL CULTURE RE-BOOT 1.5
Using Multiple Frames in School Improvement

Understanding the four frames can help school leaders better recognize the varied factors that affect—and will be affected by—their decisions. Considering how each frame would both influence and respond to a proposed change can lead to more effective and successful strategies and outcomes.

1. Separate into four groups, one for each frame: structural, human resources, political, and symbolic.

2. Ask each group to consider the implications for their frame for the following scenario:

A middle school faculty is struggling with lagging student achievement. They notice that teachers are wasting about 10 minutes at the start of each class just trying to settle the students into calm, attentive behavior. Students move through the halls between classes in boisterous groups, waving and calling to friends, shouting greetings and comments, and straggling loudly into classes as the final bell rings. Frustrated and wanting students to arrive at class ready to learn, teachers and administrators decide to require all teachers to stand at their doors in the hall between classes so they can monitor student movement and reinforce appropriate, businesslike school behavior.

- What would faculty need to consider regarding each frame in order to prepare for a successful change? What key individuals or school or district roles are represented in each frame? What possible obstacles might the individuals from each frame pose? What supports from each key constituency are needed if the change is to succeed? What might the faculty need to do to gain support from key individuals representing each frame for the change proposed?
- What might the faculty need to do to maintain support from key individuals representing each frame after the change becomes practice?

3. How can considering each of the four frames help your school design and enact effective improvement strategies?

UNDERSTANDING YOUR SCHOOL'S CULTURE

Seeing the nature of a school's culture is difficult. Our own personal experiences and values influence what we look at, what we perceive, and what we think they mean. Because our values and assumptions are usually implicit and second nature to us, we act as if the way things are is the way they should be. We comprehend school rituals, policies, activities, traditions, curricula, and pedagogy through the filters of our own—often unexamined—values and experiences within our particular society. As both participants and observers of the same structures and cultures, however, our perceptions are often incomplete, selective, and distorted. It is difficult to be neutral about the virtues and limitations of one's school culture or to notice those factors that hinder improvement.

Yet, for any change to be effective, it must be compatible with the school's culture. This requires analyzing the school's culture and bringing it to the administrators' and staff's consciousness—then, if needed, changing teachers' and administrators' attitudes and behaviors to re-boot the culture or to celebrate those cultural aspects which deserve attention and renewal.

Making Your School Culture Explicit

Before a faculty can re-boot its school culture in positive ways, it must first understand its features. Making what is largely unconscious and second nature explicit opens them for review, assessment, and reshaping.

This means first identifying the school culture's underlying assumptions, values, norms, and beliefs and determining the goodness of fit between the assumptions, the school goals, and the faculty's beliefs and feelings about each. These include the following:

- Assumptions adults hold for students
- Assumptions about leadership and decision making
- Assumptions about best practices and structures for educating all students, regardless of their family or economic background
- Assumptions about the value of change
- Assumptions about working collegially and collaboratively with other educators
- Assumptions about parents' concern for their children's education

Part of this process means examining the school's history, analyzing the school's culture, and asking (and answering) two questions:

- What aspects of the culture are positive and should be reinforced?
- What aspects of the culture are negative and harmful and should be changed?

Making a school's culture explicit also means identifying where and how each of these assumptions appears in actual observations of school practices and soliciting teachers' views and feelings about these practices. For example, do the adults in your school assume that all students have abilities to learn challenging academic content and skills—if given the necessary time and help? Do all students possess talents capable of being more fully developed, and do they believe they are people worthy of respect? Or, do teachers believe that students require instruction in basic skills before they can master higher-level ones? The answers to these questions determine whether teachers will be able to enthusiastically and faithfully implement certain reform models. For instance, the Accelerated Schools model believes that students can learn higher-order skills without first mastering lower-level ones. It may be, however, that most teachers in this school genuinely believe that students must first master basic skills (such as phonics-based reading, grammar, and usage) before introducing students to discussing complex, abstract ideas (such as a novel's character development, plot, and themes).

Similarly, a school with a culture that operates by top-down leadership and does not promote teacher involvement in decision making will have a difficult time requiring teachers to participate in new instructional programs (for which they may see no need and may lack the skills necessary) to improve their students' success. Likewise, examining a school's assumptions—about change itself, the school's "best practices" for instruction and assessment, supports for student learning, student course placement, or student movement through the halls—helps identify cultural factors that may actively support or work against any positive changes. These latter factors become targets for re-booting.

SCHOOL CULTURE RE-BOOT 1.6
Profiling Your School's Culture

Create a wall chart listing each of the 10 school culture elements listed below with enough space between and after each element for participants to vote by pasting sticky notes alongside different elements.

Profiling Our School's Culture			
Elements of a strong and supportive school culture	Extent the elements present in our school culture: 1. Very weak 2. Somewhat weak 3. Average 4. Somewhat strong 5. Very strong	Examples of where the element is present in our school	Do you want to strengthen this element or are you satisfied with it as it is?
1. An inspiring vision			
2. Leadership			
3. Innovation and risk taking			
4. High expectations			
5. Trust and confidence			
6. Referring to knowledge base			

(Continued)

(Continued)

Profiling Our School's Culture			
7. Involvement in decision making			
8. Honest, open communication			
9. Tangible support			
10. Appreciation and recognition			

1. Distribute a copy of the table above to each participant. As a group, discuss each of the 10 items, and describe what they might look like, sound like, and feel like if you were to recognize this element as an active part of your school. How would you know it if you saw, heard, or felt it?

2. Working individually, take about 10 minutes to complete the table. Then, answer the following questions for yourself, thinking about evidence or examples of school events or behaviors that support your view.

   - In what areas is your school culture very strong? In what areas is it weaker or very weak? What is the evidence of its presence, strength, or weakness?
   - Thinking of what works best for you, how would you prioritize these 10 elements so that they would support you to do your best work, gain the most satisfaction, and help all your students succeed academically and socially?
   - What are your most necessary five elements?
   - Which of these top five elements does your school culture now provide to you?
   - Which five elements need strengthening in your school culture so that you may do your best, most satisfying, and most student-successful work?

3. Distribute 10 colored paper sticky notes to each participant. Each person writes "OK" on five notes and places or draws a star ★ on five notes. Then, milling around as a group, each person votes with an OK for those culture elements that feel OK as they are and gives a star ★ to each of five elements they feel needs strengthening in order to be and do their best for themselves, their students, and their colleagues.

4. When all votes are posted, have someone tally the number of OKs and stars ★ for each culture item. Write the numbers on the large sheet next to the culture element.

5. Discuss your findings as a group:

   - Which cultural elements does this group believe to be OK as they are?
   - Which cultural elements does this group believe need strengthening so they may be more helpful to teachers and students?
   - How do your views about school culture compare with those of your colleagues?

- What should be the school culture priorities for strengthening?
- What have you learned about yourself, your colleagues, and your school from participating in this activity?
- Where do you as a school leadership team go from here to strengthen your working relationships and re-boot your school culture?

This is a highly challenging and complex activity with cognitive and affective dimensions. The group may want to think about what they experienced and learned during this activity and discuss their insights and concerns further at their next meeting.

Where We Go From Here

Organizational learning begins with school culture. At its core, school culture re-boot is about improving the instructional triad: teachers, students, and subject matter. Re-booting a school's culture develops and aligns the organizational supports for student learning and building instructional capacity.

In following chapters, we will consider the most powerful factors that can re-boot school culture—providing cultural leadership, building ethical and trusting relationships, developing teachers' professional capacity for instructional effectiveness and shared influence, establishing student-centered learning, and promoting parent–community ties—in ways that improve student outcomes. Norms that act counter to the faculty's values and goals for student learning and achievement can be re-booted from a stagnant or harmful school culture into ones that advance children's achievement within a professional, satisfying work environment. Applying the viewpoints offered by the four conceptual models can help team members identify factors that affect—and will be affected by—school changes and that must be considered when understanding problems as well as creating and implementing solutions. Chapter 7 specifically includes opportunities in the culture re-boot process to revisit and apply each of these to advance your progress.

School improvement processes are systemic, multifaceted, and ongoing. No single path is best for all schools. How development starts and moves forward in any school will largely depend on the school's base capacity, the community's characteristics, and the leadership's particular interests and concerns. Culture is organic to its community. If culture changes, everything changes. What psychoanalyst Allen Wheelis observes of individuals is also true of organizations: "Since we are what we do, if we want to change what we are we must begin by changing what we do."[5]

---

[5]Wheelis, A. (1973). *How people change.* New York: Harper Torchbooks, p. 13.

Understanding the meaning of school culture, the nature of an organization that learns, and the conceptual models that explain organizational change is the first step in helping educators re-boot it.

RESEARCH

The Impact of School Culture on Student Achievement

The articles and books listed below contain studies that consistently show school culture's key role in producing improved student achievement.

Abplanalp, S. (2008). *Breaking the low-achieving mindset: A S.M.A.R.T. journey of purposeful change.* Madison, WI: QLD Learning (Quality Leadership by Design).

Brookover, W. B., Beady, C., Flood, P., Schweitzer, J., & Wisenbaker, J. (1979). *School social systems and student achievement: Schools can·make a difference.* New York: Praiger.

Bryk, A. S., Sebring, P. B., Allensworth, E., Luppescu, S., & Easton, J. (2010). *Organizing schools for improvement: Lessons from Chicago.* Chicago: University of Chicago Press.

Bulach, C. R., & Malone, B. (1994). The relationship of school climate to the implementation of school reform. ERS SPECTRUM: *Journal of School Research and Information, 12*(4), 3–9.

Deal, T. E. (1985). The symbolism of effective schools. *Elementary School Journal, 85*(5), 601–620.

Deal, T. E., & Peterson, K. D. (1990). *The principal's role in shaping school culture.* Washington, DC: U.S. Government Printing Office.

Fullan, M. (1998). Leadership for the 21st century: Breaking the bonds of dependency. *Educational Leadership, 55*(7), 6–10.

Hoy, W. K., & Sabo, D. (1998). *Quality middle schools: Open and healthy.* Thousand Oaks, CA: Corwin.

Leithwood, K., & Louis, K. S. (Eds.). (1998). *Organizational learning in schools.* Lisse, the Netherlands: Swets and Zeitlinger.

Leithwood, K., Louis, K.S., Anderson, S., & Wahlstrom, K. (2004). *Review of research. How leadership influences student learning.* Minneapolis: University of Minnesota, Center for Research and Educational Improvement. Retrieved February 10, 2012, from http://mt.educarchile.cl/MT/jjbrunner/archives/libros/Leadership.pdf

Levine, D. U., & Lezotte, L.W. (1990). *Unusually effective schools: A review and analysis of research and practice.* Madison, WI: National Center for Effective Schools Research and Development.

Louis, K.S. (1994). Beyond "managed change": Rethinking how schools improve. *School Effectiveness and School Improvement, 5*(1), 2–24.

Louis, K.S. (2006). Change over time? An introduction? A reflection? *Educational Administration Quarterly, 42*(1), 165–173.

Payne, C. (2008). *So much reform, so little change: The persistence of failure in urban schools.* Cambridge, MA: Harvard Education Press.

Purkey, S. C., & Smith, M. S. (1983). Effective schools: A review. *Elementary School Journal, 83*(4), 427–452.

Rossman, G. B., Corbett, H. D., & Firestone, W. A. (1988). *Change and effectiveness in schools: A cultural perspective.* Albany: State University of New York Press.

Rutter, M., Maughan, B., Morrtimore, P., Ouston, J., & Smith, A. (1979). *Fifteen thousand hours.* Cambridge, MA: Harvard University Press.

Vescio, V., Ross, D., & Adams, A. (2008). A review of research on the impact of professional learning communities on teaching practice and student learning. *Teaching and Teacher Education, 24*(1), 80–91.

Waters, J. T., Marzano, R. J., & McNulty, B. (2004). Leadership that sparks learning. *Educational Leadership, 61*(7), 48–51.

RESOURCES

SCHOOL CULTURE RE-BOOT 1.7
Faculty Activity to Identify Aspects of Your School's Culture

Here is an enjoyable and provocative activity for a faculty meeting or professional development day. Its purpose is to help faculty and staff develop awareness of their school's culture, identify elements in it, share a common experience concerning their district's and school's cultural roots, and begin to think about how their school's culture influences their daily work.

Resources needed: large chart paper, colored markers, lined paper, and pens.

1. Assign teachers to groups based on the decade they joined the school district: 1960s, 1970s, 1980s, 1990s, 2000s, and 2010 and after.

2. Have teachers move to separate parts of the room, so they can talk and think in relative quiet.

3. Give each group 45 minutes to review the school and larger political, cultural, and world events of their decade, to identify that generation's legacy to the district and to your school's values and traditions, and to prepare a group presentation.

   - Have each group select a recorder and a facilitator.
   - Let the small groups consider Culture Analysis Questions and develop answers.
   - Have the teachers in these groups highlight those values and traditions that they believe help them do their jobs better—and identify those values and traditions that might no longer be effective—and incorporate these into a rap, skit, song, poster, or poem.

4. After 45 minutes, have teacher groups report back to the entire faculty and perform their assigned decade's essential features in the rap, skit, song, poster, or poem.

(Continued)

(Continued)

As a group, discuss the common themes, the unique themes, and teachers' reactions to learning about them.

Culture Analysis Questions

- *Leadership.* Who were the formal and informal leaders, and what did they stand for? Did the principals share leadership with the teachers? Did formal leaders build trust and credibility with the staff, students, and community?
- *Demographics.* What happened to the student, community, and teacher demographics during the decades considered? How did these changes impact the school? How did the school respond to these changes?
- *Crises and conflict.* What were the major crises, controversies, or conflicts that the staff faced over time? What were the sources of difficulty? How did the staff resolve conflicts? Did staff and administrators address differences directly and honestly with conflict management skills? Are these issues still a source of negative memories, toxic stories, and painful emotions?
- *Relationships.* What was the nature of people, personalities, and relationships in the school? How did principals interact with teachers? How did teachers interact with each other? How did teachers interact with students? How did teachers interact with parents and community members?
- *Change.* How were new programs, approaches, and instructional philosophies initiated, implemented, supported, and, if needed, changed or ended? How did the school address the loss of a valued leader, teacher, or student? How did the school handle past changes in the community? Are you (as individuals and as a group) willing to put up with a little discomfort in order to learn more effective ways of teaching and leading?
- *School reform.* How did each new reform wave impact the school's prior efforts? How were past changes handled or mishandled? How was the reform initiated and by whom? How was core staff involved? How did the staff deal with natural implementation dips and frustrations of new practices? How did the change process impact trust or mistrust? How did the reform end?

School Culture Surveys

The following two school culture surveys, available free online from Ohio State University at http://www.waynekhoy.com/change_scale .html, provide a means to assess faculty views about school culture issues. You may use them to study and discuss questions as small groups or as a leadership team—with or without paper-and-pencil testing and scoring— in order to derive meaning from the activity. Teachers and administrators can decide whether and how to use these with other faculty.

Faculty Change Orientation Scale

The Faculty Change Orientation Scale (FCOS) is a measure of the faculty's perceptions of change in schools. In particular, the scale focuses on teachers' perceptions of three important aspects of change in a school: faculty openness to change, principal openness to change, and community press for change.

The survey contains 19 questions that teachers and administrators answer on a Likert-type scale from "Strongly Disagree" to "Strongly Agree."

The Organizational Health Inventory

The Organizational Health Inventory (OHI), available at http://www.waynekhoy.com/ohi-e.html, surveys teachers on dimensions of institutional integrity (the school's ability to cope with outside forces), collegial leadership (extent of the principal's friendly, supportive behavior and clear expectations toward teachers), resource influence (the principal's ability to get resources for teachers), teacher affiliation (the teachers' sense of friendliness, affiliation, commitment, and accomplishment with the school), and academic emphasis (the school's press for achievement for all students who work hard, cooperatively, and respectfully).

The OHI has elementary, middle, or secondary versions. The surveys contain 37 to 45 questions to which teachers answer on a Likert-type scale from "Very Rarely Occurs" to "Very Frequently Occurs."

School Leadership as Culture Building

FOCUS QUESTIONS

- How is culture creation a leadership role?
- How does the culture re-boot process work?
- How can principals become transformational leaders?
- How does principal leadership impact student achievement?
- How do principals' five key leadership responsibilities impact school culture?
- How can principals create a culture that supports education?
- How can principals prepare their schools for culture re-boot?

LEADERSHIP AS CULTURE BUILDING

Today's school leaders work in organizations undergoing severe environmental stress. Providing access to education is no longer enough. Now, all students need to develop high-level mastery to participate competently in a fast-moving, high-information world. The new, good jobs require more than traditional skills in reading, writing, and arithmetic. Technology is automating procedural tasks. New white-collar jobs involve solving unstructured problems, demanding more complex intellectual skills: analysis, synthesis, evaluation, and creative knowledge application. Employees must be able to communicate persuasively through writing, speaking, and multimedia and work effectively in teams, often with others unlike themselves.

Many schools can no longer effectively meet the goals the larger society and community have set for them because elements of their cultures have become outdated or dysfunctional. At all levels of the organization, leaders are responsible for recognizing and doing something about this situation if future graduates are to survive in complex economic and social environments. It is no wonder that improving school leadership ranks as a high priority for school reform.

Principals make the difference between schools that serve all their children well and schools that don't. As strong instructional leaders, principals act in certain ways. They persistently communicate the "learning for all" mission to teachers, staff, parents, and the larger community. They understand the principles of effective instruction and use that knowledge to guide and monitor teaching and learning. And when necessary, they work with others to change expectations and behaviors in ways that re-boot their school cultures to better support this endeavor.

Leadership as Culture Creation

Education research shows that most school variables, considered separately, have only small effects on learning. The real bonanza comes when individual factors combine to reach a critical mass, forming a series of constructive interactions rippling throughout the school and community. The principal's job is to create the conditions for this to happen. Largely, they do this through their ability to understand and shape their schools' cultures.

Edgar Schein, an organizational development scholar, asserts that the heart of leadership is culture creation. Leadership and culture are two sides of the same coin. According to Schein, the "ability to perceive the limitations of one's own culture and to evolve the culture adaptively are the essence and ultimate challenge of leadership."[1] More importantly, Schein observes, if leaders do not become conscious of the cultures in which they are embedded, these cultures will manage them.

Leaders can create culture, in part, because they are coherence makers. They see and understand the big picture. They can identify their organizations' values, goals, strengths, and weaknesses. They see the resources, the outcomes, and the people and forces that link them. From their perspectives and experiences dealing with the whole organization, principals are in positions to create the rationality and logic to help teachers make sense of their work and see how it fits into the larger enterprise.

---

[1]Schein, E. H. (2004). *Organizational culture and leadership* (3rd ed.). San Francisco: John Wiley and Sons, p. 1.

As the school's cultural leader, principals work with others to define, strengthen, and articulate the organization's enduring values, beliefs, and cultural themes that give the school its unique identity. Culture leaders express the school's purposes and mission, tell stories to maintain or reinforce the myths, traditions, and beliefs underlying "the way we do things around here," and socialize new members to the culture. As a result, cultural leadership links students, teachers, and others as believers in the school's work who derive richer meaning from their feelings of belonging to something special.

The principal also works with others to create and reinforce culture through the symbols of culture. Symbols are outward expressions of values and meanings deeper than those we can express on a rational level. School colors, mascots, touchstones, and credos can infuse a school with meaning and influence its members' thoughts, motivations, and behaviors. Rituals, traditions, and ceremonies reinforce members' enthusiasm by cultivating identity, strengthening the ties to the school, and building a cohesive community.

Principals' attention to creating culture has positive outcomes for enhancing curriculum, instruction, professional development, and learning. First, a school with a strong, shared sense of mission is more likely to initiate improvement efforts. Second, the culture's collegiality norms are related to collaborative planning and effective decision making. Third, cultures actively dedicated to improvement are more apt to implement complex new instructional strategies that make positive differences in student learning. Lastly, schools improve best when their members recognize and celebrate small successes through shared ceremonies highlighting both individual and group contributions. In turn, all these fortify a school culture of continuous learning and improved outcomes.

As the school's cultural leader, the principal is the one who can head efforts to re-boot a school culture that no longer supports the school's mission. Effective school leaders understand the dynamics of change. Together with others, they can re-boot an organization's human, technical, educational, symbolic, and traditional aspects into a culture that embodies updated, meaningful, and enduring values—and that become the new norm.

By activating their cultural leadership, principals can leverage their schools from brick-and-mortar workplaces where teachers do their jobs in exchange for salaries into places where teachers feel part of successful teams, willing to make significant investments of time, talent, and energy in exchange for improved student outcomes, professional enhancement, and personal satisfaction. In short, cultural leadership is essential to excellent schooling.

SCHOOL CULTURE RE-BOOT 2.1
Identifying Your School's Cultural Symbols

A school's cultural symbols can visibly reinforce its core values and strengthen employees' ties to the organization as a place where they feel they are doing important work and are appreciated for their investment. In Chapter 1, School Culture Re-Boot 1.1 had the leadership team members identify items representing the three levels of culture in their school. Recalling that experience, have the leadership team look more closely at how the school's symbols express and advance the school's values.

1. Have the leadership team brainstorm the school's top five values, and write them on the board.

2. Divide the group into five smaller groups, and assign each group one of the five key school values. Each group will take 10 minutes to identify the school symbols (such as colors, mascots, icons, touchstones, credos, rituals, ceremonies, and recognition and appreciation activities) that clearly reinforce and advance the assigned value.

3. Recombine the whole group, and have each small group report their findings of which school symbols reinforce and advance their value.

4. As a group, complete and discuss the following table:

		Degree to Which Symbol Reinforces or Advances the School's Values Low–Medium–High	
School's Key Values:	School Symbols	Reinforces	Advances
1.			
2.			
3.			
4.			
5.			

5. Discuss:

- Which school values are clearly reinforced and advanced by your school's symbols (which symbols in particular)?
- Which school values are not clearly reinforced or advanced by your school symbols? Which symbols are not working as well as they should be?
- Do you need to rethink your school's core values?
- Do you need to rethink your school's symbols to express, reinforce, and advance these values?
- What refinements, repetitions, or new symbols can you identify that would reinforce and advance those values that are not presently being reinforced or advanced?

The Principal as a Transformational Leader

Many principals aspire to be respected leaders of their schools but don't know where or how to begin. Understanding what leadership entails and how to enact it can help clarify what principals can do to improve their schools.

- **Leadership is a change process.** Effective leaders figure out how to achieve what needs to be done through focused interactions and problem solving with others, providing direction and removing obstacles.

- **Leadership is a social process.** Leaders are consummate relationship builders, using their influence to persuade followers (in noncoercive ways) to become collaborators who share leading, depending on the situation.

- **Leadership is purposeful.** Leaders intend meaningful change in a particular environment, collecting, analyzing, and using data to identify goals, assess organizational effectiveness, and promote organizational learning.

- **Leaders and followers share values and purposes.** Developed together from shared values and ambitions, their mutual goals become a common enterprise that develops the widespread commitment and ownership needed to achieve better performance.

Taken together, leadership is a social process of purposeful, directed change based on shared values, goals, and accurate data capable of producing an outcome greater than the sum of its parts. The results can be substantive and transforming, while effecting continuous and sustainable improvement.

As instructional leaders, principals use these dimensions to transform their schools as cultural organizations. They understand the principles and practices of effective teaching and employ this knowledge to guide and monitor instructional programs. They persistently promote the values, beliefs, and attitudes needed to create a stable and nurturing learning environment that deems every child worthy of further effort. Additionally, they become leaders of leaders, moving from principal-centered, top-down decision making to distributed leadership. As instructional leaders, principals help teachers develop their collaborative talents, build commitment, and facilitate buy-in aimed at generating better outcomes for students. By consistently communicating and reinforcing the school's purpose in words and actions and by sharing leadership with teachers, principals create a professional environment in which everyone learns.

Principals who perform in this way can become transformational leaders. Transformational leadership entertains three main concepts.

First, the leader is a moral exemplar, a visual symbol of the organization's mission who personally embodies the organization's goals. Next, the leader articulates a vision and builds awareness of this aspirational idea while also attending to employees' other needs and concerns. Third, the transformational leader helps followers by building the team's capacity, both morally (so they *want* to) and technically (so they *can* do).

While they cannot expect to become the next Martin Luther King, Jr. or Mohandas Gandhi, individuals whose personal charisma and vision helped them lead social and cultural revolutions, school principals can use their personalities to mobilize teachers and parents toward increased student achievement. By showcasing their united expectations, principals can inspire others by developing and communicating a shared vision that motivates teachers and staff to increasingly higher levels of accomplishment. Principals can become leaders who provide intellectual stimulation, who challenge their organization's traditional assumptions, and who prompt teachers to confront their own beliefs and behaviors. Principals can become creative problem solvers who can reframe issues and use fresh insights to solve school problems. They can encourage teacher learning and resourcefulness as a means to professional and organizational growth.

Likewise, principals can become transformational leaders when they educate teachers about the school and its issues, help them challenge familiar assumptions that may block problem solving, ask teachers for their best ideas, and act on them. By helping the staff to mature their capacities, principals can make full use of the school's human capital to advance student outcomes. Principals must remember, however, that becoming a transformational leader takes time and experience to mature. It does not appear all at once.

Transformation does not come without cost, however. To become a transformational leader, principals must be willing to accept some conflict in the pursuit of school improvement. Creating change upends familiar routines and often generates hard feelings. Principals must be willing to paint outside the lines of a professional ethos that values collegiality and consensus over challenging a dysfunctional culture and ineffective practices. Leaders must be able and willing to devise smart, tough-minded solutions while also showing caring and concern for teachers. To believe that "if everyone is happy, I must not be doing my job" calls for confidence as well as consideration.

This is why culture re-boot begins with the principal. School leadership means looking beyond the urgent to concentrate on the important. It means making the time to work with others to alter the way the school does business rather than continually cope with one brushfire after the next. In the end, school leadership means creating an environment that nurtures, supports, and develops every faculty and staff members' skills in ways that make high achievement for more students a reality.

Through the force of personality, informed ideas about important issues, ample people skills, the ability to express a coherent view of what is occurring in their environment—and, hopefully, the willingness to poke and prod from many angles—principals can motivate a leadership cadre to re-boot their own cultures. In schools where norms, values, and beliefs reinforce a strong educational mission, a sense of community, relational trust among staff, and shared commitment to school improvement, positive outcomes occur for teachers and students. Over time, teachers in these schools develop a strong sense of group efficacy that generates the energy and desire to improve—even after the principal moves to the next position or retires.

Leadership and Management

While traditional school principals acted primarily as organizational managers, today's principals are expected to be organizational and instructional leaders. But, the buses, budgets, and parents' phone calls won't wait. Principals still have considerable management responsibilities for security, public relations, finances, personnel, transportation, and technology. The school still requires daily administrating. Although the terms *management* and *leadership* are sometimes used interchangeably, they mean two different things. How can principals reconcile these two seemingly competing roles?

While the leadership–management separation is not clear-cut in schools, *leadership* generally involves articulating an organizational vision, introducing major organizational change, providing inspiration, and dealing with highly stressful and troublesome aspects of organizations' external environments. *Management*, in contrast, involves implementing a leader's vision and changes and maintaining and administering organizational infrastructures. As one sage reflected, "Managers do things right. Leaders do the right things."[2]

Yet in day-to-day practice, managers can be leaders, and leaders can be managers. Managers—typically assistant principals and department heads—become leaders by providing vision, direction, strategy, and inspiration to their organizational units and acting in ways that reinforce the vision and its values. Conversely, school leaders—principals and at times assistant principals and department heads—must often perform

---

[2]Bennis, W., & Nanus, B. (1985). *Leaders: The strategies for taking charge.* New York: Harper & Row.

management functions. So, while leadership and management involve separate processes, they need not involve separate people. This is especially true in schools. In reality, principals must be able to do each, depending on the situation.

HOW PRINCIPAL LEADERS TRANSFORM THEIR SCHOOLS

Principals can impact school culture in a variety of ways. The research is clear: By directing the factors that influence the school's instructional quality, effective principals can have positive impacts on students' achievement. Similarly, the professional literature is equally clear about the key responsibilities that principal leadership entails, which lead to successful student outcomes.

Principal Leadership Increases Student Achievement

Three decades of school effectiveness research conclude that successful schools have dynamic, knowledgeable, and focused principals. Principal leadership is second only to classroom instruction among all school-related factors that influence student academic achievement. A five-year study of school reform found that "the most distinguishing feature of improving [as compared to stable or declining] schools was [that] they were led continuously by strong principals who had a vision of improvement for their school."[3]

According to one national analysis of 15 years of school leadership research, an outstanding principal exercises a measurable, though indirect, impact on school effectiveness and student achievement.[4] While indirect, the principal's role has a critical impact on teachers and, through teachers, on students. Notably, the principal controls key factors affecting a school's instructional quality:

- Attracting, selecting, and retaining outstanding teachers
- Working with the school community to establish a common mission, instructional vision, and goals
- Creating a school culture grounded in collaboration and high expectations

---

[3]Hess, A. G., Jr. (1998, September). *Strong leadership is no. 1 catalyst.* Chicago: Voices of School Reform.

[4]Hallinger, P., & Heck, R. (1998). Exploring the principal's contribution to school effectiveness, 1980–1995. *School Effectiveness and School Improvement, 9*(2), 157–191.

- Facilitating continuous instructional improvement
- Finding fair, effective ways to improve or remove low-performing teachers
- Producing high, measured student academic results aligned with state standards

Further, a meta-analysis of 30 years of research on principals' practices' effects on student achievement finds a significant, positive correlation between effective school leadership and student achievement. For the average school, having an effective principal can mean the difference between scoring at the 50th or 60th percentile on a given achievement test.[5]

Principals' behaviors have a tremendous impact on teachers' work lives. In fact, research indicates that a teacher's decision to stay at a school largely depends on the principal's leadership. Conversely, teachers cite a lack of administrator support and weak or ineffective leadership as contributing factors in the work environment that add to teacher dissatisfaction and their decisions to leave the profession. Undoubtedly, principals are the point persons in contributing to teacher satisfaction and student success.

Principals' Five Key Responsibilities

The Wallace Foundation, a national philanthropic organization that develops and shares information, ideas, and insights about how school leadership can contribute to improved student learning, has reviewed the literature and concludes that successful principal leadership entails five key responsibilities:[6]

- **Shaping a vision of academic success for all students**—based on high standards.
- **Creating a climate that supports education**—one that ensures safety, a cooperative spirit, and other foundations of beneficial interactions.
- **Cultivating leadership in others**—so that teachers and other adults assume their parts in realizing the school vision.

---

[5]Marzano, R. J., Waters, T., & McNulty, B. A. (2005). *School leadership that works. From research to results.* Alexandria, VA: Association for Supervision and Curriculum Development.

[6]Wallace Foundation. (2011).*The school principal as leader: Guiding schools to better teaching and learning.* New York: Author. Retrieved March 7, 2012, from http://www.wallacefoundation .org/knowledge-center/school-leadership/effective-principal-leadership/Pages/The-School-Principal-as-Leader-Guiding-Schools-to-Better-Teaching-and-Learning.aspx

- **Improving instruction**—to enable teachers to teach and students to learn at their best.
- **Managing people, data, and processes**—to foster school improvement.

Each of these five tasks interacts with the others—building a critical mass of clear direction and focused energies—so that everything in the school supports student learning. A vision for student success depends on a school climate characterized by high student engagement, teachers ready with instructional methods that work best for all their students, and data generated and used daily to inform teaching and learning. Orchestrating these five responsibilities well illustrates strong leadership at work. Now, let's look more closely at how principals can put these five responsibilities into action.

Shaping a Vision of Academic Success for All Students

Establishing a compelling schoolwide vision of commitment to high standards and the success of all students is a relatively new practice. Only in the last few decades has the emphasis on high academic expectations and rigorous learning been meant for all students—not merely for those heading to college. Nonetheless, the research literature over the last 25 years has consistently confirmed that having a vision of high expectations for all, including clear and public standards, is one means to closing the achievement gaps between advantaged and less-advantaged students and for raising all students' overall achievement.

Establishing a Schoolwide Vision

An essential leadership skill is the capacity to influence and organize meaning for the organization's members. Leaders articulate and define what has previously remained unsaid. They invent images, metaphors, and mental models that help direct attention and shape action. By doing this, leaders can either focus or challenge the culture's prevailing assumptions and beliefs.

An organization with a well-articulated vision can achieve a sustained competitive advantage over those organizations lacking one. *Vision* refers to a cognitive image—a mental model—of a desired future state. Vision offers a picture of what could be—a realistic, credible, attractive prospect for the organization.

An effective leader creates a compelling image that guides people's behavior. When President John Kennedy (in 1961) set the almost fantastic goal of placing a man on the moon by 1970, and when Microsoft founder

Bill Gates aimed at putting a computer on every desk and in every home, they were concentrating attention on worthwhile, highly challenging, and attainable changes. A vision provides a bridge from the present to the future. Only when you know where you want to go can you plan how to get there. Conversely, if you don't know where you are going, any road will take you there.

In schools, vision setting requires principals' skills in leadership and collaboration. The principal initiates activities that guide stakeholders to cooperatively identify better ways to educate their children and select the words and symbols by which to guide the school community toward their goal. Then, the principal brings vision into action by sharing it with a wider audience; by championing a particular image of what is possible, desirable, and intended for the enterprise's future; and by helping others understand it, refine it, and commit to it as their own.

Characteristics of a Schoolwide Vision

The principal leads the school's key leaders and stakeholders to enact culture re-boot through a schoolwide vision that includes the following:

• **A picture**—a vision creates a picture of a future that is better than the present, an ideal image of where a group or organization should be going. This picture may be outlines only and not fully developed but inspiring and attractive when presented effectively.

• **A change**—a vision represents a change in the status quo and moves an organization or system toward something more positive in the future. Changes may be in rules, procedures, goals, values, or rituals. School leaders take the best features of the prior system and strengthen them in pursuit of a new or refined goal.

• **Values**—a vision is grounded in values and advocates for positive changes in organizational and individual principles. A school leader who emphasizes that every student is important expresses the dominant ideal of human dignity and worth. A school leader who emphasizes that every student should have access and support for success in high-status courses expresses dominant values of respect, fairness, and justice.

• **A map**—a vision provides a clearly marked path or direction to follow. People often feel a sense of certainty and calm knowing they are on the right course toward their short- and long-term goals. At the same time, a vision provides a guiding philosophy that offers meaning and purpose. When people know an organization's overarching goals, principles, and values, it is easier for them to recognize who they are and how they contribute to the organization.

   • **A challenge**—a vision challenges people to transcend the status quo to do something to benefit others. Vision dares and inspires people to commit themselves to worthwhile causes.

   Frequently providing teachers and staff with the big picture—connecting the trees with the forest—gives significance and meaning to what they are doing. Picturing shared values in action; describing positive changes for the school in easily understood words, stories, and examples; using inspiring images and challenges; and clearly explaining exactly how teachers will make them a reality contribute to vision shaping. Expressing a compelling vision that mobilizes teachers into an important and shared purpose is the mark of a successful leader.

How Vision Affects the School

   A clearly articulated and widely adopted vision can help the entire enterprise make sense to its employees. It creates coherence out of separate parts. A clearly expressed vision crafts meaning for everyone in the school, showing them the big picture, so they can understand how their own roles, skills, and interests fit in. Vision provides a worthwhile ambition that energizes and motivates teachers to invest in their work, to be willing to experiment and take informed risks, and to think and act in new ways. It brings the future into the present, allowing teachers to imagine and name what can be, making future goals feel real immediately. Finally, a well-expressed vision creates a common identity, encouraging individuals to work together with a sense of joint ownership and purpose.

   Vision is the main tool leaders use to guide from the front, showing the way. The positive image of the organization as it might be allows leaders to inspire, attract, align, and energize others, empowering them to become part of a collective endeavor dedicated to achieving an attractive and valuable end. Organizations without vision begin to stagnate as forces of the status quo go unchallenged.

   To get teachers to begin thinking about a positive vision, one new Kentucky principal in a high-poverty school drew a picture of a school on a large poster board and invited the faculty to annotate it, asking them to "Create a vision of a school that's perfect." After they were finished, the principal added, "When we get there, then we'll rest."[7]

---

[7]Wallace Foundation, p. 8.

How Leaders Articulate a Vision

Principals must be able to explain and describe their vision to others. They do this by adapting the vision to their audience, highlighting its ideals, selecting the correct language and symbols, using inclusive language, and providing enough task and goal specificity so that others will have clear expectations for their efforts.

Leaders adapt the vision to their audience. Most people have a drive for consistency and will not change unless the required adjustment is not too different from their present state. Leaders express the vision to fit within others' latitude of acceptance. If the vision demands too big a change, it will be rejected. If it is articulated as fitting closely with the members' values and ideals and does not demand too great a change, it will be accepted.

Articulating a vision also requires selecting the right language. Effective leaders use words and symbols that motivate and inspire listeners. Words describing a vision should be affirming, uplifting, hopeful, and worthy. Symbols can also express a vision and bring group cohesion. For example, the image of Uncle Sam is the national personification of the United States. He appears as an elderly white man with white hair and a goatee, dressed in clothing that recalls the American flag—a top hat with white stars on a blue band and red-and-white striped trousers. The well-known "I Want You" poster of Uncle Sam pointing directly at the viewer was used extensively during World War I and World War II to recruit soldiers. Likewise, a college football team is more likely to energize its students and alumni with mascots such as Trojans, Monarchs, Cavaliers, or Volunteers rather than with bunny rabbits, hyenas, or butterflies.

Next, leaders need to describe vision to others using inclusive language that links people to the vision and makes them part of the process. Words like *we, our,* and *shared* are inclusive and enlist participation and build community around a common goal.

Likewise, schools have a rich assortment of symbols and signs throughout classrooms, hallways, and gathering places. Easily understood school mottos and credos, school banners, school mascots or logos, academic and athletic awards, and displays of students' best work and college acceptances can reinforce continually the school's essential values and core purpose. When these artifacts make sense to students and parents (without edu-jargon), they can transform schools into deeply meaningful havens for the entire school community. This is especially true when students and teachers have a hand in developing them.

Perhaps the most powerful expression of a school vision and its culture occurs when principals become living symbols of their core ideals.

How the principal spends time during the school day speaks volumes in words, deeds, and gestures about the school culture and its priorities. Greeting children and staff as they enter the school each morning, taking daily tours of the school, visiting classrooms, and speaking informally with students about what they are learning show how the leader values children and education. Mingling with students in the cafeteria at mealtimes and at extra- and cocurricular activities expresses the leader's interest in students as individuals. Similarly, joining with teachers in professional development, using faculty meetings to facilitate well-informed discussions about critical educational issues, recommending books and articles to read, and recognizing others' accomplishments with personally written notes showcase the importance of lifelong learning, collegiality, and improved professional practice. Soon, the principal's presence becomes a visible reminder of these essential values and reinforces the school culture as one of child-centered learning, collegiality, and continuous learning for all.

Finally, leaders must describe their vision with enough task and goal specification that individuals understand what they are to do in order to accomplish their goal. Direction needs to become increasingly clear and concrete the closer the leader (or the leader's agents or managers) gets to those who will actually put the vision into play through their actions in classrooms and schools. Those enacting the tasks need to know exactly what the expectations are, the time frame within which they will be completed, the resources available, and the anticipated outcomes or products to result.

If leaders can clearly express a vision that is tailored to their audience, emphasize the vision's intrinsic worth, choose uplifting words and symbols, use inclusive language, and provide enough detail that group members know what they are to do, leaders increase the chances for the vision's adoption and eventual goal achievement.

Despite the school vision's importance in mobilizing teachers, staff, and community toward valued and desired educational outcomes, the vision writing process can be extremely tedious and time-consuming. It is not our purpose to provide a template for vision writing here. Instead, we provide two highly engaging re-boot activities that principals can use with their leadership teams, teachers, students, and parents to identify and prioritize values in their school culture. These values will underpin the collaboratively developed school vision. One appears immediately below and the other, School Culture Re-Boot 2.3 Creating a School Touchstone, is in the Resources section. As collaborative activities, these re-boot exercises generate teacher buy-in and direction for future school improvement activities.

SCHOOL CULTURE RE-BOOT 2.2
Developing Symbols That Support a School Vision

Symbols can often express things in an image that words cannot express in paragraphs. Developing the foundations for a school vision can help your leadership team begin to identify their educational values and where they would like the school to go. By engaging in a conceptual and graphic activity, members with well-developed language or imaging skills can each contribute strongly.

Resources needed for each of four groups: Three sheets of large, white newsprint paper (one or two sheets for the rough draft and a third for the final product), one box of colored, washable markers, tape to hang the newsprint on the wall, and one small box of colored stars, decals, or other colorful decorations that can stick to paper without extra glue.

1. Separate the leadership team into four smaller groups.

2. Each group will have 30 minutes to discuss and create a graphic artifact high-lighted by key words and images that include at least three of the five factors listed below (one of the factors must be *values*) as they would imagine they would appear in their ideal school:

   • A picture—an image of where the group is going.
   • A change—a transformation from the status quo to a positive future.
   • Values—positive changes in the school and individual principles and standards.
   • A map—a clearly marked direction, a guiding philosophy with enough task and goal specificity.
   • A challenge—a dare that inspires people to commit themselves to a worthwhile cause.

3. After 30 minutes, have the groups post their artifacts on the wall and take turns explaining their ideas and graphics to the rest of the group.

4. Discuss:

   • What are the key images that appear in more than one graphic artifact?
   • What are the changes that appear in more than one graphic artifact?
   • What are the key values that appear in more than one graphic artifact?
   • What are the map elements that appear in the graphic artifacts?
   • What are the challenges that appear in the graphic artifacts?
   • What have you learned about what you value as a school from conducting this activity?
   • What pictures, changes, values, maps, and challenges do you want to remember and continue to use during the culture re-boot process?

How Leaders Implement a Vision

In addition to working with stakeholders to create and express a vision, leaders must translate the vision into an organizational reality—that is, find a way to have everyone walk the walk. This is when the re-boot process goes to ground. Principals must be able to continually create opportunities to express the school's values and vision to a variety of audiences and translate ideas into actions. Similarly, they must model to others the attitudes, values, and behaviors the vision expresses.

While principals may initiate and guide vision-creating actions, vision implementation also requires collaboration. Making a vision into a reality is a step-by-step process that takes continuous attention and effort. It requires supporting others' actions in day-to-day behaviors that lead to accomplishing the larger goal. One mark of successful vision implementation is that teachers, staff, students, and parents, when asked, can clearly state and act upon what the school stands for. The culture re-boot process is the means for making a vision into a reality as leaders work with others in the school community to accomplish their mutual goals.

Creating a Culture That Supports Education

Effective principals make sure that both adults and children put learning into the center of their daily activities by providing a safe and orderly environment. This is more than ensuring that the school has a friendly, business-like atmosphere in which students and teachers are free from disorder or verbal or physical assault in the halls, classrooms, or grounds. A culture that supports education builds positive relationships among teachers, administrators, and students anchored in mutual trust, respect, and ethical behavior. At the same time, teachers feel part of a community of professionals focused on high-quality instruction and worthy student outcomes.[8]

A school culture that supports leading, teaching, and learning creates a safe psychological environment. Most people want to avoid making mistakes, afraid it will make them look foolish or incompetent. The thought of trying something unfamiliar makes them anxious. Principals can help contain and reduce teachers' concerns about change when they create the conditions for teachers to share their worries in a mutually trusting and understanding group that accepts accountability for the organization's ultimate welfare, understands that adult learning takes time, and views mistakes as growth opportunities. In this way, the school leadership group provides a caring climate and affective safety to help each colleague participate in organizational learning.

---

[8]Chapter 3 will address relational trust and ethical behavior in more detail.

A psychologically safe school culture creates the conditions for teacher collaboration rather than isolation. Classroom doors are open to new ideas and to other teachers' observations. Problem solving and solutions, optimism, enthusiasm, and purpose—rather than blame, defeatism, and inertia—are regular practices. Innovation is welcomed and celebrated, while mistakes offer occasions to learn. Every member of the school community feels a sense of belonging. Everyone esteems one another for their hard work, for their genuine interest in their colleagues and students, and in their professional effectiveness in helping the group achieve their shared goals.

Providing a psychologically safe school environment begins with the principals. Unless leaders become genuine learners themselves and acknowledge their own vulnerabilities and uncertainties, they cannot set the example and help create a psychologically safe environment for others. Upending familiar beliefs and routines is disturbing to teachers. In part, their identities as competent professionals may be intertwined with these familiar assumptions, norms, and practices. Only when the principals guarantee a climate open to new ideas and the freedom to challenge current assumptions, beliefs, and behaviors can these be assessed and revised or replaced.

Principals can provide elements essential for a psychologically safe environment when they provide the following:

- Opportunities for professional development and practice
- Support and encouragement to teachers so they can overcome the fear and embarrassment connected with making errors
- Coaching and rewards for efforts in the right direction
- Norms that make it OK to make errors and learn from them
- Norms that reward innovative thinking and experimentation when aimed at improving student learning

As school culture leaders, principals must be able to create the reassuring affective environment in which teachers feel sustained and respected for engaging in and refining new behaviors rather than nervously suspect they are being forced to walk off a cliff. To make people feel safe in learning, they must have a motive, a sense of direction, the opportunity to learn, and occasions try out new things without fear of punishment or humiliation.

Cultivating Leadership in Others

Constructing a school is not about bricks but about building teachers' strengths. Leading a school is too big a job for any one person. Leaders need to depend on others to accomplish the group's purpose. To do this, principals must help develop leadership capacity across the organization.

In fact, research shows that the more willing principals are to share leadership with interested and able teachers, staff, and others, the higher the student performance on math and reading tests.

At least two factors account for shared leadership's improved student outcomes. First, providing teachers with a greater influence in school decisions improves both teacher motivation and their work setting. In turn, this generates a positive energy and focus that fortify their classroom instruction. Second, when a leadership team of principals, assistant principals, and teacher leaders work collaboratively and share responsibility for student progress, their practice represents a set of agreements and unspoken norms among the school staff throughout the building—re-booting an outdated, top-down school culture. Teachers are more likely to go along with new approaches if they have collegial support rather than be directed to change from on high. Most ironically, principals do not lose influence as others gain it. On the contrary, as respected teachers take on leadership roles, principals actually gain more control.[9]

For instance, principals can enhance teachers' leadership capacities when they encourage teachers to learn from each other. During classroom observations, principals can look for exemplary instructional practices that generate student excitement, involvement, and learning. Then, the principal can invite the teacher who uses these practices to demonstrate these approaches to colleagues to incite more success from their students. Increasing collegial learning opportunities expands leadership in several ways. First, it gives the teacher demonstrating the new approach increased confidence in his or her own instructional leadership skills. Next, it increases colleagues' respect for this teacher—and each other—as in-house experts who are willing to share their knowledge and skills. Additionally, it gives permission for other teachers to share their best practices and learn from and with colleagues. Culture re-boot is occurring as the effective practices spread improved instructional techniques to every classroom.

Improving Instruction

School improvement must be about instruction: the rigorous academic content that makes intellectual demands on students, the types of work products students are asked to produce, and the classroom pedagogies and instructional tools needed to bring these about. If culture re-boot is to make a difference, its effects must be seen largely through influencing the conditions under which teachers work and engage with students around the subject matter in the classroom.

---

[9]Chapter 4 considers the topic of building teacher capacity and sharing influence more fully.

Effective principals focus their teachers on delivering quality instruction. Intimately familiar with the *technical core* of schooling—what is required to improve teaching and learning quality—principals help define and promote high expectations, encourage teacher collaboration in planning and delivery, and connect directly with teachers and classrooms. Similarly, principals encourage continual professional learning, stress research-based strategies to improve teaching and learning, and discuss instructional approaches with teams and individual teachers.[10]

As part of improving instruction, principals keep track of teachers' professional development needs and monitor teachers' work in their classrooms. These occur through formal evaluation observations and conferences and by frequent informal visits. Some principals make 20 to 60 formative classroom observations each week, usually for brief periods of time and mostly spontaneous. To see how the teachers and students really work together, principals step behind the curtain of typical dog and pony shows, which occasionally pass for formal observations. Principals watch and comment to the teachers on what is working well and what is not, providing the specific and frequent formative feedback that helps teachers learn and grow.

For example, a principal may conduct many firsthand classroom observations and later speak with the teachers about observed examples of exemplary practice, things to think about, and next steps for improvement. The principal can also encourage teachers to build skills on their own or in collegial groups and, when ready, apply for National Board for Professional Teaching Standards (NBPTS) Certification.[11]

Managing People, Data, and Processes

Effective principals urge teachers to work with one another and with the administrators on a variety of education-focused activities. These include developing and aligning the curriculum, instructional practices, and assessments; solving problems; and participating in peer observations. School leaders collect data on classroom achievement and help teachers learn how to review and make sense of these data and use them to refine their teaching in ways that increase their students' learning and achievement. Because time is a most precious resource that teachers need in order to accomplish their goals, principals can pay attention to how the school allocates and protects time and replace some administrative meetings or teacher "duty" periods with opportunities for collaborative teacher planning.

---

[10]Chapters 4 and 5 look at this issue in more depth from the teachers' and students' perspectives, respectively.

[11]For more information about National Board for Professional Teaching Standards Certification, see http://www.nbpts.org/.

In an illustration of collegial accountability, one principal tracked academic progress across the school by using a data board that lined one wall in the school's curriculum center (off limits to students and visitors). Under photos of each teacher, staff members could view the color-coded progress lines measured at three levels: grade level, below grade level, and significantly below grade level. This semipublic moment of truth helped teachers honestly examine their students' results and take responsibility for improving their students' performance.

The reality, however, is that not all teachers will work out. Even when principals hire their teachers carefully, not every individual teacher shows competence in the classroom or the willingness to grow. These individuals must be identified, given the opportunity to improve, and either get better or be replaced. As the old saying goes, "The principal's job is to get them good or gone."

UNDERSTANDING THE DYNAMICS AND RESOURCES FOR CULTURE RE-BOOT

Re-booting school culture is a process with many moving parts. It requires principals to take a strategic approach toward enhancing teachers' capacity for leadership and instruction, student-centered learning, and parent–community ties. At the same time, principals must nurture the social relationships embedded in the daily work of schooling and its improvement. Re-booting school culture involves a smoothly working interdependence among these many variables if principals and teachers are to achieve the desired outcomes.

Re-booting also occurs within several large contexts: the school's culture, relational trust (the degree of trust, respect, and personal regard teachers have for each other and for their principal),[12] and the local situation. Throughout their daily activities, principals continually cultivate a growing group of leaders—teachers, students, parents, and community members—who can help expand the reach and responsibility for more effective beliefs, relationships, practices, and the cultural norms supporting them. Developing relational trust is an essential lubricant that makes culture re-boot easier and sustainable.

The Culture Re-Boot Process

The culture re-boot process can be understood graphically (Figure 2.1). Culture re-boot begins with the principal identifying and selecting teachers

---

[12]Relational trust will be discussed more fully in Chapter 3.

whom their colleagues respect for their instructional expertise, organizational insights, and good common sense to serve on the leadership team. As leader, the principal guides the leadership team to understand their shared values and goals and informally assess how well the school reinforces them, develop a schoolwide vision, collect data on the school's performance, learn about the change process, and reflect on organizational strengths and weaknesses. Together, the leadership team engages in reboot activities in four essential directions known for their impact on student learning: building a culture of relational trust and ethical behavior, developing teacher capacity in leadership and instruction, establishing a student-centered learning culture, and promoting and creating strong parent–community ties.

All these factors interact; changes in one aspect prompt changes in the others. For instance, unless leaders build a culture of relational trust and ethical behavior, teachers will be reluctant to make changes that might cause them to make errors and temporarily look less than skilled. Likewise, while classroom instruction depends on student motivation to learn, high-quality teaching can also increase students' eagerness to learn. And, while principals hold formal authority and the symbolic position for driving changes, expanding teacher leadership and increasing expectations for all students to master a challenging, high-status curriculum, a school already strong in these areas is easier to lead.

As illustrated in Figure 2.1, as these new approaches and practices gain momentum and popular use throughout the school, the school culture shifts (depicted as the shift from rigid line to wavy line) as teachers move from less to more functional assumptions, beliefs, and practices. Over time, with ongoing reinforcement, review, and refinement, the new "way we do things around here" leads to improved student outcomes and a more effective and sustaining school culture.

Anthony Bryk and colleagues, highly regarded school change researchers, compare school improvement to baking a cake.[13] The baker (or school culture leader) must assemble an appropriate mix of flour, sugar, eggs, oil, baking powder, flavoring, and heat to produce a light, moist, delicious cake. Without the sugar or vanilla, the cake would be tasteless. Without the eggs or baking powder, it would be flat and chewy. Without the oven's heat—in this case, relational trust—the batter would not rise and develop its proper texture or flavor. While a general cake recipe usually allows for minor adjustments—a pinch more flour, a bit less sugar—without any noticeable effects, if one of the ingredients is missing, the result is not a

---

[13]Bryk, A. S., Sebring, P. B., Allensworth, E. Luppescu, S., & Easton, J. Q. (2010). *Organizing for school improvement. Lessons from Chicago.* Chicago: University of Chicago Press, p. 66.

Source: Leslie Kaplan and Bill Owings.

cake! And, without all the components mentioned above, school culture re-boot and school improvement would not occur.

Mutually Supportive Domains

Because the re-boot factors are interactive, principals and their leadership teams cannot work on only one re-boot factor at a time. Only when mutually supporting activities occur across these various domains is school culture re-boot possible and student learning likely to improve. In contrast, student outcomes are likely to stay flat or even fall if a relevant weakness persists in any of the other factors. Thus, the ensemble of components— leadership, relational trust and ethical behavior, professional capacity for leadership and improved instruction, student-centered learning climate, and parent–community ties—taken together, are the core organizational ingredients for school culture re-boot and advancing student learning.

Although in reality, the leadership team can only focus on and discuss one topic at any particular moment, they need to think strategically about each of these domains in the short, medium, and long terms. This means attending to each re-boot area, even if they discuss them all in general at first and then plan how to sequence and possibly overlap the work of several smaller groups over one to three (or more) years' time. The bottom line is this: Each dimension will need to be addressed if students are to benefit, and as changes in one area may be undone by a lack of appropriate changes in other areas. Better outcomes will occur when plans address all areas up front.

While successful schools may not conduct culture re-boot in the same ways, they all will address the same components. No one path is best for all schools. How development starts and moves forward in any specific setting will largely depend on the school's base capacity, the community's characteristics, and the leadership's particular interests and concerns.

HOW PRINCIPALS CAN PREPARE FOR CULTURE RE-BOOT

Although school improvement can seem overwhelming, it can be approached logically, one step at a time. As the school's culture leader, the principal is the one who starts and organizes the process. Here are the steps a principal can take in preparing for a school culture re-boot.

Prepare Yourself Cognitively and Emotionally

Effective cultural leaders must build their own capacities. They must understand the concepts of school culture and organizational change and the best practices in leading, teaching, and learning. They must plan how to gain the district superintendent's support early on. They must think through how they will balance caring for others and getting things done. How will they maintain respectful relationships at the same time as they require action and change, so they don't risk fomenting an us-versus-them situation? Culture leaders must develop the skills needed to consciously orchestrate people, programs, and resources, using strategic short-, medium-, and long-term orientations with an ongoing zest for coherence making. Principals must be able to help their leadership teams make choices among competing interests and initiatives and discard those that may shift attention away from key improvement priorities. Principals must ask and answer the following:

- How will a proposed initiative complement and add value to what we are currently doing?
- Where is this initiative likely to lead in the long term?
- Is this really where we want to go?
- How can we gain the school district superintendent's support?
- How should the initiative be sequenced?

- Is the timing right for a particular activity?
- To whom can I delegate identified management responsibilities in order to give me time to think and plan for school culture re-boot?

Without this strategic—and practical—orientation and continual coherence making, school reform can resemble a scattered, uncoordinated, poorly implemented, and resource-wasting venture. Situations like this add to the staff's frustration, discouragement, and sense that "nothing really works here."

Just as importantly, leaders must be able to deal with their own anxiety before they can help others with theirs. Principals must reconcile the tension between caring for teachers and initiating change. Pushing people—including oneself—out of their comfort zones can be highly disturbing and must be balanced with sufficient encouragement. School leaders must be able to accept being respected—for their vision, their decision making, their ability to build good relationships, their clear communications, their creating the conditions for collaborative leadership, and crafting a school culture in which everyone learns—instead of pandering for popular approval by not pushing the status quo. In these varied ways, leaders build trust and confidence among colleagues. Self-awareness and self-reflection are essential companions if principals are to find the right balance to stay effective and mentally healthy.

Attending professional conferences and regularly reading professional journals and books can introduce principals to innovative ideas, other leaders, and insights into the limitations of their own school's culture. These activities also build awareness into the concepts and practices needed to improve their schools. Such knowledge, insights, and skills will not come all at once. Leadership takes time, thought, experiences, and clear feedback in order to grow. Principals must remain willing to act with informed judgment—despite their anxiety. If necessary, when they make errors, they can admit them, reflect upon their causes, refine their actions, and continue to move forward. This is why creating a safe psychological environment in which to lead is so important. Unless principals can act knowledgably but without guaranteed outcomes, neither will teachers.

Create a School Leadership Team

Fashioning a school leadership team is a complex process. Sometimes the terms *school leadership team* and *steering committee* are used interchangeably, but they can mean different things. The decision about whether to create a *school leadership team* (whose members remain in this role for several years and deal with more than school improvement) or to create a *steering committee* of school leaders (to focus solely on re-boot and school improvement with membership ending when goals are met) is the principal's to make. This section offers principals the general ideas about how to do it.

First, principals must select influential individuals to work collaboratively in leading the culture re-boot process. Both formal and informal school leaders are potential committee members. Experience tells us that those closest to the students are the most capable of making the best educational decisions. Assistant principals, teachers who represent each department, representatives from subgroups (including special education and counseling), and the larger school community who may be impacted by any changes are obvious choices. In addition to their participation and suggestions, their ownership in the re-boot process will make them want to work harder for its success.

Leadership team and steering committee sizes vary with the school size. A typical elementary school team has five or six members. A middle school team, depending on its size and the community, may have 8 to 12 members. Meanwhile, a comprehensive high school leadership team may have 10 to 15 members. Issues including budget for substitute teachers, substitute teacher availability, the number of teachers needed so the team represents the school, and the ideal number of individuals who would work efficiently as a team are also relevant concerns.

The size of the leadership team is not as important as the types of tasks they will conduct and the types of knowledge and skills the group needs. Research on the optimal team number is inconclusive. When it comes to team size, each person counts. Diversity in gender, age, and race or ethnicity is also helpful. This varied membership generates more ideas, more perspectives, and more out-of-the-box thinking for better solutions. At the same time, because many members may be unfamiliar with each other, the team may need more team-building and trust-developing activities before getting into the real work. Nevertheless, principals want to be sure the number is manageable. Groups should be large enough to involve the essential individuals but not so large that members will fail to reach consensus or sit back and let others do the work. At the same time, groups need to be small enough so people can get along with each other, speak and be clearly understood, think through problems, and identify what needs to be done.

Including influential teachers known to be persuasive school critics may be a wise choice.[14] Although principals may suspect that these skeptics

---

[14]It is important to understand the differences between a critic or skeptic and a blocker. Critics or skeptics may insist that the team think clearly, identify issues other team members might not consider, and reflect a viewpoint shared by many on the school's staff. In contrast, a blocker will try to control the agenda, call attention to self, slow group progress, and rarely work for consensus. Skeptics help the leadership team accomplish its goals. Blockers don't.

are the last folks they want on their leadership teams, they may turn out to be the best for the job. To paraphrase former President Lyndon B. Johnson's penchant for working with legislators in both political parties, it is better to have the camel's head—rather than its hind parts—inside the tent.

Many skeptical teachers gripe because they believe they have solid insights and workable ideas, but their leaders don't seek their advice or listen when it's offered. Not only do experienced teachers often have a finely honed sense for what will and will not work in their schools, but they also frequently know how to overcome obstacles to improvement and can suggest what will work. Thus, when these informal opinion leaders feel welcomed into the school leadership, understand the needs for improvement, receive the necessary data, and have input into identifying school values, creating a shared vision, and designing re-boot activities, they become invested in the re-boot's success. When they have opinions, colleagues listen. Typically, the faculty trusts their colleagues' viewpoints more than they do their administrators'. Already respected for their views and with reputations for not being pushovers, once informed, these individuals have the credibility to help the rest of the faculty accept and enact necessary changes.

What is more, this leadership team or steering committee provides a supportive environment in which the leaders can express and manage their own anxieties. These school leaders represent the organizational culture and offer an initial test of the changes possible without too much disruption of the present ethos. Typically, they know better than the principal what most teachers believe, what they do, and how most teachers will react to the initiatives. This team also creates and monitors the problem-solving groups that will address specific change programs. Finally, this team communicates to their colleagues and the community why change is needed and how it will be accomplished. By their own learning, they create psychological safety for others.

Help the School Leadership Team Learn

If they are to spread new norms throughout the school, the leadership team or steering committee must develop these new norms themselves. This usually involves sharing common mental models, having communal learning experiences, and assessing relevant school data so they can better understand their school's culture and its impact on leading, teaching, and learning. Thoughtful listening, reflecting, and having honest conversations are essential components throughout. Members' thoughts and feelings must be welcomed, respected, facilitated, and used constructively. The re-boot activities in Chapters 1 and 2, and woven throughout this text, can help build your team and educate its members.

Leading the team can give the principal occasions to ensure a safe, trusting, and respectful climate in which teachers can work together. If this group is to collaboratively identify and solve problems, they must develop a high level of mutual trust and feel accountable as a group for organizational learning. This means listening carefully to each other and trying to understand what each colleague means. Members must feel free to agree or disagree without penalty. In addition, they initially must decide on which aspects of their discussions remain confidential and stay inside the group: Later, they don't want to hear gossip about who said what to whom throughout the school. Likewise, teachers and administrators will learn to recognize and work through their own concerns (about having colleagues disagree with them, making mistakes, expressing genuine feelings about the issues discussed, or about not changing fast enough) expressed through arguments, defensiveness, and impatience. Inviting a colleague with expert skills in facilitating groups to lead or co-lead activities in which members routinely voice intense ideas and emotions will help ensure an open, safe, and trusting climate for re-boot.

Help the Team Design the Organizational Learning Process

The leadership team or steering committee must first diagnose the school's learning needs and then plan and design the organizational learning process. They may want to do this by initially addressing the major issues within the leadership team and then conducting professional development activities within grade levels or academic departments to acculturate the rest of the faculty to their experiences, findings, and plans. Or, they may want to create a set of task forces or learning groups to deal with each of the major issues. In either case, the leadership team must translate its general sense of where the organization needs to go into a set of discrete and workable problems. Generally, these include the following:

- **Assess the school's status.** What are the school's goals, and what data can tell you about how well we are meeting them?
- **Set clear measurable goals for each of the task forces or learning groups.** What topics and which aspects of the topics need serious study? What products are expected and within what reasonable yet realistic time frames?
- **Create small wins.** In addition to setting medium- and long-term goals, set a series of more modest goals that are certain to be achieved successfully and celebrated so as to boost enthusiasm and confidence.
- **Make problem solving the norm.** War stories, blaming, and scapegoating are not acceptable. All discussions are expected to lead to constructive alternatives and solutions.

- **Build partnerships with parent and community organizations.** School culture re-boot is too important to leave to teachers and principals alone.
- **Sustain communication and collaboration.** Keep clear and understandable information about findings, decisions, next steps, and accomplishments flowing among team members and between the leadership team and others in the school community, and keep lines open for feedback.

Be Alert to Obstacles

A variety of factors may stand in the way of culture re-boot and organizational learning in schools. Many well-intentioned reforms have been discarded because of a combination of negating effects that come from ignoring a school's culture. Some obstacles appear within the school context, and others fall within the principal as an individual.

After surveying the literature on failed school reforms, Andrew Hargreaves, an internationally respected expert on educational change, concludes that educational change falters or fails because the change may be one of the following:[15]

- Poorly conceived or not clearly demonstrated—it is not obvious who will benefit and how
- Too broad and ambitious, so teachers have to work on too many fronts, or too limited and specific so that little real change occurs at all
- Too fast for people to cope with or too slow, so they become impatient or bored and move on to something else
- Weakly resourced or resources withdrawn once the first phase of innovation ends—there is not enough money for materials or teacher planning time
- Lacking long-term commitment to the change to carry people through the anxiety, frustration, and discouragement of early experimentation and unavoidable setbacks—student outcomes may actually look worse in the short term as teachers discard familiar routes and experiment with new, untested practices
- Lacking committed key staff who can contribute to the change or might be affected by it—conversely, key staff might become over-involved as an administrative or innovative elite from which other teachers feel excluded

---

[15]Hargreaves, A. (1997). Introduction. In A. Hargreaves (Ed.), *Rethinking educational change with heart and mind: 1997 ASCD yearbook* (pp. vi–xv). Virginia: Association for Supervision and Curriculum Development, p. viii.

- Absent parents who support the change or presence of parents who oppose the change because they are kept at a distance from it
- Headed by leaders who are either too controlling or too ineffectual or cash in on the innovation's early success to move on to higher positions
- Pursuing goals in isolation, which are undermined by other unchanged structures

Principals and their leadership teams are well advised to refer to these obstacles—and resolve them—as they plan strategies for school change.

Other factors that limit school culture re-boot appear in the principal as an individual. The principal may lack leadership skills or be unfamiliar with the recent research and practice that informs school change, distributed leadership, teaching, and learning. The principal may lack experience and understanding of how to build a consensus or manage staff discord. Principals may be unable to prioritize and focus on what the school actually needs to advance student interests and outcomes. The tyranny of the urgent over the important may tie up principals in daily problem solving, putting out brushfires, and meeting paperwork deadlines rather than thinking long term about where they might lead their schools. Similarly, the tendency to think in terms of staff problems rather than of student needs may focus principals on single-loop rather than double-loop solutions. Finally, many principals are reluctant to leave their comfort zones and take on a seemingly monumental task where the stakes are high but success is not a sure thing.

Before principals can become school culture leaders, they must educate themselves about the tasks at hand. Before anyone else changes, leaders must overcome their own cultural assumptions and see new ways of doing things and new ways in which to do them. They must think through how they will manage the tension between caring for others and getting things done. They must deal with their own discomfort before than can help others with theirs. Pausing frequently to reconnect with their touchstone values and recommit to a schoolwide *us* will be necessary.

As principals begin to initiate change in their schools, not everyone will be happy with the idea or the process. Not everyone has an equal voice in shaping the vision for reform. Teachers who are unwilling to take on the hard work of change and align with colleagues against making needed changes to improve student outcomes must—with human resources' knowledge and help—be transitioned out of the school. It is only as participants demonstrate their commitment to engage in school improvement work and see others doing the same that a genuine community grounded in relational trust can emerge. Principals must take the lead and reach out to others, even to colleagues who don't initially reciprocate. But in the end, principals must be prepared to use their authority to re-boot the school culture and the collegial and student-centered instructional practices that flow from it.

RESEARCH

Principal Leadership and Student Achievement

Goldhaber, D. (2007, December). *Principal compensation. More research needed on a promising reform.* Washington, DC: Center for American Progress.

Hallinger, P., & Heck, R. H. (1998). Exploring the principal's contribution to school effectiveness: 1980–1995. *School Effectiveness and School Improvement, 9*(2), 157–191.

Heck, R. H., Larsen, T. J., & Marcoulides, G. A. (1990). Instructional leadership and school achievement: Validation of a casual model. *Educational Administration Quarterly, 26*(2), 94–125.

Hess, A. G., Jr. (1998, September). Strong leadership is no. 1. *Catalyst.* Chicago: Voices of School Reform.

Leithwood, K., Harris, A., & Hopkins, D. (2008). Seven strong claims about successful school leaders. *School Leadership and Management, 28*(1), 27–42.

Leithwood, K., Louis, K. S., Anderson, S., & Wahlstrom, E. (2004). *How leadership influences student learning.* New York: Wallace Foundation.

Levine, D. U., & Lezotte, L. W. (1990). *Unusually effective schools: A review and analysis of research and practice.* Madison, WI: National Center for Effective Schools Research and Development.

MacNeil, A. J., Prater, D. L., & Busch, S. (2009). The effects of school culture and climate on student achievement. *International Journal of Leadership in Education, 12*(1), 73–84.

Marzano, R. J., Waters, T., & McNulty, B. A. (2005). *School leadership that works. From research to results.* Alexandria, VA: Association for Supervision and Curriculum Development.

Sammons, P., Hillman, J., & Mortimore, P. (1995). *Key characteristics of effective schools: A review of school effectiveness research.* London: OFSTED.

Schnur, J. (2002, June 18). *An outstanding principal in every school: Using the new Title II to promote effective leadership.* National Council on Teacher Quality. Retrieved from www.nctq.org/press/2002_consumers_guide/schnur.htm

The following studies support the importance of principal leaders in building teamwork among adults.

Diamond, J. B. (2007). Cultivating high expectations in an urban elementary school: The case of Kelly School. In J. P. Spillane & J. B. Diamond (Eds.), *Distributed leadership in practice* (pp. 63–84). New York: Teachers College Press.

Sergiovanni, T. J. (2000). *The lifeworld of leadership: Creating culture, community, and personal meaning in our schools.* San Francisco: Jossey-Bass.

Smylie, M. A., & Hart, A. W. (1997). School leadership for teacher learning and change: A human and social capital development perspective. In J. Murphy & K. S. Louis (Eds.), *Handbook of educational administration* (pp. 421–441). New York: Longman.

Smylie, M. A., Mayrowetz, D., Murphy. J., & Seashore Louis, K. (2007). Trust and the development of distributed leadership. *Journal of School Leadership, 17*(4), 469–503.

RESOURCES

SCHOOL CULTURE RE-BOOT: 2.3
Creating a School Touchstone

A school touchstone is a central tool for intentionally shaping a culture. Crafted by the school community over weeks or months, it contains shared values and high expectations of universal principles that the school stands for and that can guide daily decision making, behavior, and reflection.

Specifically, the *school touchstone* is a short statement that expresses the core qualities—both academic and ethical—that a school community seeks to develop in its members. It defines how things are done at a school—its culture. It is not the mission (the school's purpose) or the vision (where the school is going). It is not a set of commandments. Instead, it is a living icon, meant to inspire, inform, and ethically guide school community members about how to go about their leading, teaching, and learning. Top universities and businesses have used touchstones for years. Properly introduced and developed, administrators, teachers, and students will start holding themselves and their peers accountable for living the touchstone's values.

Each school needs to develop its own touchstone. Because shared ownership is important, administrators, teachers, students, and parents should be involved when developing common values. This process can take time. It is important not to argue fruitlessly about the actual wording; accept what everyone can live with. The values selected should reflect a balance between academic and ethical qualities.

Consider these three examples, and then construct your own.

Example 1: "Who We Are"

- At Magruder, we take the high road.
- We sincerely care about ourselves, each other, and our school.
- We teach with vitality and caring.
- We show respect for our students, parents, and teachers.
- We expect excellence in scholarship and character.
- We deal with the root causes of our issues by engaging in courageous conversations.
- We give our best in and out of the classroom.
- This is who we are even when no one is watching!

Example 2: "The York Way"

- At York Middle School, we practice excellence in scholarship and character.
- We celebrate and honor each other by being respectful, honest, kind, and fair.
- We show our cultural appreciation for each other in all we do.

(Continued)

(Continued)

- We give our best in and out of the classroom and take responsibility for our actions.
- This is who we are even when no one is watching.

Example 3: "At Ashbury, we are connected by common goals"

- Achieving academic excellence through hard work.
- Respecting each other by using kind words and actions.
- Taking responsibility for our own learning and behavior.
- We know that it takes courage to live this creed, especially when no one is watching!

Here's a simple five-line format to use:

- Line 1: The motto, such as: "Taking the high road"; "Rigor, Relevance, and Relationships"; "Taking responsibility for our own behavior and learning"; "The courage to persevere"; "Creating a caring community of lifelong learners"; "A team of learners"
- Lines 2, 3, 4: What the motto—doing your best—looks like
- Line 5: Reminds us to be accountable: "This is who we are even when no one is watching"

Once the draft touchstone is written, take the following steps:

1. Share a draft of the touchstone with students, parents, and staff. Use valuable suggestions to make final revisions.

2. After the touchstone is finalized, post it widely throughout the school; hold an assembly (ceremony) where students and staff can share personal stories and discuss how to use the touchstone in daily life; and invite teachers and students to sign a large touchstone banner.

3. Promote the school's touchstone in many creative ways, including classroom posters, student ID cards, refrigerator magnets for parents, newsletters, or morning announcements. Teachers can often connect the touchstone qualities to their subject content and their students' behaviors.

4. Use the touchstone to orient new teachers to the school and new families to the school community.

5. Develop a rubric for each of the touchstone qualities to help students and teachers know what the touchstone's expectations look like when practiced to a high level of quality in the school. This will increase their awareness and help teachers guide student discussions and actions.

Sources: Elbot, C. F., & Fulton, D. (2008). *Building an intentional school culture. Excellence in academics and character.* Thousand Oaks, CA: Corwin, chap. 2; Peterson, K. D., & Deal, T. E. (2009). *The shaping school culture fieldbook* (2nd ed.). San Francisco: Jossey-Bass; Summit School District RE-1 III. (n.d.). *Creating a school-wide touchstone.* Summit, CO: Author, pp. 1–7. Retrieved March 21, 2012, from http://summit.k12 .co.us/specprograms/charactereducation/touchstonesinfo.pdf

School Culture, Ethical Behavior, and Relational Trust

FOCUS QUESTIONS

- How is ethics at the heart of leadership?
- In what ways are teachers and principals the moral stewards of their schools?
- Why is relational trust such an essential part of successful schools?
- What are the foundations upon which educators can build relational trust in schools?
- In what ways does relational trust support school culture re-boot and advance school improvement?
- What are attitudes and behaviors that principals and teachers can use to initiate, sustain, and repair relational trust in their schools?

"**E**thics is at the heart of leadership."[1] Communities expect those holding leadership positions to act justly and promote good as well as demonstrate moral and professional accountability. An ethical person is one who consistently tells the truth—even when concealing it might be to that person's advantage. An ethical person is one who respects all individuals for who they are and deals with others in a fair and objective manner. An ethical person has developed relatively mature qualities of autonomy, connectedness, and wholeness; acts as his or her own person

---

[1]Ciulla, J. (Ed.). (2004). *Ethics: The heart of leadership.* Westport, CT: Praeger.

within the supports and constraints of relationships; and behaves in ways that rise above immediate self-interest. These human and ethical sensibilities grow over a lifetime, hindered or nurtured by the significant people and circumstances in their lives.

At the same time, schools run on relationships. No matter who has the title or down which corridor a teacher's classroom is located, everyone in the school community depends on others to reach their desired outcomes and feel effective. Principals, teachers, students, and parents hold certain expectations about their mutual obligations. These expectations are not necessarily spelled out on paper in a formal contract or even discussed in conversation. Rather, they are implicit deals between colleagues and coworkers, educators and parents, based on assumed fairness, good faith, and reciprocity. These understandings form the basis for judging the social exchanges among people in differing roles—and comprise the foundation for relational trust.

Trust lies at the heart of strong relationships that help children learn. In schools, trust begins with the atmosphere set by the principal. Principals who can genuinely establish a trusting school environment can lead a successful culture re-boot of sustainable school improvement. As trustees of our nation's children, educators must understand the complex dynamics of ethical behavior and trust, their effects on increasing schools' effectiveness, and how to develop, maintain—and, if necessary, repair—trust in their schools.

SCHOOL CULTURE AND ETHICAL BEHAVIOR

Ethics are norms, values, beliefs, habits, and attitudes that we choose to follow—which we as a society impose on ourselves. While law regulates behavior from the outside, ethics regulate behavior from the inside. Ethics are voluntary. Professionally, ethics can be described as the rules or widely accepted standards of practice that govern members' professional conduct.

Ethical behavior and trust are related. Trust is not a feeling of warmth or affection. Rather, it is the conscious awareness that one depends on another—and the expectation that the other person will act ethically to protect our interests. Trust has been called the "mortar that binds leader to follower" and frames the basis for leaders' legitimacy.[2] Trustworthiness is an ethical behavior. In a complex, fast-paced, and ever-changing world, life seems less predictable. Trust serves as a way of reducing uncertainty.

---

[2]Nanus, B. (1989). *The leader's edge: The seven keys to leadership in a turbulent world.* Chicago: Contemporary Books, p. 101.

Ethics Are About Relationships

Ethics are about how we act in our relationships with others. It is about what we ought to do and requires a judgment about a given situation. To behave *ethically* is to choose the right behavior, while being *moral* is the ability to practice that right behavior. *Morals* refer to specific standards of right and wrong. Frequently, the two terms are used interchangeably. What is ethical is moral, and what is unethical is immoral.

Schools that display the shared values of fairness, justice, respect, cooperation, and compassion have a positive sense of community that supports both teachers and students. Typically, schools enact five ethical principles that center on respect for persons:

- Respecting autonomy, allowing another person to act independently
- Doing no harm to others
- Benefitting others
- Treating others fairly
- Being trustworthy

Complex circumstances sometimes require people to choose among competing sets of principles, values, or ideas, and ethical dilemmas result. Some of these options are not necessarily right or wrong. Nonetheless, substantial agreement exists that certain actions are better than others, and better unconditionally, regardless of situation or culture. These morally good acts are based on universal laws of truth, goodness, beauty, courage, and justice—values found in all cultures. The professional maxim—First, do no harm—is one of these.

Schooling Is an Ethical Endeavor With a Moral Purpose

People in democratic societies expect their schools to be guided by moral principles such as justice, fair treatment, liberty, honesty, equity, and respect for individual differences. Likewise, schools are supposed to serve moral purposes, including nurturing young people's human, social, and intellectual growth.

Principals and teachers have been called moral stewards, acknowledging that value judgments are central elements in educating children. In the same vein, teaching is more than a set of technical skills for delivering knowledge to students. It involves caring for children and being responsible for helping them develop their capacities to succeed as thoughtful individuals, capable employees, good neighbors, and responsible citizens in a diverse and democratic society. Teachers must consider both the ways in which they teach as well as the ends for which they are teaching. This moral responsibility is particularly important in public schools, where state laws require students to attend.

John Goodlad, a highly regarded educational researcher and theorist, plainly spells out his view of schooling as a moral enterprise with four dimensions:[3]

- **Enculturation into a political and social democracy**—schools are responsible for teaching a complex idea: In a democracy, all citizens and institutions must follow broad democratic principles—freedom, liberty, justice, equality, and fairness—balancing individual rights against the common good. Democracy is both a process and a goal. Inequalities—whether gender, racial, ethnic, or economic—cannot be justified by a majority vote. Democratic processes cannot justify undemocratic ends. This is the core of the school's moral responsibility to society.
- **Access to knowledge**—in our society, schools are the only institutions specifically tasked with giving the young organized access to the subjects that make us human: communications systems; evaluative and belief systems; physical and biological systems; social, political, and economic systems. But, providing knowledge must go well beyond memorization and recalling information. It must be fully comprehended and intelligently used, and it must be available to all students. Limiting understanding and access to essential knowledge—for whatever rationale—is morally wrong.
- **Nurturing pedagogy**—the art and science of teaching encourages and advances students' learning at their various stages of development. A teacher's failure to create an intellectually reflective, engaging classroom for learning is not simply malpractice. It is immoral, especially for students who do not have the choice to withdraw.
- **Responsible stewardship**—teachers and principals are the moral stewards of their schools, responsible for developing schoolwide excellence. Stewardship requires reflecting, studying, inventing, and rethinking what is fair and beneficial for every child. Educators must deliberately raise issues when practices are proposed or implemented—such as hiring the least qualified teachers for high-needs schools or ending arts programs and physical education to make room for test prep—that substantially interfere with the best interests of all students. Also as stewards, teachers ensure all students have access to knowledge and practice a nurturing pedagogy.

Clearly, culture re-boot is part of educators' moral responsibility. In schools, everyday decisions have moral implications for our children.

---

[3]Goodlad, J. (1990). *Teachers for our nation's schools*. San Francisco: Jossey-Bass.

How do we divide our time and attention to the students in our classrooms? What impact do our instructional grouping practices have within the classroom and across the school? Whom do we recognize or ignore, encourage or discourage, in classroom interactions? Which classrooms receive the recognized expert teachers? When educators do not question their own assumptions, norms, expectations, and actions, and when they believe school practices are neutral or simply "the way schools are," they evade their ethical responsibility to treat every student fairly. When educators do not ask themselves, "What about my thinking and actions present obstacles to children's learning?" they default on their personal responsibility for any negative outcomes that students experience as a result of teachers' decisions. And, when this lack of ongoing reflection and purposeful action becomes the school-wide norm, many children fail to learn.

Educators have a moral responsibility to be proactive about creating an ethical environment in which to conduct education. One of the ways school leaders enact this responsibility is to develop, sustain—and, when needed, repair—a school culture of trust.

SCHOOL CULTURE RE-BOOT 3.1
Assessing Yourselves as a Moral School

Many believe that schooling is a moral enterprise with four dimensions. Schools should be democratic in the way they conduct their business as well as in the ends they seek to achieve. How well do you think your school fares on being a moral school?

1. Divide the group into three smaller groups. Discuss and answer the questions below among yourselves for approximately 15 minutes. Reaching consensus is not necessary, but differing viewpoints need to be aired and considered:
   Explain why you agree or disagree with Goodlad that schools are responsible for the following:

   - Acculturating children into political and social democracy
   - Providing access to knowledge to every child
   - Providing nurturing pedagogy in which teachers create intellectual, reflective, and engaging classes for every student's learning
   - Enacting responsible stewardship that raises issues about what is fair and beneficial for every child

   On a scale of 1 to 5 (1 lowest, 5 highest), how well do you think your school is presently accomplishing each dimension? What evidence can you suggest to support this assessment?

   (Continued)

(Continued)

2. Recombine as one group. Discuss the findings from each small group. Specifically, touch on the following topics:

- How well did members feel they were heard and understood during the activity—especially in areas of disagreement?
- Are you showing the democratic process of respect for individual differences in this group here and now as you conduct our activities together?
- How would you assess the trust level among members in this group? What evidence can you show to support this view?
- Do you as a school leadership team agree or disagree that you are supposed to be addressing these four moral dimensions in your educational practices?
- Where do you agree? How well do you think your school is performing in enacting each of these moral dimensions?
- About what do you disagree?
- Which moral dimensions do you as a school need to strengthen?
- What activities, courses, programs, and practices do you need to rethink and redesign to better accomplish these desired ends?
- What evidence is sufficient for you to know if you are making progress toward these goals?

SCHOOL CULTURE AND RELATIONAL TRUST

Trust is an essential dimension of human relationships. *Trust* may be understood as an individual's or group's willingness to be vulnerable to another party—and place something they care about under the other person's protection or control—based on the confidence that the latter party is benevolent, reliable, competent, honest, and open.[4] We may care about tangible things, such as one's possessions or money, or intangible things, such as our good reputations or norms of respect and honesty. When we trust, we make ourselves vulnerable to another person who we expect to voluntarily accept the implied moral duty—or ethically justifiable behavior—to recognize and protect our rights and interests, so we can better work together in a common endeavor. Without vulnerability, there is no need for trust. As a normative ethic, trust is related to the ideas of a good and moral society in which individuals work not only for personal short-term gain but also consider the valid rights and interests of others. Ultimately, they seek to benefit each other and the larger society.

---

[4]Definition adapted from: Hoy, W., & Tschannen-Moran, M. (1999). Five facets of trust: An empirical confirmation in urban elementary schools. *Journal of School Leadership*, 9(3), 184–208 (p. 189).

Trust in Successful Schools

Trust is central to leading effective and productive schools. In fact, the *in loco parentis* responsibility, which American society has given to schools, is rooted in trust. Parents trust educators to keep their children safe and learning. Teachers must trust administrators to provide the learning climate, time, and instructional resources that allow them to teach all children well. Principals must trust teachers to act in the best interests of every child. Faculty and staff must trust one another to keep children safe and learning at schools, while they trust parents to ensure their children's daily attendance and studying at home. In addition, discussions about school culture re-boot and school improvement can only occur within trusting relationships.

Importantly, trust is not a given. In every relationship, trust must be earned through repeated interactions in which individuals always keep their word, follow through on their promises, and protect the other's interests.

Decades of research on trust in schools has found teachers' trust in colleagues as well as in their principal is linked to school effectiveness[5] and positive school climate.[6] Studies consistently find that the principals' collegial behaviors determine whether the faculty trusts the principals, while how well teachers treat each other determines how much faculty trust their colleagues.[7] The principals' authenticity, however—openness in personal relations, respecting teachers as people, accepting responsibility for mistakes and negative outcomes, the ability to see beyond stereotypes, and acting in ways consistent with one's personal self—does make a positive difference in the teachers' trust in the principal and in each other.[8] For trust to grow, it seems to require a direct connection between individuals. Openness and authenticity are key ingredients. Then, too, professionals may tend to trust other professionals who have had similar educations and hold state licenses to perform their jobs unless or until there is a reason not to.

---

[5]Hoy, W. K., Tarter, C. J., & Witkoskie, L. (1992). Faculty trust in colleagues: Linking the principal with school effectiveness. *Journal of Research and Development in Education, 26,* 38–45; Tarter, C. J., Sabo, D., & Hoy, W. K. (1995). Middle school climate, faculty trust and effectiveness: A path analysis. *Journal of Research and Development in Education, 29,* 41–49.

[6]Hoy, W. K., Hoffman, J., Sabo, D., & Bliss, J. (1996). The organizational climate of middle schools. *Journal of Educational Administration, 34,* 41–59; Tarter, C.J., Bliss, J., & Hoy, W. K. (1989). School characteristics and faculty · trust in secondary schools. *Educational Administration Quarterly, 25,* 294–308.

[7]Hoy, W. K., Tarter, C. J., & Kottkamp, R. (1991). *Open schools/Healthy schools: Measuring organizational climate.* Beverly Hills, CA: Sage; Tartar et al. (1989); Tarter et al. (1995).

[8]Hoy, W. K., & Kupersmith, W. J. (1986). Principal authenticity and faculty trust: Key elements in organizational behavior. *Planning and Change, 15,* 81–88.

Moreover, the social contexts in school greatly influence the trust that develops. Friendship networks may form based on grade level or subject taught, around instructional philosophies, location in the building, veteran teachers as opposed to novices, time of lunch break, ties with or against the principal, race, gender, or many other factors. These groups' norms may strengthen trust within each group because having mutual friends increases the likelihood of building trusting relationships. In contrast, group norms may weaken trust for others considered outsiders—even if the "outsiders" work in the next room. These ties among smaller units of teachers must be considered when working to build, sustain, and repair trusting relationships in schools.

Foundations of Relational Trust

At its base, relational trust is anchored in social respect as individuals perceive it in their interactions. Respectful exchanges are marked by a genuine sense of listening to what each person has to say and weighing this in later actions. Even when people disagree, individuals feel that others recognize the value of their opinions. Such social exchanges foster a sense of connectedness among administrators, teachers, students, and parents and promote bonds with the school as a whole.

Personal regard is another important element in determining relational trust. Social encounters in school are more intimate and continuous than those found in most other modern institutions. Many teachers work in the same schools for years, sustaining collegial relationships over their careers. Families with several children can be members of a single school's community for a decade. Powerful personal ties can form when teachers, students, and parents genuinely sense that others really care about them. Extending oneself beyond what is formally required by a job definition or an employment contract—going the extra mile (such as a teacher staying after school to work with a colleague or parent or a principal taking a genuine interest in a teacher's career development)—can be deeply meaningful for the parties involved.

Judgments about role competence also play a role in developing trust. Teachers quietly assess the likelihood of meeting their personal and professional goals when interacting with the principal, just as principals assess how well their teachers will meet the principals' goals for fostering each student's achievement. Every person in the exchange needs to determine whether their colleague has the vision, knowledge, skill, flexibility, and resources necessary to follow through on their intentions and promises.

Finally, perceptions about personal integrity shape judgments about trust. Can others be trusted to keep their word? Likewise, judgments about reliability—making certain the individual will walk the walk and not just talk the talk—is essential to trusting another. We also want to learn whether the other has an ethical perspective that guides their actions: Do they really care about children and their education?

In short, relational trust develops in day-to-day social exchanges. Through their actions, school participants express their sense of obligation toward others, and others come to perceive their intentions. Over time, as people interact and each person's statements and actions meet the others' expectations, trust grows. Even simple contacts, such as daily morning smiles and greetings by name, if successful, can strengthen a person's inclination and capacities for more complex actions later. Increasing trust and productive organizational changes reinforce each other.

Relational Trust Supports Culture Re-Boot

Increasingly, trust is acknowledged as a vital component of well-functioning organizations. When people have confidence in each other's words and actions, trust acts as an efficient lubricant, greasing the way for effective communication and collaboration. Our society provides incentives to behave in ways that are trustworthy, to develop a reputation for trustworthiness, and to collect the benefits of trusting relationships.

Trust is central to school improvement. To be effective and produce high levels of student learning, schools must be cooperative, cohesive, efficient, and well managed. Shared decision making requires administrators to trust the teachers they invite to participate. Trust in teachers is key to the relationships that connect students and their families to schools. Including parents in school government requires trust that they are motivated to work for the common good rather than the narrow interests of their own child. As principals ask teachers to challenge and revise their basic assumptions, beliefs, and instructional practices, teachers need a community of trust to help them learn new skills.

Relational trust provides the space and resources for school culture re-boot because it results in these benefits:

- **Supports open communication**—people with high degrees of trust are more likely to disclose more accurate, relevant, and complete data about school issues. They also are more willing to share their thoughts, feelings, and ideas essential to better identify, diagnose, and correctly solve problems that interfere with student learning.
- **Supports mutual respect about controversial issues**—when trust and mutual respect are high, group members can listen considerately and think calmly during heated conversations about hot topics

or *nondiscussables.*[9] As passionate colleagues' voices grow louder and more excited, listeners can continue to show genuine sensitivity to their colleagues' views, feelings, and hopes—even though the expression's passionate intensity may make listeners feel uncomfortable or they may disagree with what is said. Trust and mutual respect prevents politeness from being used as a cover to engage in veiled actions that undermine the group's goal.

- **Increases commitment**—widespread teacher and parent buy-in on school re-boot efforts occur more readily in schools with strong relational trust. When trust is high, teachers believe they will be supported in revising their thinking and instructional practices, and parents believe the educators are still looking out for their children's safety and learning despite the new ways of doing things.
- **Motivates efforts**—relational trust creates an encouraging energy for taking up the difficult work of school improvement. Reform asks teachers who are already working hard to take on more work as they engage with colleagues in planning, implementing, and evaluating school improvement initiatives. It asks teachers to confront the inevitable conflict that stems from organizational change. Trusting that colleagues share their vision of a better future for all their students—and will work conscientiously with them to make it a reality—provides a powerful catalyst for action.
- **Increases collaboration**—providing real opportunities for teachers to make decisions jointly with principals highlights teachers' competence in contributing valuable knowledge and insights to decision quality—and gives them influence over decisions that affect them. When teachers trust each other, they are more willing to collaborate in a spirit of professional community.
- **Reduces individual vulnerability**—teachers with strong relational trust are able to speak honestly with colleagues about what's working and what's not without seeming judgmental, confused, or weak. Relational trust reduces the risks associated with change— allowing teachers to feel safe to experiment with new practices in the classroom, find occasions to learn from one another in the trial-and-error phase common to learning new behaviors, and begin reaching out to parents.

---

[9]*Nondiscussables* are the elephant in the room, those topics discussed frequently but so filled with anxiety and fear that conversations about them occur only in the parking lot, the restroom, the carpool, or around the dinner table. Nondiscussables may include subjects such as the principal's leadership, underperforming teachers, or how the school makes decisions. The fewer the nondiscussables, the healthier the school. See Barth, R. (2002). The culture builder. *Educational Leadership, 59*(8), 6–11.

- **Increases the zone of acceptance**—paradoxically, even as principals' trust in teachers invites them into shared decision making and joint control of important school issues, so do teachers' increased trust in their principals grant them the authority to make unilateral decisions by which teachers will abide.
- **Enhances school climate and culture**—as a school's climate becomes more open, it reinforces trust. The higher the trust that principals and teachers share, the healthier their interpersonal relationships. Continued over time, the unguarded, respecting, and trusting climate become part of the school's culture—"the way we do things around here"—further sustaining openness, collaboration, shared decision making, continuous learning, and improved practice. Anything less is viewed as a violation of the norm.
- **Improves organizational citizenship**—organizational citizenship describes employees' behaviors when they freely go beyond formally prescribed job requirements and engage in voluntary acts without expecting recognition or reward. These behaviors are more likely to appear when teachers trust their principals. Repeatedly performing in these ways over time makes them part of the school's culture. Likewise, educators who conduct themselves with altruism, courtesy, conscientiousness, sportsmanship, integrity, honesty, and moral behavior display personal qualities essential for healthy work environments but which cannot be written into job descriptions.
- **Fosters higher trust, fewer rules**—when trust is absent, organizations tend to develop more contract specifications, job descriptions, and rules to enforce minimal compliance with expectations. Rules act as safeguards against opportunistic behavior. A plethora of procedures, guidelines, and instructions sends the message to employees that the organization does not trust them to do their jobs well or respect their professionalism. Ironically, such practices further undermine trust and interfere with achieving the goals they were written to serve.
- **Encourages collective efficacy, achievement, and school effectiveness**—over the past two decades, research has offered compelling evidence on the role of trust in school effectiveness and student achievement. The greater the faculty's trust in students and parents, the higher the school achievement in reading and mathematics—even after controlling for socioeconomic status. Teachers' collective sense of efficacy—the extent to which they perceive they can make a positive contribution to student learning—has also been powerfully linked to student achievement.[10]

---

[10]The references that support the relationship between trust in schools and student achievement appear in the Research section toward the end of this chapter.

In sum, the evidence of trust's importance for smoothly functioning, effective schools is sharp and irrefutable. Trust is related to positive school climate, to productive communications, to participative decision making, and to teachers' willingness to go beyond the minimum job and contract requirements. Trust makes a difference in student achievement, teachers' collective efficacy, and overall school effectiveness. In contrast, when trust is absent, organizations substitute rules to keep their members in tow, even when this may be counterproductive to schools' purposes. If schools are to function well, they need relational trust as a foundation for all else.

The processes of school improvement and relational trust development occur together over extended time and actually fuel each other. The higher the relational trust, the greater the efforts to enact and assess school improvement initiatives. In turn, the more small wins in school improvement, the greater the relational trust becomes. With each success, teachers, principals, and parents can look at each other and think, "I knew I could depend on you!" At the same time, as trust grows in schools, so does teachers' work orientation, the school's involvement with parents, and the sense of safety and order that students experience.

Lastly, when the trust among leadership team members is high enough to deal directly and respectfully with the values, beliefs, and assumptions that undergird educators' behaviors, the school climate and culture become more professional. Dissenters gain respect for asking the most important questions, and teachers come to see the benefits of direct conversations to improve their abilities to work with students.

Relational Trust and Student Learning

Relational trust among adults in a school community does not directly affect student learning. It has no impact on curriculum alignment, for example. Rather, relational trust creates the basic social network and school culture within which school professionals, parents, and community leaders can initiate and sustain the essential supports for school improvement. Trust facilitates the school re-boot processes, which in turn makes teachers more effective in generating student learning.

In contrast, the lack of trust can be very damaging to student learning. Without trust, teachers and students engage in self-protective actions. They become increasingly unwilling to take risks. Teachers may withhold information or act deceptively to protect their interests. Administrators and teachers may fall back on rules and contractual agreements to protect themselves. Students, keenly alert to teachers' feelings of discomfort and defensive behaviors, begin to feel unsafe, too. When students feel unsafe, they focus their energies on protecting themselves rather than learning. All these behaviors are counterproductive.

And what is worse: Once distrust takes hold, it tends to grow. Individuals continually view and interpret with suspicion even innocent actions by those they distrust, constantly reconfirming their misgivings. Schools with falling trust experience significant declines in teacher capacity, student-centered learning, and strong parent–school connections essential to effective school functioning.

Developing Relational Trust

Trust is a dynamic phenomenon that has different characteristics at different stages of a relationship. The trust that a novice teacher has for a principal is not as strong as the trust a veteran teacher has for a principal who has been a cooperative and supportive colleague for a dozen years. Several levels of trust appear in schools:

- **Provisional trust**—at the start of a relationship, provisional trust assumes that, because one party wants to keep the relationship going, the other will meet expectations in order to do so. This type of trust may be uneven and vary with the situation. Relationships may remain at this level if continued interactions do not generate increased trust.
- **Knowledge-based trust**—this connection takes hold as individuals get to know each other and begin to feel able to predict how the other is likely to act in a given situation. Ongoing communication; respectful, pleasant exchanges; and keeping one's word help foster this type of trust. This type of trust may be uneven and vary with the situation.
- **Identity-based trust**—a mature relationship builds empathy and strengthens the identification between two individuals. Identity-based trust rests on complete empathy with the other person's wishes and goals so that each can effectively represent the other when that individual is not present. This type of trust tends to be unconditional.

Notably, more trust is not always better. Remember Jim Jones?[11] Trusting too much provides too few incentives to discourage one person from taking advantage of the other and too few costs or unacceptable risks if they do. Meanwhile, trusting too little limits opportunities for people in organizations to show the vulnerability needed to engage in improvement

---

[11]Jim Jones (1931–1978) was founder and leader of the Peoples Temple (located in San Francisco), who in 1978 led 909 temple members in a mass murder and suicide in their Jonestown, Guyana, colony. Members, including more than 200 children, were told to (or forced to) ingest a liquid containing cyanide.

processes. The optimal level of trust depends on the persons, their relationship, and the situation.

Recognizing that trust grows in stages helps school leaders understand that they have a key role in fostering its development. Megan Tschannen-Moran and Wayne Hoy, two educational leadership professors and researchers, have studied trust in schools and find the following common facets of organizational and interpersonal trust.[12] Principals and teachers who want to build and sustain relational trust can look to see if these facets are apparent in their own behaviors—and in those with whom they interact.

Features That Make One Willing to Trust Others

- **Willingness to risk vulnerability**—interdependence means that the interests of one party cannot be achieved without relying upon another. For example, when principals invite teachers to share in decision making, principals risk losing control of the outcome but still remain responsible for it. Where there is no interdependence—and no risk—there is no need for trust.
- **Confidence**—trust depends on the degree of certainty one holds in the face of risk. The degree to which a person can accept uncertainty with some amount of faith is the degree to which that person can be said to trust. Principals must have confidence that teachers will work collaboratively to learn, practice, and use more effective instructional techniques. In turn, teachers must feel confident that principals will not judge them unfairly as they are learning.

Features That Make Others Trustworthy

- **Benevolence**—a belief in the other person's goodwill or kindness that will protect and not harm another's well-being or something one cares about. Teachers must rely on the principal's goodwill as they try out new teaching methods and make inevitable mistakes.
- **Reliability**—the predictability or consistency of a person's behavior that suggests the individual will be generous and compassionate toward another. Given the principal's past behavior, teachers are confident that their needs will be met. Principals who consistently take time to listen to teachers' concerns are considered reliable.
- **Competence**—the other person has sufficient knowledge and skills to perform a given set of tasks to a level that fulfills expectations. Good intentions are not enough. Teachers are rightfully wary of having a

---

[12]Tschannen-Moran, M., & Hoy, W. K. (2000). A multidisciplinary analysis of the nature, meaning, and measurement of trust. *Review of Educational Research, 70*(4), 547–593.

principal observe them for evaluation when they believe that principal does not have a clear knowledge of effective instructional practices.

- **Honesty**—a person's word—verbal or written—can be relied upon as true, accurate, and a commitment to future actions. When principals accept responsibility for their own actions and avoid twisting the truth in order to shift blame to another, it speaks to the principal's character, integrity, and authenticity.
- **Openness**—the extent to which relevant information is not withheld as well as a process by which people make themselves vulnerable to others by sharing personal information. Principals who share complete and accurate information with teachers rather than express the party line, which colors the truth to make the organization—or the principal—look good, are showing openness. Such openness signals a reciprocal trust, a shared confidence that neither the information nor the individual will be exploited.

While all these facets of trust are important, their relative weights depend on the individuals' degree of interdependence and vulnerability in their relationships. For instance, when visiting an eye surgeon about correcting a cataract, the physician's competence is highly significant. We trust the physician to use enough knowledge and skill to keep us from going blind or appearing disfigured. To a different extent, principals trust their teachers to work successfully with all children based on the instructors' competence, reliability, and integrity. Teachers, in contrast, feel more trust for their principal based on the principal's perceived kindness, friendliness, and integrity. Nonetheless, educators consider all aspects of trust—caring, reliability, competence, honesty, and openness—as vital.

Additional Factors That Influence the Inclination to Trust

In addition to willingness and confidence, additional facets affect an individual's bent to develop trusting relationships. Principals have the capacity to influence some—but not all—of these and should consider them when constructing a school leadership team and increasing teacher buy-in to innovations. They include the following:

- **Emotions about the individual they trust**—is the trust based on competence and reliability or another factor that might not be relevant to getting the job done? For instance, a principal may trust a teacher for his or her professional skills even though the principal may not like the teacher personally.

- **Assumed shared values**—if a new principal directly challenges a school's fundamental assumptions and values, teachers may perceive their new leader as operating under such a different world view that feelings of trust may grow more slowly—if at all.
- **Diversity of the group**—people tend to extend trust more readily to those they perceive as similar to themselves. Trust is more difficult to establish in situations of diversity because people are unsure about others' cultural norms and may be biased in favor of those like themselves. Differences may occur in age, gender, class, education, race, ethnicity, disability, or some other factor.
- **Rational calculations of the relative costs**—various factors play into whether to keep or end a relationship. For instance, teachers who serve as union representatives in their buildings may question the principal's benevolence but also expect (trust) that he or she will not act in unprincipled ways because of the threat of initiating a union grievance procedure and facing the ensuing fallout.
- **Institutional factors**—schools may engender trust because all administrators and teachers are required to have licenses or certifications, which serve as quality control in professional practice. Schools also have norms, rules, and regulations that clarify expectations and reinforce trust.

For trust to form, teachers and principals do not need high levels of trust in every aspect of that person's behavior. Instead, educators need confidence only in those areas in which they share a critical interdependence—where people rely on each other and when bad things happen as a result of unmet expectations. Basically, if a person's actions and intentions are perceived as benevolent, that individual can be trusted even if his or her credibility is imperfect. Competence, however, is the bottom line. It would be foolish to trust someone who clearly lacks the knowledge and skills to do the job well. Trust levels need to be appropriate to the context, the persons, and the situation. Likewise, trust needs to be moderated by a willingness to punish exploitive behavior.

Starting, Sustaining, and Repairing Relational Trust

The nature of relational trust changes over time. At first, teachers may trust a principal solely on the basis of his or her higher position in the organization. With months of firsthand experience working together, the individuals get to know each other better, and the relationship deepens. The parties know the other's typical motives and actions. Mutual empathy and understanding grow. Knowledge-based or identity-based trust may develop.

The social context also imposes constraints, values, and penalties that affect the trust relationship. Principals and teachers who typically interact only at school and school events do not have opportunities to see each other as complete people beyond the professional boundaries. In fact, difficulties may arise if they do.

Similarly, trust in relationships ebbs and flows as the individuals decide how to respond to occasions when their expectations for protection and care are not met—and their trust is broken. Do they ignore the breach, seek to fix the relationship, or try to get even?

In work relationships, trust develops in stages: initiating, sustaining, and repairing. Understanding each can help school leaders deliberately work to strengthen trust in their relationships and their school culture.

How Principals Initiate Trust

Research demonstrates that principals can effectively initiate and sustain their faculty's trust when leaders and managers engage in behaviors that communicate consistency, integrity, concern, communication, and sharing control. These actions reflect the broader facets of trust discussed earlier:

- **Consistency**—principals' personal beliefs, organizational goals, and work behaviors must match. Teachers and staff have greater confidence when they feel they can predict their superiors' conduct.
- **Integrity**—principals act in an evenhanded manner, tell the truth, keep their promises, accept responsibility for their actions, and avoid shading the details in order to shift blame to others.
- **Benevolence**—principals show consideration and sensitivity to teachers' and staff's needs and interests, act in ways that protect employees' rights, and do not exploit others for personal or professional gain. Principals gladly apologize for their actions that may have caused teachers, students, or parents unpleasant consequences.[13]
- **Communication**—principals speak accurately and openly, giving teachers adequate explanations and timely feedback. They exchange ideas and thoughts freely with teachers—and they encourage teachers to voice their own ideas and frustrations

---

[13]One story tells of a principal's willingness to apologize for an unfair comment to a teacher was so well known among the school's faculty that it helped to build widespread trust in the principal, even among those who had not received the apology. See Tschannen-Moran, M. (1998). *Trust and collaboration in urban elementary schools.* Unpublished doctoral dissertation, Ohio State University—Columbus.

candidly to the principal (in the appropriate setting, of course), including criticism of the principal's own decisions (without fear of repercussions).

- **Sharing control behaviors**—principals who share control and decision making with teachers increase teachers' perceptions of the principals' trustworthiness and respect for them. Distributed influence gives teachers greater opportunities to express and act upon their interests and allows teachers increased responsiveness to students' needs.

How Teachers Initiate Trust

While principals' behaviors are important to setting the general tone of school trust, teachers' behaviors have a greater impact on the degree to which they trust each other and their influence on student learning. To build trust in their colleagues, teachers want to see other teachers showing these qualities:

- **Benevolence**—when teachers cover each other's classes in emergencies, when they socialize with each other outside school, when they take meals to families experiencing illness, and when they donate sick days to allow a seriously ill colleague more time to recover, they express a caring that generates relational trust.
- **Openness**—when teachers share professional ideas, successful teaching strategies, and materials and equipment in the interest of helping students learn, they build trust among colleagues.
- **Honesty**—when teachers tell the truth, even at risk to themselves (rather than bend the facts to make a colleague look bad), and when they refuse to spread negative gossip about colleagues, they increase others' trust in them.
- **Competence**—especially as teachers are expected to collaborate in school leadership roles and to improve instructional practices that increase student learning, the competence of one's colleagues becomes an increasingly important element of trust.

To strengthen trust in schools, principals and teachers are well advised to reflect honestly on the factors above, which colleagues need to see and hear in order to trust them and strengthen their relationships. In addition, principals and teachers may want to solicit honest feedback from others in their school to see if others actually are seeing them as they wish to be perceived. Asking for such direct and intimate feedback—and thinking about it—are, by themselves, authentic acts that strengthen trust.

Principals and leadership teams can complete School Culture Re-Boots 3.3 and 3.4 in the Resources section of this chapter. Re-Boot 3.3

allows the team to assess their school culture for evidence of trust-promoting behaviors and identify areas in which more trust is needed. Re-Boot 3.4 generates feedback for each leadership member on how well he or she is communicating these facets of trust to others—and how to strengthen trust among team members.

Sustaining Trust

Although principals and teachers have a range of behaviors that they can use to initiate and build trust in relationships, maintaining trust in the schools is more complicated. While certain organizational dynamics—such as the differences in power and authority between principals and teachers—make it difficult to keep high levels of trust in schools, research suggests that principals' and teachers' sensitivity to the following areas can either reinforce or destroy trust:

- **Trust in principal–teacher relationships**—to sustain trust, teachers tend to look for their principal's benevolence, openness, and fairness (especially in relation to the principal's role as a supervisor who evaluates teachers' performance), but principals are more concerned with teachers' competence and reliability.
- **Trust in school attributes**—school leaders can positively shape the school's structure, policy, and culture when they facilitate shared decision making and accountability; encourage parties to interact frequently, face-to-face, in positive ways; and demonstrate caring, support, and concern. For instance, principals routinely walking through the halls, smiling and greeting teachers and students by name, help keep an upbeat learning environment. In contrast, negative gossip or simply bad news spread by word of mouth, e-mail, or the public media can magnify the destructive impact of broken trust and make the school seem an unsafe place.
- **Trust in ongoing cooperative interactions**—when the school culture encourages people to interact in cooperative—rather than competitive—ways and grow strong professional communities, teachers maintain greater trust in their leaders and school.
- **Building collective trust**—trust not only occurs among individuals but also within and among groups. Educators and school staff can develop trust for entire academic departments or work units who continually demonstrate competence, reliability, and caring for others.
- **Reputation**—relationships inside schools tend to be ongoing. Except for newcomers and retirees, people expect to keep interacting with the same people over time. This creates an incentive for individuals to act in ways that develop a reputation for trustworthiness and to benefit

from trusting relationships. Similarly, when a principal or teacher stands in good repute, it is more difficult for a negative event to substantially reduce others' trust in that individual. In contrast, a reputation developed for unfairness, dishonesty, and opportunism is difficult to undo. A network of mutual friends and colleagues further locks in, or reinforces, the trust—or the distrust—among these individuals.

Betraying Trust

Trust is not always justified. Expectations that placing something that one cares about into another person's control are not always met. Accidents happen. People are misused. A trusted person may act in ways that exploit—rather than protect—a colleague's vulnerability. A simple insensitive comment, a broken confidence, a decision that violates the sense of care one expects from another can leave the victim feeling stunned, confused, and angry. Likewise, parents trust that teachers will keep their children safe and learning. When a child is harmed at school, even when the injury is unintended, parents feel let down. In an instant, a trusting relationship can be jeopardized—or destroyed.

Betrayal involves actual behaviors rather than disloyal thoughts. Betrayal is voluntary: The trusted person either lacks the motivation or ability to meet the other's expectations or is motivated to defy them. Betrayal marks the loss of perceived benevolence and integrity, two critical components in trusting relationships.

Trust violations in schools stem from two sources: a damaged sense of civic order (that is, broken rules that govern behavior and what people owe each other in a relationship) or a damaged identity. Broken rules include unkept promises, lying, dodging job responsibilities, stealing ideas or acclaim from others, disclosing private confidences and secrets, and changing the rules after the game is over. Abusive authority, corruption, coercive or threatening behavior, sexual harassment, improper dismissal, and favoritism also violate trust. Principals—and central office administrators—need to use their power wisely if they are to maintain the civic order essential to successful school life.

Damaged identity results from public criticism, incorrect or unfair accusations, blaming other employees for one's personal mistakes, and insults. Students and teachers each feel betrayed when they are victims of unfair or public criticism. Although principals don't enjoy being victims of unjust or public censure, they can rationalize that taking the heat is part of being a strong leader. Principals also have more resources available for correcting any unjust criticism.

Incidents of betrayal can affect how well the school functions. When broken promises lead to lost trust, teachers' performance erodes, and they express more intentions to leave the organization. Likewise, betrayal's effects are long lasting. One study on betrayal in the workplace found that 50 percent of the incidents that participants remembered had occurred more than 20 years earlier, and 25 percent had occurred more than 30 years earlier.[14]

The school's culture can influence the likelihood of betrayals occurring. School norms that stress ethical behaviors and a work environment of openness, trust, and respect discourage abuses of trust. In contrast, schools characterized by competing goals, internal politics and conflict, and shifting coalitions lend themselves to more betrayals.

Sometimes, the school's culture and norms do not match the individual teacher's personal expectations of what a trusting relationship entails. Occasionally, a breach of personal trust is not necessarily unethical or antisocial. Consider the situation in which a teacher inadvertently finds a colleague deliberately taking monies from a school account for personal use and listing the expense under another budget category. The observing teacher must decide whether to disclose (betray) the colleague's indiscretion or act within professional and organizational norms (tell the principal and keep the principal's trust).

SCHOOL CULTURE RE-BOOT 3.2
Reflecting on Incidents of Betrayal in Your School

Betrayal occurs when individuals feel that their trust in another person has been broken. Trust takes a long time to develop but only moments to damage. Sometimes, our insensitive actions can harm a relationship and spoil the trust that two persons share.

1. Individually, think about the examples of betrayal above, and consider times when you might have inadvertently—or deliberately—said or done something that would injure another colleague's trust in you.

2. In pairs, without naming names, tell about a time that you may have betrayed another colleague's trust in you, what happened, how the two of you restored the trust—or didn't—and what you have learned about maintaining trust that you were not fully aware of before. If you could not restore trust, what do you suspect might have prevented it?

3. In the larger group, discuss what you have learned about keeping trust that you were not fully aware of before.

---

[14]Jones, W., & Burdette, M. P. (1994). Betrayal in relationships. In A. Weber & Y. J. Harvey (Eds.), *Perspectives on close relationships* (pp. 243–262). Boston: Allyn & Bacon.

Getting Even

People who feel their trust betrayed are likely to respond in some way. Whether that response leads to restored trust or to more conflict depends on the choices the individuals make. Their perceptions about how the breach occurred are likely to influence their decisions.

For instance, if a teacher feels let down by a colleague who did not attend a scheduled 8 a.m. parent–teacher meeting with an angry mother—but the no-show occurred because the colleague's car broke down on the way to school—the offending action may be perceived to be outside the colleague's control. As a result, the upset teacher chalks it up to "that's life!" and lets it go. But, if the dismayed teacher concludes that the colleague's selfishness or unkindness deliberately caused a betrayal—the absent teacher actually took a personal day and had not planned to attend the meeting at all—the betrayed teacher could easily blame the absent colleague and look for opportunities for payback. The offended teacher may even blame the school secretary or the school as a whole for not informing the present teacher that the absent colleague would not be at the meeting. A cycle of disappointment, reduced trust, revenge taking, further disappointment and anger, and more lost trust may fuel a negative and disruptive cycle.

Revenge behaviors may be emotional and impulsive or rational and deliberate. When the trust is broken between principal and teacher, the betrayed individual may become overly cautious and watchful. He or she may withdraw from any contact with the affronting colleague, may have revenge fantasies, or may try to extract punishment or get even. Betrayed individuals may arrange for private confrontations or seek to restore their reputations. In schools, revenge behaviors occasionally appear as teachers sabotaging each other or the principal, filing union grievances, refusing extra duties, withholding effort, and working to the contract. They may prompt a self-perpetuating cycle of suspicion, competition, and retaliation, which undermines the school's effectiveness. In the best circumstances, however, the aggrieved person may do nothing or offer forgiveness.

Betrayed persons have choices about how to respond to a breach in trust—and this choice gives them some control over if and when they will ever offer their trust again. But, while payback may give its user more power in the immediate situation, it can lead to increased conflict and irreversible harm to themselves and their school.

Repairing Trust

Repairing trust is a challenging and time-consuming process. First, each party must genuinely want to restore the relationship. Without the sincere desire to improve the affiliation—as evidenced in words, actions, and body language—all attempts at trust building will be discounted as phony. Next, each must perceive that the short- or long-term benefits of rebuilding trust are valuable enough to invest the time and energy into healing the break. Then, to rebuild trust, the individuals must engage in a cooperative search for a mutually favorable, win-win solution. Only in this way can they reverse the destructive cycle. But, without at least some modicum of trust, the repair cycle is not likely to begin.

In the real world, overcoming the serious hurt from betrayal is more complex, cognitively and emotionally, than the steps depicted here, but the outline of necessary actions remains the same. To start repairing broken trust, the offending party must take the following steps:

- Recognize and acknowledge that he or she has violated a colleague's trust.
- Determine the nature of the violation, and admit that the violator has caused the break.
- Admit that the act was destructive.
- Accept responsibility for the effects one's actions has caused (and ask for forgiveness).

In turn, the victim can choose one of four alternate courses to repair the trust:

- Refuse to accept any actions, terms, or conditions for restoring the relationship.
- Allow forgiveness, but require unreasonable acts for making amends.
- Allow forgiveness, but identify reasonable acts for making amends.
- Allow forgiveness, and indicate that no further acts of making amends are necessary.

An example of how broken trust may be restored illustrates this point. One afternoon, a new assistant principal asked a French teacher and a student to leave a conference room they were using for tutoring. The assistant principal wanted to use that spot to meet with a school improvement committee and assumed it easier for the single teacher and student to relocate than to redirect an eight-person committee to another location. Although the French teacher and student gracefully left, the assistant principal knew from the teacher's unsmiling expression that she was not pleased. The next morning, the assistant principal went to the French teacher's room during a planning period and apologized. The assistant principal admitted to acting thoughtlessly: The teacher already had the room in use, and the administrator could have found another meeting location. The assistant principal said it would not happen again, and she regretted having inconvenienced and embarrassed the teacher in this way. The French teacher listened, still unsmiling. She agreed that the administrator had not handled yesterday's situation well but accepted the apology. Before the day was over, most of the faculty knew what had happened and were pleased at how it had been resolved. And, the French teacher became one of the assistant principal's strongest advocates.

Acts of making amends—whether reasonable or unreasonable—are usually intended to test the violator's sincerity and commitment to rebuilding the relationship. They show the offending party's willingness to accept a degree of personal loss in the interest of restoring the relationship. At the same time, amends provide the violator with the occasion to work out any guilt over the incident.

Constructive attitudes and actions can help repair broken trust. Trying to understand and accept the other party's interests, attitudes, and beliefs is a good start. Communicating clearly in a conciliatory way with an authentic desire to reestablish trust without sacrificing either party's values or interests—and then carrying it out reliably—helps. Using persuasion rather than coercion also creates a more trusting environment. Give others the benefit of the doubt: Assume that they do not see themselves as bad people seeking immoral ends through illicit means. They usually believe they have a good reason for doing as they do. At the same time, extending blind trust—accepting excuses that seem completely unreasonable given the information available—is ill advised. Rather than advance trust, it strengthens distrust.

If, however, after several attempts to rebuild trust, the other party remains hostile, it is important not to overreact. Honest communications of cooperative intentions foster a better outcome than no attempts to cooperate at all. Although principals have the authority to punish inappropriate behavior, they must use this power carefully if they are to encourage and sustain trust within the school community. If it can be done, restoring trust is the best solution for individuals who must work together—for their own sake, for the school's functioning, and for the children's well-being.

Understanding the dynamic nature of trust is essential in schools. School structure, policies, culture, and the involved individuals' personalities all play significant roles in developing and sustaining trust. With a greater understanding of trust's importance and the costs of distrust, principals and teachers may be more willing to invest the effort to initiate, maintain, and repair trust that has been damaged.

BUILDING RELATIONAL TRUST WITH PARENTS

Parents send schools their children, and they trust educators to keep them safe and learning. Yet, many educators are uncomfortable with parents and have difficulty developing trusting relationships with them. Many parents feel the same way about teachers. Nonetheless, it is essential that educators move beyond their assumptions and discomfort about parents and find ways to build the mutual trust needed to actively support children's learning and achievement.

Sometimes, principals and teachers hold mistaken stereotypes of parents, which limit their abilities to form robust school–home ties. One study found that educators tended to classify parents into one of three groups: committed partners, meddlesome intruders, or distracted absentees.[15] The educators assumed that parents did not become involved because they were either apathetic about their children's education, too lazy to get involved, or both. Or, they were overinvolved *helicopter* parents, constantly hovering over their children's activities, who thought they knew more about education than the teachers.

Unsurprisingly, parents vigorously disagreed with these conclusions. In fact, all the parents strongly valued education, they wanted to help their children with school, they wanted to help the schools, and they wanted to feel comfortable at school activities. Parents were just uncertain of what they were supposed to do. They were, however, sure that they were not always welcomed or listened to in their children's schools. Mutual trust was lacking.

Teachers' trust in students and parents appear related to students' socioeconomic status. The cultural differences associated with poverty seem to negatively influence the social relationships among students, parents, and their teachers. Because trusting relationships are essential to academic achievement, it is especially important to guard against lowered expectations, mistaken assumptions, and reduced trust for these students' capacities for high academic achievement. In fact, trust can foster a milieu that supports student achievement even in high-poverty schools: The higher the trust, the higher the achievement. Similarly, the cultural differences between teachers and highly affluent students can create occasions for misreading parents' desires for their children to have assignments tailored to their personal interests and strengths. Well-to-do parents are not trying to "control" the teacher or tell the teacher how to teach. Rather, they want to help the teacher to keep their children motivated about learning.

---

[15]Smrekar, C. (1966). *The impact of school choice and community: In the interest of families and schools*. Albany: State University of New York Press.

When teachers believe their students are competent and reliable, they create learning conditions that enable students' academic success.

Respect for parents—a deep sensitivity and appreciation of their core beliefs and values, circumstances, needs, ethnic traditions, and hopes for their children—is an essential foundation for gaining parents' trust. Parents want to believe that the school will do what is in their children's best interest, regardless of socioeconomic status, race, ethnicity, gender, religion, or prior school achievement. Trust cannot be required. It must grow in the natural give-and-take of genuine and caring interactions. Only as teachers, principals, and parents can get to know each other as people—such as at school conferences, sports events, school concerts and plays, picnics, and reading groups—can their confidence in each other's concern and truthfulness grow. This takes time and repeated opportunities for meaningful exchanges.

If educators and parents want trusting relationships with each other, they must actively look for or fashion occasions for it to develop. The school's culture should encourage deep ties to the community through interactions, relationships, and activities. Principals need to create occasions for parents and school personnel to talk, listen, tell stories about their children, laugh, and worry together and build relations that last through times of celebration and trial. Too often, schools' typical outreach events, such as back-to-school nights, principal chats, assemblies, newsletters, fundraisers, and parent centers, go through the motions without fostering meaningful parent–school ties or common purpose. Making it part of the school culture to reach out with genuine interest and connect with parents in ways that are meaningful to them as well as to the educators is essential, especially when the community is diverse and collective purposes and approaches to students' learning cannot be assumed.

Trust is a reciprocal process. It must be built throughout the school community by clearly demonstrating teachers' concern for students' well-being and their competence in fostering student learning. In addition, principals and teachers need to be kind, understanding, reliable, open, and honest in their dealings with one another if they are to foster mutual respect and support. Without trust, principals, teachers, and parents actually reduce their opportunities for working together to limit their vulnerability. Without trust, students lose an essential form of social support. Without trust, disengagement from the educational process and reduced student achievement result.

When distrust is rampant in a school culture, it is unlikely that the school will be effective. And, once distrust is established, it is difficult to restore.

Teachers, principals, students, and parents depend on each other. Their interdependence makes them vulnerable and in need of trusting relationships. More than any other factor, a high level of trust provides the foundation for the professional talk, openness, and work needed to re-boot a school culture, improve professional practices, and generate better outcomes for students. As Michael Fullan, the international education scholar and researcher, writes, "High-trust cultures make the extraordinary possible, energizing people and giving them the wherewithal to be successful under enormously demanding conditions—and the confidence that staying the course will pay off."[16]

RESEARCH

Trust and Student Achievement

Bandura, A. (1993). Perceived self-efficacy in cognitive development and functioning. *Educational Psychologist, 28*(2), 117–148.

Bandura, A. (1997). *Self-efficacy: The exercise of control.* New York: Freeman.

Bryk, A. S., & Schneider, B. L. (2002). *Trust in schools: A core resource for improvement.* New York: Russell Sage.

Bryk, A. S., Sebring, P. B., Allensworth, E., Luppescu, S., & Easton, J. Q. (2010). *Organizing schools for improvement: Lessons from Chicago.* Chicago: University of Chicago Press.

Goddard, R. D., Hoy, W. K., & Woolfolk Hoy, A. (2001). Collective teacher efficacy: Its meaning, measure, and impact on student achievement. *American Educational Research Journal, 37*(2) 479–508.

Goddard, R., Tschannen-Moran, M., & Hoy, W. (2001). A multilevel examination of the distribution and effects of teacher trust in students and parents in urban elementary schools. *The Elementary School Journal, 102*(1), 3–17.

Goddard, R. D., Tschannen-Moran, M., & Hoy, W. K. (2002). The relationships of trust to student achievement in urban elementary schools: A multilevel analysis. *Elementary School Journal, 102*(1), 3–17.

Hoy, W. D., Tarter, C. J., & Witkoskie, L. (1992). Faculty trust in colleagues: Linking the principal with school effectiveness. *Journal of Research and Development in Education, 26*(1), 38–45.

Hoy, W. D., & Tschannen-Moran, M. (1999). Five faces of trust: An empirical confirmation in urban elementary schools. *Journal of School Leadership, 9*(3), 184–208.

Tarter, C. J., Sabo, D., & Hoy, W. K. (1995). Middle school climate, faculty trust and effectiveness: A path analysis. *Journal of Research and Development in Education, 29*(1), 41–49.

Tschannen-Moran, M. (2004). *Trust matters: Leadership for successful schools* (1st ed.). San Francisco: Jossey-Bass.

Tschannen-Moran, M., & Hoy, W. K. (2000). A multidisciplinary analysis of the nature, meaning, and measurement of trust. *Review of Educational Research, 70*(4), 547–593.

---

[16]Fullan, M. (2005). *Leadership and sustainability.* Thousand Oaks, CA: Corwin, p. 73.

RESOURCES

SCHOOL CULTURE RE-BOOT 3.3
High-Trust and Low-Trust School Cultures

School cultures can support or discourage relational trust. In this cognitive and affective trust-building activity, teachers and administrators will assess their school's culture of trust on a range of practices and create a respectful environment to share their views. The groups should focus their attention on sharing openly, honestly, and respectfully with each other.

1. In groups of three, discuss what behaviors of trust and respect you would need to see and hear from the others in this room in order for you to honestly and openly express your ideas and feelings about your school and its culture and about what you think is working well and what you think is not. Also, what attitudes and behaviors from colleagues would discourage you from being honest and open?

2. Next, in your small group, review and discuss Table 3.1 and circle or check the box that best reflects how you believe that trust is shown in your school.

3. Briefly give examples of the attitudes, events, or behaviors that led you to your viewpoint.

4. Gather as a whole group. Discuss (and be aware and respectful to each other's ideas and emotions):

   • How easy or uncomfortable was it for you to ask and answer these questions about your school?
   • How easy or uncomfortable was it for you to speak honestly and openly with colleagues about your views?
   • What supportive attitudes and behaviors do you need from your colleagues in this room and in this school that would enable you to think fully and answer honestly and openly about your observations and reactions to subtle yet powerful aspects of your school?
   • What attitudes or behaviors from colleagues would discourage you from being honest and open about your observations and reactions to events in your school and ideas for improvement?
   • What can this group do to make certain that each member receives the necessary supportive behaviors from colleagues, so they may thoughtfully and openly address improving your school?
   • What can you do to make certain that each member receives the necessary supportive behaviors from colleagues, so they may thoughtfully and openly address improving your school?

5. On a scale of 1 to 5 (1 as the lowest score, 5 as the highest), ask the group to rate the school on the extent to which it encourages or discourages relational trust in each dimension in Table 3.1.

6. Which examples were judged as the highest trust-building and school culture-supporting characteristics (scores of 4 and 5)?

7. Which examples were judged as the trust-discouraging school culture characteristics (scores of 1 and 2)?

8. Which examples were judged weak but not encouraging or discouraging school culture characteristics (score of 3)?

9. What do these findings suggest about how well and in what areas your school culture builds and sustains relational trust?

10. Identify the priority order in which you would like to strengthen trust in the areas rated the weaker and weakest, so your leadership team can build and sustain—and perhaps repair—relational trust in your school.

11. Identify what you can do starting now to strengthen relational trust in your school. What can you stop doing now to strengthen relational trust in your school?

Table 3.1 Examples That Build and Sustain or Discourage Relational Trust

Examples That Build and Sustain Relational Trust	Examples That Discourage Relational Trust
Principals invite teacher discussion and input into important decisions that affect them.	Principals make important decisions affecting teachers without getting teacher input.
When principals and other school leaders make mistakes, they admit it and apologize directly to those affected.	When principals and other school leaders make mistakes, they ignore, deny, or blame others for the error.
Principals and teachers give each other the benefit of the doubt.	Principals and teachers are quick to assign blame without getting a full explanation of the circumstances from those involved.
Principals, school leaders, and most teachers are trustworthy, reliable, kind, open, and honest and share teachers' concerns.	Most school leaders or teachers in this school are not trustworthy, reliable, kind, open, or honest and do not share teachers' concerns.
The principal's actions and beliefs are consistent; he or she walks the talk.	The principal's actions and beliefs are not consistent; he or she does not walk the talk.
Principals and school leaders act on their belief that most teachers in the school are competent professionals.	Principals and school leaders do not always act as if most teachers in the school are competent professionals.

(Continued)

Table 3.1 (Continued)

Examples That Build and Sustain Relational Trust	Examples That Discourage Relational Trust
Teachers are confident that they can make any student academically successful and seek to work with students of varied abilities.	Teachers compete to instruct a small group of elite students and discourage others.
The school has an open-access policy toward high-challenge, high-status classes and provides multiple supports to have all enrolled students succeed.	Regular students are discouraged from enrolling in high-challenge, high-status courses.
Teachers are friendly, collegial, and cooperative with other educators throughout the school.	Small teacher cliques are antagonistic to other teacher cliques.
Department and faculty meetings are occasions for group discussion about important school issues.	Department or faculty meetings are occasions for hostile attacks, bickering, or disinterest.
Academic and social innovators are welcomed, encouraged, and supported.	The faculty ridicules those colleagues who suggest or try new ideas to make the school better.
Communication is open, honest, and mutually respectful and flows in all directions.	Mistrust is widespread.
Interpersonal frictions are clarified and resolved privately in mutually satisfying ways.	Faculty and staff gossip about other members.
All teachers like teaching their children and respect and work with parents as partners.	Many teachers express dislike for their students or their parents.
Other examples:	Other examples:

12. Discuss how leadership team members might prepare their own departments or groups to conduct this activity successfully.

SCHOOL CULTURE RE-BOOT 3.4
Assessing and Getting Feedback on Trust-Ability

Principals and teachers need to develop high levels of trust in each other if they are to work together successfully in school culture re-boot and school improvement. This activity requires trust. It gives principals and teacher leaders an opportunity to self-assess on key factors that allow others to trust them—and also gives each individual feedback on how well the rest of the leadership team perceives them as demonstrating these trustworthy qualities. The ultimate goal is for each member to be able to actively show the qualities that generate and sustain trust in their actions at work.

1. Prepare two 3″ × 5″ index cards (or paper sheets) for each individual on the leadership team using the format below:

Name:	High	Medium	Low
Benevolence			
Reliability			
Competence			
Honesty			
Openness			
Integrity			
Sharing control/Teamwork			

Note: *Sharing control* refers to the principal. When considering a teacher, think of *teamwork*.

2. Each member will take two cards and write his or her name on each card.

3. Take a few minutes to assess yourself honestly on these seven dimensions and generate trust, rating yourself as high, medium, or low, marking this assessment on Card 1. Think about occasions when you believe you showed this quality in action within the past month. Keep Card 1 for yourself (confidential).

4. Each member passes Card 2 (blank, except for the teacher's or administrator's name) to the next person on the right. That member will complete Card 2 by placing a check in the column that best describes how well that member perceives the named person has demonstrated each trust dimension in the past month: high, medium, or low. The person filling out the card should think about incidents when he or she saw this quality in action in the person named on the card. Do not sign or initial the card.

(Continued)

(Continued)

5. After a minute, each person passes the completed Card 2 to the next person on the right, who completes the card the same way. Continue completing and passing Card 2 until it is back to the individual to whom it belongs (the named person).

6. Each person will take a few minutes to review silently the feedback received on Card 2 and see what it means to that individual. Then, each member answers the following questions to himself or herself:

   • Do the card owner's perceptions closely match the feedback given by the rest of the leadership team?
   • Does the card owner trust the individuals who gave this feedback to be fair and accurate (to the best of his or her experience)?
   • How much vulnerability did the card owner experience during the activity?
   • Which item rankings are a little off—and which are far off? What does this feedback mean to the card owner?
   • Does this feedback make the card owner feel good or disappointed in his or her ability to communicate trust to others through his or her behaviors?
   • What issues does the feedback suggest the card owner think about and perhaps work to strengthen?

7. After completing the individual reflection (about 5 to 10 minutes), each member will take a turn describing the value of this experience to him or her as a professional and identifying what they plan to do as a result of this experience. These comments must be sincere, but they can be generalities. No one needs to be specific unless they choose to be; and one person's sharing details does not mean that everyone must share details. The goal is for each individual to work on having others perceive their dimensions of trust as always active and perceptible in school interactions—and for each person to do the work needed to make this a reality.

8. As a group, ask and answer: What does this activity tell you about the amount of trust you hold for each other in this leadership group? If it is high, how do you sustain and strengthen it? If it is low, how do you build or repair it?

9. Discuss how leadership team members might prepare their own departments or groups to conduct this activity successfully.

Wayne K. Hoy is the Fawcett Chair and Professor in Educational Administration at Ohio State University. A prolific researcher and writer, Hoy makes his surveys available to education professionals at no fee to help school leaders and school leadership students gain a fuller understanding of the factors that make them effective instructional leaders. If the school leadership team wishes to survey their faculty on trust and related dimensions to use for professional development and school improvement, the following three scales are available from Hoy's website.

The Omnibus T-Scale

This survey, available at no cost from http://www.waynekhoy.com/faculty_trust.html, measures teachers' views on faculty trust (26 questions) using a six-point, Likert-type scale to determine the school's profile on five facets of trust (benevolence, honesty, reliability, competence, and openness) as well as three types of faculty trust: trust in the principal, trust in colleagues, and trust in clients (students and parents).

Examples of statements include the following: Teachers in this school trust the principal; teachers in this school typically look out for each other; and students in this school can be counted on to do their work. The survey is appropriate for elementary or secondary schools.

Reliability and construct validity are high. Teachers complete the survey anonymously. A faculty meeting is recommended as a good time to administer the instrument. It takes less than 10 minutes to complete. Scoring directions are provided, and schools can compare their profiles to those of other schools.

The Organizational Climate Description Questionnaires

This survey, available at no cost from http://www.waynekhoy.com/ocdq-re.html, http://www.waynekhoy.com/ocdq-rm.html, and http://www.waynekhoy.com/ocdq-rs.html, comes in three versions: elementary, middle, and high school (42 questions for elementary, 50 questions for middle, and 34 questions for high schools) using a four-point, Likert-type scale. Teachers and administrators indicate the extent to which each statement characterizes their school. Subtests include supportive principal behavior, directive principal behavior, collegial teacher behavior, intimate teacher behavior, and disengaged teacher behavior.

Examples of survey questions include the following: The principal rules with an iron fist; the principal uses constructive criticism; the principal goes out of his or her way to help teachers; and teachers are proud of their school. The surveys have relatively high reliability and strong construct validity. Teachers complete the survey anonymously. A faculty meeting is recommended as a good time to administer the instrument. It takes less than 10 minutes to complete. Scoring directions are provided. The survey yields six scores, which represent the school's climate profile. Schools can compare their profiles with those of other schools.

Organizational Health Inventory

The Organizational Health Inventory (OHI), available at no cost at http://www.waynekhoy.com/ohi-e.html, http://www.waynekhoy.com/

ohi-m.html, and http://www.waynekhoy.com/ohi-s.html, comes in three versions: elementary, middle, and high school (37 questions for elementary, 50 questions for middle, and 44 questions for high schools) using a four-point, Likert-type scale. Teachers and administrators indicate the extent to which each statement characterizes their school. Subtests include institutional integrity, collegial leadership, resource influence, teacher affiliation, and academic emphasis.

Examples of statements include the following: The principal explores all sides of topics and admits that other opinions exist; teachers in this school like each other; teachers identify with the school; and students respect others who get good grades.

Reliability is relatively high, and construct validity is strong. Scoring directions are provided. Teachers complete the survey anonymously. A faculty meeting is recommended as a good time to administer the instrument. It takes less than 10 minutes to complete. Scoring directions are provided. The survey yields six scores, which represent the school's climate profile. Schools can also compare their profiles with those of other schools.

Developing Professional Capacity for Shared Influence

FOCUS QUESTIONS

- Why should principals develop their teachers' professional capacities for leadership and instruction?
- How does principal leadership affect teachers' professional capacity and student learning?
- What improved school outcomes for teachers, students, and school culture result from increased professional capacity in leadership and instruction?
- What school culture factors support developing professional capacity?
- How can professional learning communities be vehicles for increasing teachers' professional capacities?
- What are the characteristics of effective professional learning communities?

A ccording to Kenneth Leithwood and colleagues, internationally recognized authorities on school leadership, "Leadership serves as a catalyst for unleashing the potential capacities that already exist in the organization."[1] A leader's central task is to help improve employee performance. Because employees' work effectiveness depends on their beliefs, values, motivations, skills, and knowledge—and the conditions in

---

[1]Leithwood, K., Harris, A., & Hopkins, D. (2008). Seven strong claims about successful school leadership. *School Leadership and Management, 28*(1), 27–42 (p. 27).

● 103

which they work—understanding and developing people is a key leadership responsibility. In schools, principals can advance student learning through initiatives directed at fostering the school's—that is, the teachers'—professional capacity in instruction and distributed leadership.

School culture re-boot encourages human resource development and moves schools away from traditional top-down decision making. When principals "mandate" that teachers make instructional changes, teachers may appear to comply. But in reality, they may ignore it and shut their classroom doors. Or, they adapt the new techniques to meet the directive's letter but not its spirit. Resistant teachers may alter their behaviors until they can safely return to their former ways; they don't revise their preferences.

In contrast, re-booted cultures operate through spheres of influence in which consensus replaces much of principals' unilateral decision-making power. In settings of shared authority, peers—not supervisors—persuade colleagues to do things differently. Hiding teaching practices from peers is more difficult. As a result, teachers and principals in a re-booted culture work together, generating a collective ability to do things on behalf of student learning that teachers are not able to do while working alone.

Teaching is already a full-time job, but teachers do not necessarily work at full capacity. Many have time and energy to engage with their schools if their schools provided meaningful opportunities to extend teachers' impact and increase their professional learning. If teachers are to take on additional roles, they need to be able to perform at their best in each role, and each role needs to complement the others in integrated and synergistic ways. To create a milieu that supports teacher growth, principal leadership must help shift the school's culture and structure to better support adult and child learning. All teachers need to expand and refine their instructional practices to successfully engage all students, and potential leaders must be identified and encouraged to take on additional roles within the school.

Or, as Casey Stengel, the legendary Yankee baseball manager, once noted, "Getting good players is easy. Getting 'em to play together is the hard part."

WHY SCHOOLS SHOULD DEVELOP PROFESSIONAL CAPACITY

Because principals as leaders primarily work with and through other people, one of their most important jobs is building the capacity of their administrators, teachers, and staff to effectively enact the important aspects of educating children. *Capacity* is not a term teachers tend to use when thinking about their professional development. Typically, teachers refer to *capacity* when asking how many students or parents the school's auditorium can seat for a band concert or how many people can fit safely into the gym for a basketball game. Lawyers refer to a defendant's mental fitness, or mental *capacity*, to stand trial. In a work context, however, *capacity* is a general term referring to the power, ability, qualifications, or competency to accomplish some particular task.

Professional capacity is the combination of teachers' skills, beliefs, outlooks, and work arrangements that help them share responsibility for student learning and support each other's continuous improvement. *Capacity building* can be understood as helping teachers to acquire the skills and attitudes to learn new and more effective ways of thinking and acting. When principals help teachers develop their instructional and leadership skills, schools increase their organizational capacity.

School culture re-boot requires developing broad-based and skillful teacher participation in the school's work—increasing their capacity. Accomplishing this requires significant teacher and principal collaboration.

Why Principals Build Their Schools' Professional Capacity

Principals build teachers' capacities because principals cannot do it all alone. Principals play leadership, managerial, political, instructional, and symbolic roles in their schools. For one person to be everywhere in a school and do everything well all the time is simply an impossible and unreasonable expectation. Instead, schools need leaders throughout the organization nurturing the commitment for sustainable improvement every day and up close in the ordinary behaviors that make schools run. This means helping teachers develop the willingness, knowledge, and skills to improve their instructional practices and to take on leadership responsibilities. Roland Barth, education author and founder of the Harvard Principals' Center, predicted that the future of public education depends upon the majority of teachers extending their work as educators to the entire school, not just the classroom.[2]

Critics have long claimed that for principals to focus narrowly on instructional leadership in an effort to improve student achievement would be dysfunctional for both the principal and the school. Principals must adjust their leadership to the realities at hand. For instance, the direct involvement in teaching and learning that principals can carry out in small elementary schools—where principals may know the names and reading levels of the schools' 250 students—is clearly an unrealistic possibility for

---

[2]Barth, R. (2001). *The teacher leader.* Providence, RI: The Rhode Island Foundation.

larger schools. In addition, working to improve teaching one teacher at a time—through the observation and evaluation process—is neither efficient nor effective.

At the same time, many secondary school principals have less instructional and curricular expertise than the teachers they supervise. For this reason, teachers are more likely to take instructional advice from classroom colleagues they respect than from their principal. Even if principals had the necessary will and skill to conduct hands-on instructional leadership, they may find that their schools' basic structural and normative conditions work against it.

In short, it is naive to think that principals can carry the burdens of school leadership and school improvement by themselves. Such an approach is not sustainable and does not promote organizational improvement. Instead, if leadership for school improvement is to reach every hallway, it needs to be spread more widely throughout the organization.

Instead, if principals and teachers set up professional learning communities (PLCs) in which teachers work together collaboratively on a regular and frequent basis to build their instructional capacities, principals can monitor their ongoing work. By asking teacher learning teams to submit products that result from their collective inquiry and dialogue—items such as clarifying essential curriculum, developing consistent pacing guides and common assessments, documenting analysis of student results and using these to plan for improved outcomes, naming the students needing extra learning time and help to become proficient and providing a calendar for giving them extra assistance, generating schedules of peer observations on specific pedagogical techniques, and offering evidence of student attainment—principals can generate far more teacher and student learning. At the same time, teachers learn how to direct their own professional growth. Organizing people into teams in which they work together to achieve common goals for which members are mutually answerable is a robust way to promote individual and collective accountability. We will look more closely at PLCs later in this chapter.

While remaining the central agents of change, principals can recognize teachers as essential partners in this process, acknowledge their professionalism, and benefit from their knowledge and skills. In the complex workings of today's schools, principals' success will be determined by their ability to inspire a culture that develops and draws upon their colleagues' resources for improving teaching and learning—by acting as "hero-makers" rather than heroes.[3]

---

[3]Slater, L. (2008). Pathways to building leadership capacity. *Educational Management Administration and Leadership, 36*(1), 55–69 (p. 55).

Capacity Building and Improved School Outcomes

Developing teachers' capacity helps the organization. Teachers possess critical information about their students and how they learn. They have experiences inside and outside the classroom that can significantly contribute to improved student achievement as well as enhanced work life quality. By improving their instructional effectiveness and generating more student learning—and by acting in leadership roles such as lead teachers, instructional coaches, or school improvement team chairs—teachers can reshape their school's goals and culture while retaining ties to their classrooms. In these ways, teachers develop greater legitimacy as leaders, and principals become the leaders of instructional leaders.

Most importantly, a growing body of evidence affirms that teacher capacity building is central to both classroom and school improvement. One of the most congruent findings from recent studies of effective leadership is that authority to lead need not be located in the person of the leader but can be dispersed throughout the school among other people. With the proper development and support, teachers can help improve schools. In fact, research finds that teacher leadership far outweighs principal leadership in school improvement because it has a direct and significant impact on student engagement.

Additionally, focusing on developing human potential opens the door for people to experience the autonomy, job enrichment, achievement opportunities, and affiliation that bring commitment, fulfillment, and satisfaction. Collaborative activities in which individuals lead, learn, and influence others by building on their personal strengths and passions may satisfy higher-level needs and tap greater levels of personal motivation and competence. Also, having leadership roles increases teachers' knowledge and influence over curricular, instructional, and administrative decisions. Job satisfaction results when individuals feel energized and purposeful in their work.

Likewise, enhancing teachers' professional capacity enhances their self-esteem, skills, motivation, commitment, and beliefs about their working environment even as it improves the school's quality. Teacher leadership improves teachers' confidence in their own abilities and teaches them to activate, influence, and encourage other adults. It improves their attitude toward teaching. They become invested in "their" school and its success. Some data suggest that teachers taking on school leadership roles not only leads to higher levels of performance, but it also decreases teacher absenteeism, reduces their alienation, and possibly encourages them to remain in the teaching profession.

Researchers find connections between teachers' emotions, their leadership behaviors, and student learning. A recent synthesis of evidence about the emotions that shape teachers' motivations (levels of commitment, sense of efficacy, morale, job satisfaction, stress, and the like) and the effects on student learning indicates strong effects of teachers' emotions on their practices and strong effects of leadership practices on those emotions.[4] As illustrated in Figure 4.1, when principals build teachers' capacity and adjust the working conditions to support teacher learning, teachers' motivation and commitment grow, and they change their instructional practices in ways that directly influence student achievement.

Figure 4.1 How Principal Leadership Affects Teacher Capacity and Student Learning

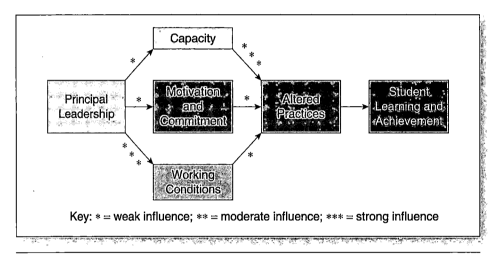

Key: * = weak influence; ** = moderate influence; *** = strong influence

Source: Adapted from Leithwood, K., Harris, A., & Hopkins, D. (2008). Seven strong claims about successful school leadership. *School Leadership and Management, 28*(1), p. 33.

Finally, research highlights that an organization's ability to improve and sustain progress depends on its ability to foster and nurture PLCs, or *communities of practice.* Teacher leadership is central to generating a schoolwide culture where all educators participate in leadership activities and decision making, have a shared sense of purpose, engage in collaborative work, and accept joint responsibilities for their outcomes.[5] Only then can school culture generate and uphold improvements.

[4]Day, C., Stobart, G., Sammons, P., Kington, A., & Gu, Q. (2006). *Variations in teachers' work and lives and their effects on pupils: VITAE Report.* DfES Research Report 743. London: Department for Education and Skills.

[5]Citations for studies that support increasing teachers' capacity having a positive effect on student and school outcomes are listed in the Research section of this chapter.

School Culture Factors That Nurture Professional Capacity

Generally speaking, teachers will not want to take on additional responsibilities unless their school culture supports these endeavors and encourages shared learning opportunities to build knowledge and use skills. Schools whose culture actively assists distributed leadership and organizational learning share the following norms:

• **Supportive and knowledgeable leadership**—the most important thing school leaders can do is to create the conditions that foster professional community. Encouraging and respecting teachers as learners include letting teachers know that they have the expertise to make student learning happen—if they work together and keep their knowledge and skills fresh through collective study, practice, feedback, and reflection. It also helps to provide teacher teams with effective facilitators and adequate support.

• **Unity of purpose**—principals and teachers develop a sense of common purpose and values and a collective sense of responsibility for all students. They agree on their priorities, share norms about practice, and hold each other accountable for results. Improving pedagogy by gaining and using new knowledge and skills is a professional obligation; becoming a great teacher is a career-long endeavor.

• **Trust and respect**—healthy professional communities are safe places in which to examine practices, voice disagreements, take risks, try new ideas, and acknowledge mistakes. Teachers are willing to risk a public display of their practice and thinking and can speak to each other frankly about the core issues of school improvement. Teachers feel honored for their expertise, are ready to share their resources, and are willing to engage in respectful disagreement to identify and resolve difficulties.

• **Focus on learning**—all school activities are clearly directed toward improving student outcomes. All teachers share ideas and resources about how to best generate student learning. Classroom practice is public; teachers and administrators routinely visit classrooms and provide specific and timely feedback to colleagues about instructional improvements. Everyone understands and discloses measures of student progress.

• **Collaboration and sharing**—a strong professional community encourages collective actions, values mutual aid rather than isolated, individual efforts and privacy, and shares responsibility for instructional improvement. The focus is always on how this activity helps students learn. Establishing group norms—such as coming prepared for meetings, no *bird-walking* (sticking to the topic or task), and *honoring the time* (being prompt and present, physically and mentally)—helps members believe that they are using their time meaningfully and ensuring all voices are heard.

• **Varied perspectives welcome**—the school culture supports principals and teachers sharing leadership roles and appreciates diverse ways of thinking about problems. Respectful disagreements stimulate better solutions. Individuals' contributions may vary—some mentoring, others coaching or collecting and analyzing data, a few in formal governance roles—but each promotes shared success. Collegiality is authentic and beneficial to teachers and students.

• **Continuous improvement**—principals and teachers expect to renew their knowledge and skills through up-to-date study and practice. Reviewing current research and exemplary approaches is essential. Taking risks and trying new ideas are encouraged and expected. Mistakes in the search for improved teaching and leadership are viewed as learning opportunities. Colleagues continually prompt each other to examine and improve what they are doing.

Re-booting culture to build professional capacity dismantles the traditional school culture of parallel "egg crates" in which teachers were interchangeable parts in a larger organization, and principals made unilateral decisions. Instead, principals and teachers build a climate of trust, mutual respect, and collegiality in which they share a common purpose and collective responsibility for all students' achievement. Professional learning and increased competencies in instruction and leadership are ongoing concerns focused on improving outcomes for all students.

BUILDING TEACHERS' INSTRUCTIONAL CAPACITY

Because a school's purpose is to educate all children—and children in today's schools are more diverse in backgrounds and learning needs than ever before—improving teachers' instructional capacities has big payoffs for student success. Researchers, principals, and parents alike agree that teachers' effectiveness is the most important school factor in student learning.

Keeping teachers' competencies in sync with preparing students for today's fast-paced, information-rich world is essential. The knowledge and skills needed for employment in the 21st century require teachers to develop new ways of organizing and presenting curriculum and instruction—and new ways of engaging students in learning. If our students are to keep pace with those national and international peers who will vie with them for tomorrow's best employment opportunities, their teachers must keep up, too.

Teaching Quality and Student Achievement

Teaching quality matters. Aside from a well-articulated curriculum and a safe and orderly environment, the individual teacher is the most influential school factor in student learning. Consistently working with highly effective teachers can overcome the academic limitations placed on students by their family backgrounds. And, successful teaching experiences count. With a few years of successful classroom experience in which teachers continually reflect on their effectiveness and refine their practice, they can boost their students' learning more than colleagues without this experience.

The long-term outcomes of having high-quality teachers are also positive. A 2012 National Bureau of Economic Research study finds that adults who had high-quality teachers when they were students were more likely to attend college and have increased their cumulative earning potential.[6] In contrast, consistently working with weak teachers can keep students from making academic—and earnings—gains.

While teachers' knowledge of their subjects' content and strong verbal skills have been linked to higher student achievement, they are not enough to create an effective teacher. Both evidence and experience show that effective teaching requires a set of professional practices different from but connected to the content taught. Teachers who clearly understand the learning process and who adapt their instructional behaviors accordingly have students who learn more. Teachers who show they care about their students as individuals by understanding their backgrounds, interests, and learning preferences and who use these insights to motivate students' efforts have students who learn more. When teachers systematically study how students learn and develop more effective instructional behaviors, their students' achievement increases. And, regardless of how much content teachers know, those who cannot effectively manage their classrooms and provide safe and supportive learning environments have students who learn less than their peers.

Pedagogy matters. Research and experience confirm that knowing how to teach content to students with a range of backgrounds, interests, motivations, prior knowledge, and future goals is what makes a measurable impact on student achievement.

Teaching 21st-Century Skills

Throughout most of human history, people lived and organized their lives around limits of geography, family and kinship, community, religions,

---

[6]Chetty, R., Friedman, J. N., & Rockoff, J. E. (2012). *The long-term impacts of teachers: Teacher value-added and student outcomes in adulthood.* NBER Working Paper No. 17699. National Bureau of Economic Research. Retrieved September 15, 2012, from http://www.nber.org/papers/w17699

and local worldviews. Most never traveled—or spoke with others who lived—more than a few miles from where they were born. This is no longer true. Today's world is global, not local, and our understanding of what it means to be educated is changing. Today, youth grow up linked to economic realities, social processes, technology and media practices, and cultural movements that spill over regional and national borders. As a result, education's challenge has become one of shaping the cognitive skills, interpersonal sensibilities, and cultural awareness of children and youth whose lives will be engaged in both neighborhood and transnational settings.

Technology is visibly changing the workplace, connecting people together in virtual environments. Thanks to computer networks, people no longer have to sit in adjoining cubicles to work together. Standardized protocols can now connect everyone's machines. Software applications encourage the development of standardized business processes for how certain kinds of commerce or work will be conducted, allowing people in Mumbai, India, and Raleigh, North Carolina, to work together seamlessly.

Globalization—the trend of de-territorializing skills and competencies so that people working anywhere in the world can collaborate with those working elsewhere—affects what students worldwide need to know and be able to do. Learning that enables students to develop high levels of knowledge and skills and the ability to use them flexibly to solve real-world problems is a necessary condition for obtaining well-paying employment when—or where—students are ready to join the workforce.

We do not know what the world will be like in 5 years, let alone in 60 years when today's kindergartners retire. We do know that our economy is generating fewer jobs in which workers engage in repetitive, assembly line-type tasks throughout their day and more information-rich jobs that challenge employees with novel problems that require critical analysis, resourceful problem solving, and teamwork.

To be successful in the 21st century, our students will need more than a factory-model education based on the needs of Industrial Age employers. Through the late 19th and early 20th centuries, good preparation for factory employment meant school children sat and listened while teachers stood and delivered textbook lessons. Students changed classrooms to ringing bells. Today, companies have altered how they organize and do business. Workers have more responsibility and contribute more to productivity and innovation. Advanced economies, groundbreaking industries and firms, and high-growth jobs require more-educated workers with the ability to respond flexibly and knowledgeably to complex problems, communicate effectively, manage information, work in teams, and produce new knowledge. Many of these workers can work in any country with Internet connectivity.

To move confidently into this economic and social milieu, students need a broader and deeper array of knowledge and skills, and the capacity to apply their learning to solve real-world problems, such as the following:

- **Deep understanding of core subject matter**—knowing the facts and how they fit together
- **Critical thinking**—solving complex, open-ended problems and making judgments tied to content
- **Collaboration**—with peers, teams, and experts across several networks
- **Cognitive flexibility and adaptability**—to use information and skills in new ways and to adjust oneself to new realities, new roles, and lifelong learning
- **Effective oral and written communication**—interacting competently and respectfully with others across cultural and geographic boundaries
- **Accessing and analyzing information**—to find necessary resources, critique their accuracy and value, make reasoned decisions, and take purposeful action
- **Curiosity, imagination, and creativity**—thinking outside the box to design new and better solutions
- **Initiative and entrepreneurialism**—making well-reasoned decisions and taking action

These are not habits of mind or skills that students can learn by sitting passively at their desks listening to teacher lectures within their four classroom walls.

Twenty-first-century teaching also will include certain nonnegotiables: high-quality curricula with clear goals and that students find relevant and meaningful, the capacity to diagnose and remedy student learning needs, the use of data to monitor and provide feedback on student learning, the ability to recognize when an instructional technique isn't working and adjust it to fit the student, and an environment that challenges and supports students.

Increasingly, 21st-century students will be assessed on what they can do with what they have learned—how they can solve actual problems and what fresh knowledge they can produce—rather than on what they can memorize and recall or by accumulated seat time. Teachers' expectations for all students' learning will be high. Lessons will include occasions for students to analyze, synthesize, evaluate, and create rather than merely comprehend information or practice context-free skills. Students will be actively involved in making choices about study topics and projects rather than on receiving teachers' accumulated wisdom.

Likewise, 21st-century students will work collaboratively with classmates—on-site and around the world—rather than alone at their desks. The curriculum will be thematic, interdisciplinary, and project-based as it is in authentic situations rather than artificially fragmented into separate departments. Literacy will expand from the three Rs to the multiple communications platforms now available. Learning and assessments will include student performances, projects, and many forms of media rather than relying primarily on textbooks and standardized tests.

Our nation's governors are supporting this effort. In March 2010, the National Governors' Association released the Common Core State Standards blueprints, giving K–12 schools a clear and consistent framework about what students are expected to learn in English language arts and mathematics to prepare them for college and the workforce regardless of where they live. Standards include rigorous academic content, comprehension of information-rich text in varied disciplines, and application of knowledge in authentic situations using critical and creative thinking, collaboration, problem solving, research, inquiry, and presentation and demonstration skills. To ensure that all students will be prepared to succeed in a global economy and transnational society, the standards are evidence based and informed by other top-performing countries. As of late 2012, 46 states and the District of Columbia have adopted these standards.

Some wonder, however, whether teachers will be able to make profound changes needed in how they teach. Will they be able to create the dynamic, engaging, high-level learning experiences for students necessary to successfully meet these standards? Basically, teachers will have to reframe their roles from information provider to inquiry facilitator. They will have to know more content and use it more flexibly. Recent reports from the Bill & Melinda Gates Foundation and Consortium on Chicago School Research find that, although many teachers score well on procedural tasks like planning and behavior management, they perform relatively low on things like analysis and problem solving, using investigation or problem-solving approaches, student participation in making meaning and reasoning, and relevance to history and current events.[7] The Chicago study also found that principals were not much better at using these techniques than teachers.

To sum, the concept and practice of 21st-century education will need to be different from the one most teachers experienced earlier in their

---

[7]Sawchick, S. (2012, February 22). The challenge of teaching higher-order skills. *Education Week, 31*(21),12.

education careers. Many teachers will have to learn how to teach very differently than they were taught. This will not be easy. Clearly, to effectively teach students how to use higher-order thinking and meaning making, teachers and principals will have to be able to do it themselves: They will become lifelong learners. The academic and cognitive demands on both educators and students will be substantial. Making this shift successfully will require a majority of schools to undergo a culture re-boot.

Meeting 21st-Century Teaching Standards

If teachers are to ensure that every K–12 student will become a high school graduate ready to enter college or the 21st-century workforce, all teachers need to know and be able to perform those common teaching principles and foundations that cut across all subject areas and grade levels and that are essential to improve student achievement. Professionally, what veteran and novice teachers know and do differs only in their degree of sophistication. A conceptual model that engages learners and enables them to take ownership of their own learning, emphasizes the learning of content and application of knowledge and skill to real-world problems, and values the differences each learner brings to the learning experience exists. Using this model as a benchmark for assessing, building, and refining K–12 teachers' classroom skills and establishing a collaborative culture can boost their instructional—and leadership—capacities.

The Interstate New Teacher Assessment and Support Consortium's (InTASC) Standards for licensing new teachers, updated in 2011, represent the common core of teaching knowledge, skills, dispositions, and behaviors that will help students learn the high-level capacities needed for a knowledge-based, global economy.[8] These standards include the essence of what effective teachers need to know and do. Areas of professional knowledge and skill include learner development, learning differences, learning environments, content knowledge, application of knowledge, assessment, planning for instruction, instructional strategies, professional learning and ethical practice, and leadership and collaboration.

Compatible with other national and state standards—including the National Board for Professional Teaching Standards (NBPTS), our highest recognition of teaching excellence—the InTASC standards are relevant to all teachers regardless of their years in the classroom. School Culture Re-Boot 4.1 describes these standards and allows educators to assess themselves on these dimensions. The resulting discussions can help identify areas for growing a school's instructional and leadership capacities.

[8]Council of Chief State School Officers. (2011, April). *InTASC model core teaching standards. A resource for state dialogue.* Washington, DC: Author.

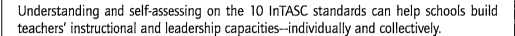

SCHOOL RE-BOOT 4.1
Assessing Your Capacity for 21st-Century Teaching

Understanding and self-assessing on the 10 InTASC standards can help schools build teachers' instructional and leadership capacities—individually and collectively.

Resources: Two sticky notes for each person and a large classroom board for writing. Each member should have a copy of the standards table (below) to use as a reference and worksheet.

1. As group, read each standard. Discuss examples of what each standard looks and sounds like if practiced effectively in the classroom—and what each looks and sounds like if not practiced effectively. Members can write key words next to each standard on their copies to help them remember what they mean in their classrooms.

2. After the discussion, take a few minutes for individuals to self-assess on each standard, finding examples from one's own classroom practice within the past two weeks as evidence that it is (or is not) a regular practice. Also reflect on each teacher's core beliefs about teaching and learning.

3. Reconvene as a large group. Write each standard number and its two-word descriptor on the board. Pass out two sticky notes to each person. Each person writes "Need More" on one note and "Strong" on the other. Have each member place the "Need More" sticky note next to the standard in which they would like professional development and the "Strong" sticky note next to the standard in which they believe they already have effective and frequently used skills.

4. Count the "Strongs" and the "Need Mores." Rank the top three "Strong" areas in which the team believes they are most effective and those "Need More" areas that should become the first focus for professional development. It may help to prioritize the professional development targets.

5. Discuss:

- What are the school's strengths in instructional and leadership capacities?
- What are the areas needing growth?
- What are the core beliefs about teaching and learning that this leadership group holds?
- How do these fit with the school's identified strengths in instructional and leadership capacities?
- How accurately do these findings reflect the skill sets of all teachers in the school?
- How would this group conduct this or a similar activity within each academic department to get a more accurate assessment?

Self-Assessment Key: **N** = needs improvement; **H** = high-level knowledge and skill		
InTASC Standard	*Looks, Sounds Like*	*Self-Assessment*
Standard #1: Learner Development The teacher understands how learners grow and develop, recognizing that patterns of learning and development vary individually within and across the cognitive, linguistic, social, emotional, and physical areas, and designs and implements developmentally appropriate and challenging learning experiences.		
Standard #2: Learning Differences The teacher uses understanding of individual differences and diverse cultures and communities to ensure inclusive learning environments that enable each learner to meet high standards.		
Standard #3: Learning Environments The teacher works with others to create environments that support individual and collaborative learning and that encourage positive social interaction, active engagement in learning, and self-motivation.		
Standard #4: Content Knowledge The teacher understands the central concepts, tools of inquiry, and structures of the discipline(s) he or she teaches and creates learning experiences that make the discipline accessible and meaningful for learners to assure mastery of the content.		
Standard #5: Application of Content The teacher understands how to connect concepts and use differing perspectives to engage learners in critical thinking, creativity, and collaborative problem solving related to authentic local and global issues.		
Standard #6: Assessment The teacher understands and uses multiple methods of assessment to engage learners in their own growth, to monitor learner progress, and to guide the teacher's and learner's decision making.		

(Continued)

(Continued)

InTASC Standard	Looks, Sounds Like	Self-Assessment
Standard #7: Planning for Instruction The teacher plans instruction that supports every student in meeting rigorous learning goals by drawing upon knowledge of content areas, curriculum, cross-disciplinary skills, and pedagogy, as well as knowledge of learners and the community context.		
Standard #8: Instructional Strategies The teacher understands and uses a variety of instructional strategies to encourage learners to develop deep understandings of content areas and their connections and to build skills to apply knowledge in meaningful ways.		
Standard #9: Professional Learning and Ethical Practice The teacher engages in ongoing professional learning and uses evidence to continually evaluate his or her practice, particularly the effects of his or her choices and actions on others (learners, families, other professionals, and the community), and adapts practice to meet the needs of each learner.		
Standard #10: Leadership and Collaboration The teacher seeks appropriate leadership roles and opportunities to take responsibility for student learning, to collaborate with learners, families, colleagues, other school professionals, and community members to ensure learner growth, and to advance the profession.		

Principals, too, have professional capacity building to do. Effective instructional leadership requires that principals develop their own knowledge and skills about student and teacher learning. Principals must know and understand, for instance, the principles of learning theory and curriculum. They must be able to analyze instruction and provide timely, clear formative and summative feedback to teachers. In addition, principals must be able to articulate high standards for student learning and support teachers' innovations to reach these standards. Principals' work should be routinely guided by a steady focus on evidence of student learning gathered through data reports and recurring classroom visits. The bottom line for principals should be, "What is working and what is not working—and why?"

Professional Learning Communities

Research finds that the most useful professional development emphasizes active teaching, assessing, observing, and reflecting rather than abstract discussions. Collaborative and collegial learning environments—a PLC—can build a critical mass of enhanced practice that extends beyond the individual classroom.

A *PLC* is systematic process in which teachers work together and engage in continual dialogue to analyze and improve their classroom practice. Taking individual and collective responsibility to improve every child's learning, teachers work in teams to develop norms and protocols to clarify expectations about their roles, responsibilities, and relationships. Together, they engage in an ongoing cycle of questions about their students' work and develop more effective instructional approaches. Teachers focus on strengthening the school's instructional guidance system[9] through a process of critical dialog about issues such as these:

- What is and is not happening in our classrooms?
- How do we know that something is actually working?
- How will we know when each student has learned?
- What do we do when our students don't learn?
- Are there other practices that might work better?

Deep team learning and higher levels of student achievement result.

What Professional Learning Communities Do

PLCs have certain attributes and conduct a variety of collaborative, job-embedded professional learning activities that can improve teaching practice and student achievement. These include the following:

- **Collaborative teams**—with a focus on student learning, teachers work together interdependently to achieve common goals. Each team member has access to the entire team's ideas, materials, techniques, and talents. They regularly visit one another's classrooms and provide feedback and assistance. Observers may use protocols to structure their

---

[9]Bryk, A. S., Sebring, P.B., Allensworth, E., Luppescu, S., & Easton, J. Q. (2010). *Organizing for school improvement. Lessons from Chicago.* Chicago: University of Chicago Press, pp. 55–56.

observations and comments. Teachers may videorecord their teaching to make aspects of their practice open to peer review, to analyze aspects of their practice that are difficult to assess on the fly, and to try out and refine new strategies. Research has found that building collective—rather than simply individual—capacity can change teachers' practices, knowledge, and effectiveness and provide organizational growth.

• **Collective inquiry**—teachers analyze student work together to determine the current reality and the best practices around their students' existing achievement levels. Teachers have opportunities to develop a common understanding of what high-quality work is and looks like, what common misconceptions students have, and which instructional strategies are—or are not—working. Likewise, PLC teams turn data into useful information to pinpoint what students need and inform future instruction.

• **Action orientation and experimentation**—teachers accept that they may need to do things differently if they want different (improved) results. Engagement and experimentation are valued ways to reach new awareness and achieve meaningful learning.

• **Continuous improvement**—ongoing inquiry about what's working and what's not, frequently using common assessments and student work, to identify instructional strengths and remedy weaknesses, and refining teaching practices to generate more student learning build teachers' instructional capacities. Innovation and experimentation to increase student learning become "the way we do business." Change occurs as teachers learn to describe, discuss, and adjust their practices according to the collectively held standard of teaching quality and successful student outcomes.

• **Focus on results**—PLC members realize that everything they do must be judged by their outcomes rather than their intentions. All initiatives are linked with ongoing assessments tied to school and district goals and based on concrete, timely, relevant, and user-friendly feedback about student learning. In turn, these findings drive new initiatives in a spiraling circle of continuous improvement.

• **Study groups**—when teachers in PLCs study educational practices and research together, they make new strategies and concepts visible by trying out new ideas. Teachers can use what they learn in study groups to improve assessment practices, raise expectations for traditionally underperforming students, and design curricula that students find engaging and relevant. Teams also generate products that reflect their learning focus, such as lists of essential outcomes, different kinds of assessments, analyses of student achievement, and strategies for improving results.

Learning in PLCs occurs in four related ways. First, teachers gain new ideas by reading and discussing books or articles, viewing instructional and locally produced videos of colleagues' teaching, personally observing effective classroom practice, or receiving expert presentations in an area of interest. Second, teachers transfer this information to their own settings by preparing lessons, materials, activities, and assessments to use with their students. Third, PLC members observe and reflect on the effects of student learning, asking themselves, What worked? What is the evidence? What do I need to learn more about? Fourth, PLC members meet with others to discuss, problem solve, and create. They share what they learned, what they tried, what they observed, what happened with students, and what they might want to fine-tune for further use. The results are changed teacher behaviors that lead to greater student learning.

Why Professional Learning Communities Work

PLCs build teachers' instructional capacity because they recognize and take advantage of the complex nature of teachers' classroom involvement. The PLC places teachers within a common instructional system where analysis of evidence from shared practices provides a common ground for honing and improving instructional behaviors. Teachers are committed to transforming the learning that is responsible for results. They value each other as people in relationships of care, respect, and challenge. They use quantifiable evidence and shared experience to probe into teaching and learning issues and make judgments about how to improve them. Perhaps as important, the same teacher who easily dismisses a principal's recommendation to include a new instructional strategy cannot as easily discount repeated evidence that his or her students are not being as successful as their peers in learning the knowledge and skills the teacher agreed were essential and as measured on multiple assessments that he or she agreed were valid.

In turn, the PLC's efforts and outcomes further strengthen the school culture's norms about individual and collective responsibility for educating every child and the continuous improvement of teachers' professional capacity. Both individual and collective growth ensue, and the PLC becomes a significant resource to individual teachers'—and their students'—learning and improvement.

School Culture Supports for Professional Learning Communities

Despite their obvious benefits to teachers and students, creating effective PLCs requires time, trust, and learning. These factors can be strengthened with the school culture re-boot factors already discussed as well as with these additional culture supports:

- **"Our kids," not "My kids"**—PLCs expand teachers' responsibilities from "my kids" to "our kids." Teachers share, observe, and discuss one another's practices on a near-daily basis and collaborate to find and use the most effective instructional practices and common assessments essential for teachers' own learning.

- **Open and reflective dialogue**—members continually talk to each other openly and thoughtfully about their situations and challenges, their subject contents, the nature of adult learning, and their own thinking. Sharing weaknesses creates opportunities for building strengths.

- **Community renewal**—a vibrant PLC reinforces community and membership with ceremonies, symbols, and celebrations. Participants celebrate important professional events and socialize new members into the desired culture. Teachers feel supported, valued, and respected for their professional contributions and effectiveness.

Collaborative school cultures are associated with increased student success and improved retention among new teachers. Ironically, while the teachers' collective capacity depends on the quality of the staff recruited into a school, a school with strong PLCs becomes an attractive place for teachers to work. In turn, this strengthens the school's ability to recruit and keep such quality faculty—a virtuous circle, indeed.

Getting Professional Learning Communities Started

Effective PLCs do not develop overnight, and no one size fits all. Building a strong and effective PLC may take months or years. Early meetings are often slow and filled with tensions and conflicts, silences and misunderstandings. Each group will have its unique characteristics. Persistently working through these challenges by accepting shared responsibility for individual growth, creating small-step opportunities to develop trust and negotiate values and beliefs about teaching and learning, evolving a group identity and norms of interaction, and productively using differing viewpoints will lead to positive outcomes for teachers and students.

Then, too, PLCs benefit from up-front and ongoing planning. It helps to start by choosing content anchored on a foundation of research that supports instructional effects on learning and translates it into everyday classroom practice. Likewise, it helps to find curricular materials that are teacher friendly and suitable to use in a learning team model of professional development. Also, surveying all the programs or practices that teachers are being asked to learn—and then paring down the targets to those that directly impact student learning (and for which teachers have the time to learn, practice, discuss, reflect, and retry) and the resources available—are essential. Teachers must clearly and realistically define their scope of learning for a semester, a year, and beyond in a multiyear time-frame. Covering a lot of material does not equal learning, even for teach-ers. Similarly, communicating clear expectations for PLC members' responsibilities for learning to occur inside and outside meetings is critical.

Education leaders can support PLCs in varied ways. Superintendents can alter the yearly and daily school calendars to provide dedicated time for pro-fessional learning and teacher collaboration on a continuing basis. They need to provide the interactive technologies to support capacity building across media platforms and geography. Principals need to provide PLCs with unin-terrupted time—such as with common planning periods or release time—to meet together during the workday and workweek, so they can collaborate and learn on a regular basis. Principals can also meet with PLC leaders and facilitators regularly to understand what their teams are doing, plan together for team activities, and identify topics for professional development. Likewise, leaders can provide articles, videos, taping equipment, or other resources to support team learning. Providing these collegial growth opportunities and resources is still the exception in U.S. schools, however, because most U.S. teachers' days are spent directly teaching students.

SCHOOL CULTURE RE-BOOT 4.2
Identifying Areas for Instructional Improvements

Identifying areas for instructional improvements is an essential step in deciding on a focus for PLC activities.

1. As a group, read the list of common problems of practice. Discuss what a teacher might see and hear if he or she walked into any classroom and answered "Yes" or "No" to each question—or provide a short answer when indicated.

"Yes" or "No":

- Are students engaged in high-level (analysis, synthesis, evaluation, and creativity) or low-level tasks (recognition and recall)?
- Do teachers frequently ask high-level or low-level questions?
- Do teachers enact a high-level curriculum in a low-level way?
- Are students able to transfer learning from one content area or grade level to another?

(Continued)

(Continued)

- Are some students—such as students with special needs, English language learners, students from minority groups, boys and girls—performing as well as they might? If no, what does this look like in the classroom?
- Do teachers do most of the talking and thinking in the classroom?

Short Answer:

- Which students get opportunities to engage in cognitively ambitious tasks?
- To what extent are teachers explicitly making the curriculum relevant and personally meaningful to all students? Which students would agree—or disagree—with your answer?
- To what extent is student understanding in mathematics conceptual or only procedural?
- To what extent are teachers explicitly teaching all students to read with comprehension dense informational text in English language arts, history and social studies, and science? To what extent are the students succeeding? What do teachers do with students who are not succeeding?
- To what extent are teachers explicitly teaching all students able to integrate their knowledge and skill and apply their learning to critical thinking and problem solving? How often are most students using these skills to complete their assignments? Which students would agree—or disagree—with your answer?
- To what extent are teachers explicitly teaching all students developing skills to express their thinking in effective oral and written communication? How often are students using these skills to complete their assignments? Which students would agree—or disagree—with your answer?
- To what extent are teachers explicitly teaching all students to develop skills in accessing and analyzing information? How often are students using these skills to complete their assignments? Which students would agree—or disagree—with your answer?
- To what extent are teachers giving students opportunities for self-direction on open-ended, complex, sustained, highly challenging, cognitive performance tasks? Which students are not receiving such learning opportunities? Which students would agree—or disagree—with your answer?
- To what extent are teachers giving students opportunities to do work that is interesting and valuable to them? Which students would agree—or disagree—with your answer?
- To what extent are teachers giving all students occasions to learn to persist, to think flexibly, to be comfortable with ambiguity, to manage their time well, and to accept setbacks as learning opportunities? Which students would agree—or disagree—with your answer?
- To what extent are teachers giving students increased responsibility for more intellectually rigorous tasks and their own learning and growth? Which students would agree—or disagree—with your answer?

- To what extent are teachers explicitly teaching students to collaborate effectively in teams to learn and produce learning projects together? Which students would agree—or disagree—with your answer?
- To what extent are teachers explicitly teaching students how to use technology to increase their learning and their demonstration of their learning? Which students would agree—or disagree—with your answer?
- To what extent are most students active or passive participants in class?
- How do teachers know what students know?
- How do students know the quality of their work?
- What role do students play in assessment?
- How do students talk with one another about classwork?

2. Individually, reflect on your own classes for the "Yes" and "No" questions. Can you answer yes to each question above? If yes, does the behavior appear several times each week?

3. Individually, reflect on your own classes for the short answer questions. Can you say these conditions reflect your classroom at least half or more of the time? What would you need to help you learn how to teach in this manner better or more often?

4. Discuss which of the above teaching practices are realistic—or unrealistic—for your students, and why. What do you see as the learning curve between where you are now and where you would like to be?

5. How do you think teachers in the separate departments would answer these questions? What do you think would be their priorities for improving their professional skills?

6. What can your school do to help you make your teaching 21st-century relevant?

7. Discuss findings as a basis for future planning. How would you prioritize professional development for the desired instructional practices over the next 3 to 5 years?

8. Consider inviting a trusted colleague to observe your class and give you feedback about areas in which you appear effective and areas in which you may need additional work.

9. Consider using this survey within each school department to increase faculty awareness of the pedagogical skills necessary for 21st-century teaching, to let them assess themselves against them, and to gain the faculty's views about their instructional practices and their wishes for professional development.

BUILDING TEACHERS' LEADERSHIP CAPACITY

While principals are legally responsible for recommending faculty to be hired, evaluating personnel, managing resources, and implementing laws and regulations related to students, school programs, and curriculum, successful schools need teachers to work with principals to affect the school culture, policies, and practices related to better student learning. By supporting each other in their work and by sharing responsibility for results, educators can transform the relationship between authority and influence in schools in ways that drive positive change.

Teachers can also learn how to lead outside the classroom. In a role different than—but in tandem with—formal school leadership, teachers can enhance their own (and their principals') capacity to create cultures of success. Such collective leadership has been shown to have a stronger influence on student achievement than individual leadership. In addition, if teachers are to be held more accountable for student learning, they must be given more sway over their work environments.

Many avenues prepare teachers to become leaders. Some teachers learn how to be leaders through professional experiences and mentoring in their schools. Some gain leadership experience in their local or state professional associations. Others pursue more recognized training through advanced course credits and degrees in educational leadership. Likewise, many teachers become leaders in their schools by earning their peers' respect, being lifelong learners, being approachable, and using people and group skills to influence and improve their colleagues' educational practices. They model effective techniques, exercise their clout in formal and informal settings, and support collaborative team structures within their schools.

Many teachers who plan on remaining in the profession for the long term do not want to become principals or administrators. They don't want what they see as the huge burdens and 24–7 responsibilities that principals carry, which threaten to undermine their work–life balance. They do want opportunities to contribute to school decision making and occasions to work more collaboratively with their colleagues. When new leadership roles are connected to the classroom and their work with students—as opportunities for professional development—teachers are more motivated to assume them. Overall, teachers taking on leadership roles prefer to work as partners rather than as superiors with other teachers. Actually, when teachers find their new roles conflict with classroom teaching or create tensions with colleagues, stress and confusion often result.

Areas for Teacher Leadership

Schools have many arenas within which teachers can build their professional capacities for leadership and instruction. Formal teacher leadership is visible in three main areas:

• **Leadership of students or other teachers**—serving as facilitator, coach, mentor, trainer, curriculum specialist; becoming a union representative;

creating new approaches for instruction, parent engagement, or professional development; and leading study groups

- **Leadership of operational tasks**—keeping the school organized and moving toward its goals through roles such as department head, action researcher, and school improvement team member

- **Leadership through decision making or partnership**—serving on school committees or instigating partnerships with businesses, higher education, local school districts, and parent–teacher–student associations

Teachers also lead when they enhance their skills in less formal leadership roles, like the following:

- **Translating school improvement into classroom practice**—as they work with students, teachers transfer their PLC learning into the classroom, ensuring a link between school improvement planning and behaviors that maximize positive student outcomes.

- **Participating in leadership**—by working collegially, teachers feel ownership of the change as they shape school improvement efforts and guide other teachers toward a shared goal.

- **Mediating**—with a deep understanding of teaching and learning processes, teachers are important sources of expertise and information about the curriculum, instructional practices, and students' learning needs.

- **Fostering a collaborative culture**—teachers work with colleagues to support mutual learning and continuous improvement in ways that enhance student achievement.

- **Improving outreach and collaboration with families and community**—understanding that families, cultures, and communities have significant impacts on student learning, teacher leaders work with colleagues to promote ongoing, systematic collaboration with families and key stakeholders to expand opportunities for student learning and improve their organization.

In these ways—and others—teacher leadership can transform schools to better support teacher and student learning. As they empower their colleagues to become closely involved in decision making within the school, they contribute to both their school's improvement and its democratization. And, an assortment of teachers becomes a team.

Identifying and Developing Teacher Leaders

Teacher leaders are individuals who are or have been teachers (or school counselors) with meaningful classroom experiences, are known among their colleagues as being excellent educators, and hold their peers' esteem. Likewise, teachers attracted to leadership positions are achievement and learning oriented and are willing to take risks and assume responsibility. While transitioning to leadership tasks, these teachers come to know their school's culture, how to work effectively within the system, and how to persuade their colleagues.

Eight factors indicate a teacher's readiness to assume leadership roles and responsibilities:

- Excellent professional teaching skills
- A clear and well-developed personal philosophy of education
- Have reached personal and career stages that enable them to give time, energy, and attention to others and to assume a leadership role
- Interest in adult development
- Cognitive and affective depth and flexibility—he or she enjoys thinking abstractly, tying the conjectural to the concrete, and showing sensitivity and receptiveness to others' thoughts and feelings
- Strong work ethic
- Excellent people skills
- Strong organizational and administrative skills

Many teachers become leaders without planning to do so. Rather, they find themselves doing something that feels like leadership—chairing school committees; building collegial relations with principals; designing improved instructional approaches; developing insights into what people want, mean, think, and feel; and having other teachers ask for their opinions. Learning to lead requires performance, cognitive, and emotional learning.

SCHOOL CULTURE RE-BOOT 4.3
Identifying Potential Teacher Leaders in Your School

Using the table below, generate examples of formal and informal leadership for your school in each area listed (include more than two roles for each area if needed). Identify possible teachers or school counselors (or other educators) from your faculty for each one. Also, consider whether these potential leaders currently have the readiness factors that will make them available and potentially successful school leaders. Principals may want to collaborate with formal teacher leaders to cast a wide and diverse net to identify possible leaders.

Area of Teacher Leadership (list examples)	Potential Teacher Leader (name him or her)	Readiness Factors (identify at least four of the eight factors listed above)
Leadership of students, teachers * *		
Leaders of operational tasks * *		
Leadership through decision making * *		
Translating school improvement into classrooms * *		
Participating in leadership * *		
Mediating * *		
Fostering a collaborative culture * *		
Improving outreach * *		

After identifying potential teacher leaders, brainstorm the ways in which you might include them to further develop their instructional and/or leadership capacities.

If promising candidates lack readiness, how might members of your leadership team help each individual candidate to become ready?

Developing Teachers' Leadership Capacities

Principals and teacher leaders have many ways of helping teachers build their professional capacity. Much of this growth occurs within caring professional relationships involving conversations, coaching, mentoring, inducting new teachers into the organization, and other means. Likewise, principals can arrange the school structure in ways that support teachers' professional learning and leading.

Conversations

Capacity-building conversations have common factors: shared purpose, a search for understanding, remembering and reflecting on beliefs and experiences, revealing ideas and information, respectful listening, and identifying increasingly skillful actions. In informal one-to-one talks, principals and teachers can share ideas, review classroom or school data together, or discuss long-range planning. Principals can return a teacher's question about how to handle a particular situation with, "What do you recommend?"

Coaching

Performance coaching includes clearly identifying what the teacher wants to learn, providing opportunities to experiment with new leadership and instructional strategies, giving detailed and timely feedback on effectiveness, and sustaining a relentless comparison of the present performance to the ideal state. Principals can ask teacher-centered questions that expand teachers' focus from self to others and outcomes, such as these: What is your desired result for working with your team? What role will you play? What evidence will you look for that will tell you that you have been successful? Throughout coaching, the principal or teacher leader as coach is consistently available for support and practical guidance.

Mentoring

Addressing a wider scope of behaviors than coaching, mentoring by principals and teacher leaders involves coaching and feedback, modeling, educating, and providing occasions to enact emerging leadership skills outside the classroom and school. Mentoring teachers may involve helping them learn how to set priorities, create agendas, and run effective meetings. Mentoring pairs may consider and evaluate the potential moral and legal consequences of decision making and offer encouragement and challenge. Discussions may also include generating ideas about how to move into leadership roles and finding occasions to increase instructional or leadership skills. Benefits accrue to the mentor, too, with increased job satisfaction, engagement with the school's professional community, as well as more leaders with whom to share energies and accountability toward meeting common goals.

New Teacher Induction

Induction programs help new-to-the-job teachers begin their careers in a culture that supports adult learning and teacher leadership. Acculturating fresh faculty to the school's vision, welcoming teachers into a community of adult and young learners, and identifying the various legitimate roles and responsibilities for teachers to play as classroom and schoolwide leaders help sustain the teacher leadership culture. Placing new teachers into supportive PLCs can help ensure a successful transition into the profession as well as increase their classroom effectiveness from their earliest days. Such induction activities and ethos can help new teachers emerge as leaders early in their careers.

Additional Means

Principals can also expand teachers' leadership capacity by offering job-embedded, ongoing professional development that is intellectually stimulating and practice based. They can be patient and reassuring as teachers accept new leadership roles and make early missteps. Leaders can offer occasions for teachers to read, think about, and frankly discuss important educational issues that affect their school and their students—and consider views that may conflict with their own. Lastly and perhaps most importantly, principals and teacher leaders can be the appropriate role models upon whom developing teacher leaders can benchmark their own progress.

Leaders build their schools' professional capacity when they create conditions that encourage teachers to grow as instructors and leaders. Capacity building involves bringing people together so they can construct and negotiate meanings and arrive at shared purpose. It means teachers taking responsibility for both individual and collective growth, looking at students as "ours" rather than "mine," and accepting individual and collective accountability for increasing their achievement. Capacity building enables more teachers to develop their own informal authority and display leadership in areas that affect teaching and learning.

When whole grade levels, departments, or schools are involved in collegial professional learning, they create a critical mass for changed instruction—and sustained improvement—at the school level.

Apart from family factors, teacher leadership—inside and outside the classroom—has a far greater impact than principal leadership on student achievement. School improvement changes are better accepted, used, and sustained as compared with schools without shared leadership. The message is clear: School culture re-boot and improvement are more likely to occur when leadership is distributed and when teachers have a vested interest in improving their professional capacities in ways that benefit themselves and their students.

RESEARCH

How Building Teachers' Capacity Improves School Outcomes

Day, D., Harris, A., & Hadfield, M. (2000). Grounding knowledge of schools in stakeholder realities: A multi-perspective study of effective school leaders. *School Leadership and Management, 21*(1), 19–42.

Fullan, M. (2001). *Leading in a culture of change.* San Francisco: Jossey-Bass.

Goddard, R. D., Hoy, W. K., & Woolfolk Hoy, A. (2000). Collective teacher efficacy: Its meaning, measures, and impact on student achievement. *American Educational Research Journal, 37*(2), 479–507.

Harris, A. (2004). Distributed leadership and school improvement: Leading or misleading? *Educational Management Administration and Leadership, 32*(1), 11–24.

Harris, A., & Lambert, L. (2003). *Building leadership capacity for school improvement.* London: Open University Press

Holden, G. (2002). *Towards a learning community: The role of teacher-led development in school improvement.* Paper presented at the CELSI British Council Leadership in Learning Conference, London, UK.

Hopkins, D., & Jackson, D. (2002). Building the capacity for leading and learning. In A. Harris, C. Day, M. Hadfield, D. Hopkins, A. Hargreaves, & C. Chapman (Eds.), *Effective leadership for school improvement* (pp. 84–105). London: Routledge.

Leithwood, K., & Jantzi, D. (1998). *Distributed leadership and student engagement in school.* Paper presented at the Annual Meeting of the American Educational Research Association, San Diego, CA.

Leithwood, K., Louis, K. S., Anderson, S., & Wahlstrom, K. (2004). *Executive summary: How leadership influences student learning.* New York: Wallace Foundation.

Morrissey, M. (2000). *Professional learning communities: An ongoing exploration.* Paper presented as the Southwest Educational Development Laboratory, Austin, TX.

Mujis, D., & Harris, A. (2003). Teacher leadership: Improvement through empowerment? An overview of the literature. *Educational Management Administration and Leadership, 31*(4), 437–448.

Ogawa, R. T., & Bossert, S. T. (1995). Leadership as an organizational quality. *Educational Administration Quarterly, 31*(2), 224–243.

Seashore Louis, K., Leithwood, K., Wahlstrom, K. L., & Anderson, S. E. (2010). *Learning from leadership: Investigating the links to improved student learning. Final report to the Wallace Foundation.* Minneapolis, MN: University of Minnesota. Retrieved April 2, 2012, from http://www.wallacefoundation.org/Knowl edgeCenter/KnowledgeTopics/CurrentAreasofFocus/EducationLeadership/ Documents/Learning-from-Leadership-Investigating-Links-Final-Report.pdf

Spillane, J. P., Halverson, R., & Diamond, B. (2001). Investigating school leadership practice: A distributed perspective. *Educational Researcher, 30*(3), 23–28.

RESOURCES

Survey of Core Indicators That Support Professional Capacity

This informal survey asks teachers and administrators to answer "Yes" or "No" to their school's core indicators of professional capacity. This can be taken by leadership team members as well as by the teachers on faculty. It might be useful to see how the principal's answers compare to those of the leadership team and to compare leadership team members' with those of their teachers. By reviewing and discussing results, school leaders can assess how their faculty perceives their school as supporting professional capacity and suggests areas for school culture re-boot and changed practices.

Essential Support	Core Indicators of Professional Capacity To what extent is each core support present and effective on a 1–5 scale (1 = low and 5 = high)?	1 2 3 4 5
	School Leadership	
Inclusive leadership–the degree to which teachers view their principal as an inclusive, facilitative leader, focused on parent and community involvement and creating a sense of community in the school		
	• The principal is committed to shared decision making.	1 2 3 4 5
	• Teachers have formal and informal leadership roles in this school.	1 2 3 4 5
	• Teachers have influence in determining books and materials.	1 2 3 4 5
	• Teachers have influence over how school funds are used.	1 2 3 4 5
	• The school improvement team has been a positive influence on teaching and learning.	1 2 3 4 5
	• The school improvement team has made a contribution to improving parent involvement.	1 2 3 4 5
	• The principal promotes a professional community for teachers.	1 2 3 4 5
Instructional leadership–the degree to which teachers view their principal as setting high academic standards, visiting classrooms, carefully tracking students' progress, pressing teachers to use what they learn from professional development, and exercising leadership for instructional reform		
	• The principal carefully tracks student progress.	1 2 3 4 5
	• The principal presses teachers to use what they learn in professional development to improve student learning and achievement.	1 2 3 4 5
	• Once the school starts a program, the principal and faculty make sure it is working.	1 2 3 4 5
	• The professional development in the school has led to meaningful changes in teachers' teaching practices.	1 2 3 4 5
	• You are involved with my school's improvement team.	1 2 3 4 5

(Continued)

(Continued)

Essential Support	Core Indicators of Professional Capacity To what extent is each core support present and effective on a 1–5 scale (1 = low and 5 = high)?	1 2 3 4 5
Teacher influence–a measure of the extent of teachers' involvement in school decision making		
• Teachers have influence in determining books and materials.		1 2 3 4 5
• Teachers have influence over how school funds are used.		1 2 3 4 5
• Teachers helped develop the improvement plan for the school.		1 2 3 4 5
• The school improvement team is a positive factor in the school.		1 2 3 4 5
• Teachers help each other become more effective instructors.		1 2 3 4 5
Relational trust–a measure of the degree of confidence members have that others will act with integrity, will not take advantage of your vulnerability, and will look after your interests		
• You trust the principal's word.		1 2 3 4 5
• The principal has confidence in teachers' expertise.		1 2 3 4 5
• You trust most of your colleagues to keep their word.		1 2 3 4 5
• Teachers respect other teachers who take the lead in school improvement efforts.		1 2 3 4 5
• Most of your colleagues see you as a competent professional.		1 2 3 4 5
Professional Capacity		
Professional dispositions–teacher orientation toward innovation; teachers' assessments about whether their colleagues are continually learning, seeking new ideas, and have can-do attitudes; and school commitment		
• Most teachers are eager to try new ideas.		1 2 3 4 5
• Teachers are encouraged to stretch and grow as teachers and leaders.		1 2 3 4 5
• If you wanted to be a more effective teacher, your colleagues would help you.		1 2 3 4 5
• You would recommend this school to parents seeking a place for their child.		1 2 3 4 5
• Your colleagues invite each other to visit their classrooms and give feedback about instructional practices.		1 2 3 4 5
• You feel loyal to this school.		1 2 3 4 5
Quality of professional development–frequency and quality of opportunities to continue adult learning related to your work		
• Your professional development experiences in this school have deepened your understanding of subject matter.		1 2 3 4 5
• Your professional development experiences in this school have been sustained, focused, and directly tied to what you do in your classroom.		1 2 3 4 5
• You frequently take courses at a college or university to improve your teaching.		1 2 3 4 5

Essential Support	Core Indicators of Professional Capacity To what extent is each core support present and effective on a 1–5 scale (1 = low and 5 = high)?	1 2 3 4 5
Professional community—the teachers' assessment of their capacity to work together on improvement initiatives (public classroom practice, reflective dialog, peer collaboration, focus on student learning, teacher socialization, and collective responsibility)		
• This year, teaching colleagues have observed your classroom at least twice.		1 2 3 4 5
• This year, you have received useful instructional suggestions from colleagues.		1 2 3 4 5
• You often speak with colleagues about what helps students learn best.		1 2 3 4 5
• Together with your colleagues, you do a good job talking through views, opinions, and values.		1 2 3 4 5
• Principals, teachers, and staff collaborate to make the school run effectively.		1 2 3 4 5
• Teachers make conscious efforts to coordinate teaching with others in their grade levels.		1 2 3 4 5
• When making important decisions, the school focuses on what's best for student learning.		1 2 3 4 5
• This school has well-defined learning expectations for students.		1 2 3 4 5
• Experienced teachers invite new teachers into their classrooms to observe.		1 2 3 4 5
• The faculty makes conscious efforts to help new teachers feel welcome.		1 2 3 4 5
• Most teachers feel responsible to help colleagues do their best.		1 2 3 4 5
• Most teachers take responsibility for improving the school.		1 2 3 4 5

Source: Adapted from Bryk, A. S., Sebring, P.B., Allensworth, E, Luppescu, S., & Easton, J. Q. (2010). *Organizing for school improvement. Lessons from Chicago.* Chicago: University of Chicago Press, p. 82.

Collective Efficacy Scale

Collective efficacy is the shared perception of teachers in a school that the efforts of the faculty as a whole will have positive effects on students. The Collective Efficacy Scale (CE-Scale) is a 21-item scale, which measures the collective efficacy of a school. Teachers answer a five-part, Likert-type scale from "Strongly Disagree" to "Strongly Agree." The CE-Scale is available free on-line from Ohio State University at http://www.waynekhoy.com/collective_efficacy.html.

Sample questions include the following: Teachers in the school are able to get through to the most difficult students. Teachers here don't have the skills needed to produce meaningful student learning. If a child doesn't learn something the first time, teachers will try another way. The lack of instructional materials and supplies makes teaching very difficult. Teachers in this school think there are some students that no one can reach.

Results from the pilot study suggest that the 21 items offer a valid and reliable measure of collective efficacy. The instrument provides content, criterion-related, and predictive validity evidence for scores on the collective efficacy and reliability scales.

Establishing a Student-Centered Learning Culture

FOCUS QUESTIONS

- Why is it essential that public schools educate every student to high levels?
- What are the components of a student-centered learning environment?
- How does a safe and orderly environment contribute to student learning?
- How do high teacher expectations contribute to student learning?
- How do academic press and supports contribute to student learning?
- How do supportive peer norms contribute to student learning?
- How do strong and caring relationships contribute to student learning?

O ur era is one of increasing personalization. Rather than everyone listening to the same radio stations, we personalize our playlists through Rhapsody and iTunes. We read the *New York Times* on our iPads or with a newspaper spread flat on the kitchen table. We take our politics through Fox News, CNN, MSNBC, or Twitter. Customized, person-centered services have become expectations—except in education.

Ideally, the goal of schooling is to educate each student as an individual, meeting his or her specific needs to prepare for whatever academic and life challenges lie ahead. Along with a high-quality curriculum that every student must learn, focusing on one student at a time is what the best teachers have always done intuitively. This vision, however, is more rhetoric than practice. Given the heavy toll that today's tight education funding is taking on class sizes and educator employment, it is difficult to remember that teachers do not teach a class but each child in a class. Twenty-first-century schooling challenges teachers to balance competing goals for education: equity and excellence, standards and customization, efficiency and relationships. This is easier said than done.

Good teachers are able to take a high-quality curriculum with clear goals and create an environment that both stimulates and supports each student. Teachers hold high expectations for each student's achievement. They provide a safe, organized, and nurturing classroom milieu in which students can take risks to learn. Good teachers are able to recognize when something isn't working well and can promptly modify the curriculum or instruction to fit the student. They develop caring relationships with students that encourage and sustain persistence in learning and appropriateness in behavior. And, teachers can customize learning opportunities to cultivate individual achievement. When these student-centered practices characterize the school's culture, they create a psychosocial environment that profoundly affects student motivation, involvement in learning, behavior, and achievement.

This chapter focuses on how teachers can use their professional capacities to provide a student-centered learning culture with a safe and orderly environment, high expectations for student achievement, academic press and supports (including supportive peer norms), and caring relationships. All these variables work together to affect how well each student succeeds. As the popular saying goes, "Effective schooling requires rigor, relevance, and relationships."

WHY WE NEED TO EDUCATE EVERY CHILD TO HIGH LEVELS

The United States is currently undergoing one of the most acute demographic transformations in our history. Our ability as a nation to make this transition constructively depends in large measure on how well we can educate every child to high levels.

Demographic Changes

The U.S. Census Bureau predicts that Latinos, African Americans, Asian Americans, Native Americans, Native Hawaiians, and Pacific Islanders will collectively become the majority population in the United States by 2042. By 2050, minorities are expected to account for 54 percent of the U.S. population. Non-Latino whites will represent the remaining

46 percent, down from their current 63.7 percent share.[1] However, African-American students are nearly three times as likely as white students to be retained in a grade, while Latino students are twice as likely to be held back—a valid predictor for dropping out.[2] Research finds that slightly more than half of students from historically disadvantaged minority groups are finishing high school with diplomas.[3]

Failing to successfully educate large numbers of minority children has major implications for the American workforce. The National Center for Public Policy and Higher Education predicts that, by 2020, the white working-age population will have declined to 63 percent of the total U.S. population (down from 82 percent in 1980). Because large numbers of younger workers will be members of ethnic minorities, while larger numbers of white workers are retiring, the workforce will shift from a majority of white workers to include more people of color.[4]

Unless this upcoming workforce has the high-quality education and skills to provide national, statewide, and local leadership and to earn strong and consistent wages, our whole society will suffer. This workforce will shape our society through its political, social, economic, and artistic influences. It will stimulate our economy through consumer purchases and taxes as their wages contribute to the Social Security and Medicare Trust Funds, which support retirees, disabled citizens, and ailing seniors. If tomorrow's workers have lower capacities for offering societal vision and governance and lower personal incomes than do present and retiring workers, our body politic and social networks may not be able to meet their obligations.

Likewise, the typical sorting of students into high- and low-challenge courses based on their presumed abilities and life goals is highly problematic. Frequently, these placements are closely correlated with the learners' race and socioeconomic status, and they both predict and contribute to student outcomes. Less-privileged students tend to occupy

[1]Bernstein, R., & Edwards, T. (2008, August 14). An older and more diverse nation by midcentury. U.S. Census Bureau News, Washington, DC: U.S. Census Bureau. Retrieved April 18, 2012, from http://www.census.gov/Press-Release/www/releases/archives/popula tion/012496.html; U.S. Census Bureau. (2012). USA QuickFacts from the U.S. Census Bureau. Washington, DC: Author. Retrieved April 18, 2012, from http://quickfacts.census.gov/qfd/states/00000.html

[2]Robelin, E. W., Adams, C. J., & Shah, N. (2012, March 7). Data show retention disparities. Education Week, 31(23), 1, 18–19.

[3]Education Week. (2011, June 7). National graduation rate rebounds. 1.2 million students still fail to earn diplomas. Diplomas Count 2011. Washington, DC: Author. Retrieved April 23, 2012, from http://www.edweek.org/media/diplomascount2011_pressrelease.pdf

[4]Lewis, A. (2006, February). A new people. Phi Delta Kappan, 87(6), 419.

lower-track or group classes, while more privileged students tend to enroll in more advanced ones. Students in higher-level classes typically have better teachers, curricula, and achievement levels than peers in lower-level classes.

Educators forget that the human brain is amazingly malleable and— when motivated to do so—individuals can nearly always outperform expectations set for them. Research finds that virtually all students would benefit from the kinds of meaning-making, problem-solving, logical-thinking and transfer-of-learning curriculum and instruction usually reserved for advanced learners.[5] And, because low-level classes are largely comprised of students from groups that are soon to become the majority of our citizens, the social and financial costs of not educating all students to high levels become immediately clear.

Unless we focus on educating each child to high levels and close the achievement gaps between affluent (largely white) and low-income students (largely students of color), the most highly educated generation in U.S. history could be replaced by a generation with far lower education levels (as measured by high school and college completion rates). Many people's well-being and lifestyles will be reduced as a result—as will our nation as a whole. Plainly, it is in every teacher's and principal's best interests as future retirees to make certain that traditionally underserved students are underserved no longer. Establishing a student-centered learning culture in every school is one promising means to successfully address this issue.

A Student-Centered Learning Environment

Since the 1980s, education reform has pressed for uniform curriculum standards, common assessments, and rigorous accountability rules for schools, teachers, and students. Presently, nearly all states have adopted common core standards in English and mathematics; the reading expectations will also affect science, history, and social studies teachers. Along with having all students meet challenging common standards, however, it is possible to tailor learning to meet students' interests, ambitions, and learning needs. While the curriculum tells what to teach, teachers have choices about how they teach. If they are to help each student learn to high standards, teachers must include varied approaches that are responsive to both the class as a whole as well as to students as individuals.

Although gearing instruction to students' common learning characteristics instead of individual differences can increase efficiency, the

---

[5]National Research Council. (1999). *How people learn: Brain, mind, school, and experience.* Washington, DC: National Academies Press.

cost of total uniformity is student failure. And, while it is unrealistic to think that a teacher can teach 20 to 35 different lessons to as many students in one class, a certain amount and type of individualization are necessary if every student is to reach challenging standards. Rather than ignore these individual differences, effective teachers learn how to address them in ways that enable each student to meet the school's learning goals.

Establishing a *student-centered learning culture* means creating the conditions and ethos that best support every learner's ability to master a high-challenge, standards-based curriculum. Through a variety of means—including developing high teacher expectations for each student, creating a safe and orderly learning environment, providing academic press along with meaningful academic and social supports, affording supportive peer norms, and fostering helpful and respectful relationships—teachers and principals can re-boot their school's culture in ways that advance the likelihood of every child's academic success.

A student-centered learning culture asserts an appreciation and support for young people's capacity to grow and develop, intellectually, socially, and behaviorally. Through the daily interactions of educators and students, the school culture affirms these views:

- Young people do well if they can.
- Students are smart and can be encouraged to learn.
- Teachers have the skills—and are accountable—for ensuring that each child learns to high levels.
- The school will provide resources to help teachers and students meet this goal.
- Behind every defiant behavior is a lagging skill and a need for that skill.
- Problems should be solved proactively (rather than in the heat of the moment or immediately afterward) and collaboratively with the student.

This positive and growth-oriented frame motivates educators to work with students to ensure student development—educationally and personally.

What a Student-Centered Learning Culture Looks Like

In a school with a well-established student-centered learning culture, everyone expects to learn and expects everyone else to learn. Academic prospects are high for every student, and the supports are present to help each reach them. Teachers are willing to make the time to go back and fill in the learning gaps for students who are not progressing well. Educators understand that securing a strong cognitive foundation is more essential than racing through the curriculum and ignoring students' learning needs. At the same time, students assume more control over what and how they learn and how they demonstrate what they know and can do. Classrooms and school halls highlight many samples of high-quality student work. Depending on how an individual student learns best, many opportunities exist to learn in multiple ways and at varied rates.

In student-centered learning cultures, teachers focus on "they learned it" rather than "I taught it." The cultural emphasis shifts from teaching to learning. Starting with what the school offers, teachers also look to what the student needs. Teachers come to know their students— their learning capacities and paces, their interests, their concerns, and their personal and family assets and resources, and use these insights to make the curriculum relevant and personally meaningful to each learner.

In student-centered learning cultures, each student has constructive relationships with other students and with many teachers and adults in the community. Successful learning is celebrated and emulated. People work together on interesting projects in small and large groups. Across the school, conversations buzz with thought-provoking and relevant topics. People listen respectfully and carefully to one another, feeling free to disagree respectfully, take risks, be wrong, and try something new. Interpersonal trust is widespread and visible. Newcomers are welcomed, and diversity is an asset to make the community stronger. It feels good to be there. Students feel known and respected, surrounded by others who care for them and have their backs. What is more, "this is the way we do things around here."

A SAFE AND ORDERLY LEARNING ENVIRONMENT

What happens between teachers and students in everyday classroom interactions affects students' academic functioning. Effective teachers create and sustain a safe, organized, caring, and intellectually challenging environment. It is essential that teachers and students feel physically and emotionally safe, comfortable, and cared for if they are to have the psychological energy needed for teaching and learning. Without a minimum level of security and calm—if children feel frightened, humiliated, or discounted by their teachers (and vice versa)—a school has little chance of positively affecting student achievement.

Benefits of a Safe and Orderly Environment

Many studies find that, the more safe and orderly the school climate,[6] the higher the students' math and reading achievement levels. A secure and organized environment is significantly correlated with less student fear, lower dropout rates, and higher student commitment to learning. Research supports the general conclusion that, the greater the school's academic quality and more positive its emotional climate, the lower the level of school crime and violence. An encouraging, helpful, and culturally conscious school climate can make a significant difference between students' academic success or failure.[7]

It is easy to understand why. Worry about safety shifts the brain's attention. When students and teachers worry about their personal safety, their focus insistently turns to protecting themselves. They become cautious and watchful, and they stay hyperalert to potential dangers. At such times, the emotional parts of their brain are more fully aroused, and their cognitive areas become less active. In these situations, they cannot find extra energy to pay attention to teaching and learning. Achievement suffers.

Conversely, in a school with a safe and orderly environment, teachers and students feel no personal danger. Because their emotions are calm, their cognitive capacities can become more fully engaged. The learning environment is well structured and organized. Teachers are committed to teaching and learning. They set high but achievable goals for students. Likewise, students are highly motivated, put effort into their schoolwork, and respect peers who achieve academically.

In safe and orderly schools, teachers clearly describe and model their expectations for appropriate student behaviors, and they encourage students to practice good citizenship with their peers and teachers. In safe and orderly schools, staff will frequently be visible in student restrooms, hallways, unlikely corners, and occasionally riding the school bus. Their active and friendly presence is a visible reminder for students to act in mature and accountable ways. In these schools, educators help students understand that meeting their civic responsibility means looking out for the welfare of their classmates and their school. Telling an adult when

---

[6]*School climate* is the overall psychosocial ambiance—the school's culture, personality, or feel—in which teachers' and students' behaviors occur. A safe and orderly environment is an aspect of school climate. Climate reflects a school's teaching practices, student and faculty diversity, and the quality of relationships in the building, as well as the facility's cleanliness, attractiveness, and state of repair; the academic performance expected and received from all students; and the feelings of trust and mutual respect shared by educators, students, and parents.

[7]Several key studies on how school safety affects academic achievement appear in the Research section of this chapter.

trouble is brewing gains campuswide respect as responsible behavior; it is not viewed as ratting out their friends.

These climate and culture factors can have positive influences on the learning environment—or they can create significant barriers to learning.

SCHOOL CULTURE RE-BOOT 5.1
Assessing for a Safe and Orderly Learning Environment

1. Read and discuss the characteristics of a safe and orderly school learning environment listed below. Discuss other examples of what this might look like, and add them to the list. Separate into pairs, and use the list to discuss and assess your school's safe and orderly environment. After the discussion, honestly assess your own classroom on these dimensions.

Ratings Key: 1–Unsatisfactory   3–Needs Some Improvement   5–Very Good

	Rating for School			Rating for Own Classroom		
Safe and Orderly School Characteristic	1	3	5	1	3	5
The school is clean, inviting, and comfortable. Graffiti or disorder is promptly noticed and removed.						
Teachers and students at the school say that they feel safe, and smiles are evident everywhere.						
Students and parents say that teachers and administrators really care about them.						
Students sit in mixed race and gender groups in the cafeteria and classrooms.						
Teacher–student interactions are positive.						
Rules and expectations are clearly and visibly communicated (and frequently reviewed and enforced) to students (and parents), stressing mutual respect and responsibility.						
Teachers, administrators, and other adults are visible in the halls and common areas whenever students are using them from morning entry through afternoon dismissal.						
The principal and administrators are aware of the school's details and undercurrents and use this information to prevent and solve problems.						

Safe and Orderly School Characteristic	Rating for School			Rating for Own Classroom		
	1	*3*	*5*	*1*	*3*	*5*
Students breaking rules receive fair and consistently administered consequences.						
Early recognition systems identify students with high potential for violence and extreme behaviors, and educators intervene to help prevent and solve problems.						
Challenging students have in-school adult mentors with whom they regularly discuss concerns and solve problems.						
Additional example:						
Additional example:						
Additional example:						

2. Pairs report their school assessments to the whole group. One person tallies the whole group's points for each characteristic.

3. Discuss as a group:

- How do teachers' own classroom's safe and orderly characteristics compare with the overall school's characteristics? How do you explain this difference—or similarity?
- How is maintaining a safe and orderly learning environment evidence of educators caring for students?
- Which aspects of this school's safe and orderly environment are strong?
- Which are the three characteristics most in need of improvement?
- What can members of this group do to begin improving the school's safe and orderly environment?

The leadership team might want to give this survey to all teachers in their grade levels or departments to assess their views on this topic and to heighten their awareness of how safe and orderly environments impact student learning.

The leadership team might also want to give a version of this brief survey to students— in one of their classes or homerooms or to student leaders to see how safe and orderly they perceive their school—and share findings with the leadership team.

A school's safe and orderly environment is more than the absence of undesirable behaviors, such as students fighting or bullying. Rather, it is the pervasive presence of desirable actions and attitudes showing respect for and appreciation of human diversity and democratic values.

TEACHER EXPECTATIONS

Teachers form expectations for student performance and tend to treat students differently depending on these expectations. Research strongly supports this assertion.[8] To establish a student-centered learning culture, teachers must adjust their expectations and instructional practices so that all children can learn to high levels.

Evidence That Expectations Influence Performance

The classic Hawthorne study at Western Electric's plant in Cicero, Illinois (1927–1932), provided data that suggested that teachers' expectations can greatly influence students' performance. Like the workplace, the classroom is a powerful social network, and students' feelings about both their teachers and classmates have important implications for how much they are willing to exert themselves to succeed at learning. As with adult employees, students' aptitudes are less important than their attitudes about schoolwork in predicting their academic achievement.

Likewise, in *Pygmalion in the Classroom,*[9] investigators (a Harvard University professor and an elementary principal) told elementary school teachers that, based on their students' standardized test scores, certain children were "late bloomers" and could be expected to be "growth spurters." In truth, the tests did not exist, and the children designated as "spurters" were chosen randomly. Nonetheless, findings showed that changes in teacher expectations can produce changes in student achievement. When teachers expect students to do well, students tend to do well; when teachers expect students to fail, they tend to fail.

Studies by Jeannie Oakes,[10] a University of California at Los Angeles education professor, and James Coleman,[11] a Johns Hopkins sociology professor, also confirmed that teachers' expectations about their students strongly affect how teachers treat these students in ways that create self-fulfilling prophesies. Students treated as if they were high achieving acted

---

[8]Studies connecting high teacher expectations and high student performance can be found in the Research section of this chapter.

[9]Rosenthal, R., & Jacobson, L. (1968). *Pygmalion in the classroom: Teachers' expectations and pupils' intellectual development.* New York: Rineholt and Winston.

[10]Oakes, J. (1985). *Keeping track: How schools structure inequality.* New Haven, CT: Yale University Press.

[11]Coleman, J. S., Campbell, E. Q., Hobson, C. J., McPartland, F., Mood, A. M., Weinfeld, F. D., et al. (1966). *Equality of educational opportunity.* Washington, DC: U.S. Government Printing Office.

in high-achieving ways. Students treated as if they were low achieving performed as low achievers.

Expectations can create reality. In a circular fashion, students' and teachers' perceptions and expectations both reflect and determine their achievement goals. They influence the strategies they use to meet these goals; the skills, energy, and other resources they use to apply these strategies; and the rewards they expect from making—or not making—this effort. And as research shows, teachers' behaviors reflecting these expectations are related to measures of student academic achievement.

Developing teachers' instructional capacities pays off because, the more effectively teachers teach, the higher all their students achieve—and the less accurate teachers' initial predictions become about who will or will not achieve well. Each player's positive expectation influences the other in a mutually reinforcing manner. As observed in *Pygmalion in the Classroom*, when teachers treat all students as high achievers—providing them with similar rigorous academic content, similar praise, and similar feedback and making similar demands for actual effort and products—students perform and achieve well.

SCHOOL CULTURE RE-BOOT 5.2
Teacher Expectations and Student Achievement

Teachers' expectations for students' achievement influence students' learning and achievement.

1. Review the research findings below, and discuss as a group the extent to which each finding is true to your own experiences. Describe what each finding might look like or sound like in an actual school. What are the benefits—or disadvantages—to students of teachers holding these beliefs?

   - Teachers' perceptions of current students' performance as well as their judgments for students' future performance are generally accurate. Once set, teachers' expectations change little. In school, first impressions matter.
   - Student characteristics such as physical attractiveness, socioeconomic status, race, use of standard English, and history of grade retention are all related to teachers' expectations for academic achievement.
   - Teachers overestimate the achievement of high achievers, underestimate the achievement of low achievers, and predict least accurately low achievers' responses.
   - The better the teachers know their students, the more accurate their expectations for student academic success, especially in the early elementary grades (grades 1 and 2).

(Continued)

(Continued)

2. Identify_ways that teachers in your school can monitor their expectations for students, so they don't underestimate any child's ability to learn to high standards.

Consider conducting this activity with teachers in their grade levels or departments to advance the ideas about how teachers' expectations influence their behaviors toward students and their students' achievement.

Re-Booting Teachers' Expectations

Re-booting—that is, refining and expanding—teachers' expectations for all students' achievement is an essential aspect of establishing a student-centered learning culture. Carol Ann Tomlinson and Edwin Lou Javius, two educators concerned with classroom equity and high standards, identify seven interrelated principles that inform teachers' beliefs when they want to help all children learn to high levels.[12] When enacted in classroom practices schoolwide and over time, these expectations can re-boot the school culture in ways that increase every student's learning.

• **Accept that human differences are not only normal but also desirable**. Each person has something of value to contribute to the group, and the group is lessened without that contribution. As a microcosm of our world, the classroom should be culturally and economically inclusive and support students in making meaning in multiple ways.

• **Develop a growth mind-set**. Teachers must logically challenge the pre-conception that mainly affluent students have high ability levels. When teachers expect student growth—and provide students with clear learning targets, guidelines, feedback, a safe learning environment, and the message that each student has the capacity to do what is required for success (and teachers will support their labors)—they can create learning experiences in which student effort—rather than background—is the greatest determiner of success. Students who work hard and intelligently can accomplish their goals.

• **Understand students' cultures, interests, needs, and perspectives**. People are shaped by their backgrounds. Respecting students means respecting their backgrounds, races, and cultures. To this end, teachers need to understand how each student approaches learning and craft an environment

---

[12]Tomlinson, C. A., & Javius, E. L. (2012, February). Teach up for excellence. All students deserve equitable access to an engaging and rigorous curriculum. *Educational Leadership, 69*(5), 28–33.

that respects and responds to what each student brings to the classroom. Treat others as they want to be treated. Through conversations with students and observations of them at work, teachers develop a learning profile about the way he or she likes to learn, personal interests, and varied ways of reaching the goal. Then, teachers purposefully select instructional approaches that respond to them to ensure high-level success for each student. All learning activities align with essential learning targets and have intellectual rigor: They are both standards friendly and student friendly.

• **Create a base of rigorous learning opportunities**. Teachers begin with clear ideas about what learning should occur as the result of a lesson or unit aligned with assessments and standards. Then, teachers connect students with the curriculum by transforming student-boring topics into student-friendly concepts that have enduring value beyond the classroom, lie at the heart of the discipline, require analysis, have the potential to engage students, and span various cultures. Give students a reason for studying the curriculum.

For instance, instead of teaching about butterflies, teach about life cycles in which all living things share similar development. Instead of studying the Industrial Revolution, teach about the concept of human progress and who wins or loses. Instead of pollution, study interdependence and the relationships between humans and their environment. In these ways, teachers help students form conceptual understandings of the disciplines, connect what they learn to their own lives, and use essential knowledge and skills to address meaningful problems. Exploring these ideas creates occasions for collaborating with peers, examining varied viewpoints, and creating authentic products for relevant audiences. Teachers also incorporate a range of resources that elicit students' interests, help students make sense of what they are learning, and support struggling learners. These classroom cultures value and encourage excellence, and students gain satisfaction from accepting and spending their best efforts on worthwhile challenges.

• **Understand that students have differing points for entering and moving through the curriculum**. For students to take intellectual risks, classrooms need to feel safe to students from a wide range of cultural, racial, and economic backgrounds. Effective teachers seek multiple ways for students to show what they know, and every student needs occasions to shine as intellectual contributors. When students fall behind, misunderstand, or move beyond expectations, teachers are ready to take appropriate instructional actions—scaffolding for students who need extra work with prerequisites and extending depth and scope for students who surge quickly ahead. Formative assessment provides ongoing data for personalizing learning for both struggling and advancing students.

• **Create flexible classroom routines and procedures that attend to learners' needs.** Teachers provide occasions for a range of student needs and differences. Teachers select times when the class works as a whole, when students work independently, and when they work in groups. At key times in the learning cycle, teachers decide when they need to work with part of the class more intensively. They teach students when and how to help one another as well as how to direct their own work effectively. Such flexible approaches can increase each student's achievement.

• **Be an analytical practitioner.** Teachers who create student-centered learning cultures consistently reflect on their practices for evidence that these are working for each student and adjusting when they are not. Keenly attuned to their students, teachers notice when they show positive behaviors and new learning. Then, teachers provide helpful, descriptive feedback so students can successfully recall or repeat the skill, knowledge, or behavior that serves them well. They ask students to help teachers understand what will help make the students most successful, and they shape a classroom atmosphere that maximizes each individual's growth and growth of the group as a whole.

Of course, as much as they may care for each student, teachers cannot personalize every part of the curriculum. Expecting each student to develop high-level skills in literacy, numeracy, communication, and critical thinking is not negotiable. Learning outcomes linked to learning standards and grade-level benchmarks cannot be compromised. Although receptive to students' interests and needs, teachers cannot personalize the desired learning outcomes. And, for students enrolled in courses with high-stakes exit exams, such as international baccalaureate (IB) or advanced placement (AP) tests, teachers cannot jeopardize the students' success on the exam by omitting required content. Effective teachers can, nonetheless, hold to the expected learning outcomes while still permitting many occasions for personalization. Insightful teachers learn where the flexibility exists to customize the curriculum or the instructional approaches to connect with individual students—and then do it.

For example, if the learning outcome is composing a well-organized, coherent, five-paragraph essay, teachers can emphasize different skills and expected levels of complexity for different students in a class according to the present skills levels and interests so that all students progress toward the goal successfully. Certain students will need more time to reach the standard; during this time, those who have already mastered the objectives can extend and deepen their learning to the standards in agreed-upon ways. Similarly, while the form of assessments can occasionally be personalized, the evaluation criteria for quality work should not.

Community expectations also matter. Investigators have found that, when a community pressures its schools to set higher expectations, students' performance improves.[13] Whether the push for high student achievement comes from parents or from teachers and principals, when the community and school share high expectation for student achievement in a clear and focused mission and accompanying behaviors, it has a positive impact on student achievement.

Likewise, high teacher expectations for students' achievement work best when they are shared and reflect a school's cultural norms. Students thrive when they are immersed in an environment defined by shared, growth-enhancing values. When students attend schools where beliefs and expectations differ from classroom to classroom and hallway to hallway, they become confused. At the same time, inconsistent values classroom to classroom demoralize teachers who suspect that their colleagues are undermining them. Without consensus on high academic and behavioral expectations and high supports for all students, students may comply (at least minimally) with each teacher's expectations. But, students do not develop the internalized habits of mind and consistent behaviors unless teachers and administrators reinforce these same principles and expectations all day long and in varied settings. This helps explain why students can behave so poorly outside their own classrooms or when a substitute is in charge. When their teachers—the embodiments of these positive values and expectations—are out of sight, their norms disappear, too. Children are likely to take values seriously when they perceive at least a general consensus on them among the adults whom they respect.

SCHOOL CULTURE RE-BOOT 5.3
Teachers' Expectations in a Student-Centered Learning Culture

1. Divide the large group into three or four smaller groups with at least three or four members in each unit. Each unit will consider and discuss Tomlinson and Javius's seven principles.

   • What does each mean?
   • What does each look and sound like when practiced in a school?
   • To what degree does each member agree with each principle?

   (Continued)

---

[13]Hallinger, P., & Murphy, J. F. (1986). The social context of effective schools. *American Journal of Education, 94*(3), 328–355.

(Continued)

- What parts can members enthusiastically support—and why?
- Which aspects make any members uncomfortable—and why?

2. After 15 minutes, recombine into a whole group and review and discuss each group's answers to these questions:

- How well does this school already believe and practice these seven principles daily?
- Which principles are practiced daily by most teachers in the school, and which need additional attention? Give examples.

The leadership team may want to conduct this activity within grade level or departments to have teachers discuss how these learning-supportive behaviors might appear in their classrooms and school and to increase their awareness about how they can boost student learning and achievement.

SCHOOL CULTURE RE-BOOT 5.4
High Expectations and School Characteristics

1. Read and discuss the characteristics of a school with high teacher expectations for all students' achievement as identified below. Discuss other examples of what this might look like, and add examples to the list.

2. Separate into pairs and discuss and assess your school's teacher expectations for every student's achievement.

3. After the discussion, honestly assess your own classroom on these dimensions.

Ratings Key: 1–Unsatisfactory   3–Needs Some Improvement   5–Very Good

High Teacher Expectation for Every Student's High Achievement Characteristic	Rating for School			Rating for Own Classroom		
	1	3	5	1	3	5
The school has developed a shared vision of all students achieving at high levels, regardless of family backgrounds.						
The school has standards and practices in place to avoid both grade retention and social promotion by keeping all students learning apace with peers.						

High Teacher Expectation for Every Student's High Achievement Characteristic	Rating for School			Rating for Own Classroom		
	1	3	5	1	3	5
Teachers, administrators, and parents expect all students to learn a full range of skills—from basic mastery of needed skills to higher-level, complex problem solving—and they act on this belief.						
Teachers have confidence in their skills to help all their students master the basic and higher-level skills, regardless of their family background—and teachers act on this belief.						
Teachers clearly inform students and parents of what students are expected to know and be able to do by the end of the unit or semester.						
Teachers help students use what they already know to learn new knowledge, develop new skills, and expand their understanding.						
Teachers use a variety of effective instructional approaches to ensure that all students learn.						
Students and teachers work together during class time and before or after school (when needed) to master the expected content and skills.						
The school has ongoing, collegial professional development tied to the classroom curriculum to help every teacher improve his or her instructional effectiveness.						
Students and teachers believe that their efforts are more important than their ability to produce their final achievement.						
Students and parents believe that their teachers have confidence in their ability to master the curriculum and expect them to do well.						
The school has a very low dropout rate and a very high promotion or graduation rate.						
Additional example:						
Additional example:						

4. Pairs report their school assessments and one member tallies points for group as a whole for each characteristic.

(Continued)

(Continued)

5. Discuss findings as a group:

- How do teachers' individual expectations for every child's achievement compare with the school's overall expectations? What does this mean to you?
- How do you explain the differences between the individual and school ratings?
- Which aspects of teachers' high expectations for every student's high achievement are strong?
- Which three aspects of teachers' expectations need improvement? What can members of this group do to begin improving teachers' expectations for every student's high achievement?

The leadership team might want to conduct this activity with teachers to gain their views about teachers' expectations for student achievement in their school and to deepen their thinking about how their attitudes affect student learning.

The leadership team might also give a version of this brief survey to students—in one of their classes or homerooms or to student leaders—to see how they perceive teachers' expectations for their academic success—and share findings with the leadership team.

Underestimating students' abilities and desires to learn a high-challenge curriculum hurts them. When students enter classrooms with skills and life experiences different from those that teachers expect, many educators mistakenly conclude students cannot—or don't want to—do complex work. When students fall short because they don't understand teachers' vocabulary or the schools' unwritten rules, teachers conclude that they lack motivation. When teachers allow pupils to sit silently during lessons or praise them for earning high grades by performing at a level that requires neither risk, stretch, nor struggle—educators underrate them. It would be better for every child if teachers thought of student potential like an iceberg—most of it hidden from view—and act upon the belief that high trust, high expectations, and high supports will reveal what lies beneath.

ACADEMIC PRESS AND SUPPORTS

Academic press refers to the extent to which students, teachers, and administrators feel a strong emphasis on scholastic success and meeting specific achievement standards. *Academic supports* refer to the actions that teachers and students take to ensure that students succeed scholastically. *Social supports* refers to personal relations that students have with people in and out of school, including teachers, parents, relatives, and peers, which may help them do well in school.

Academic press, academic supports, and social supports are interactive and mutually reinforcing. Research finds that both high levels of academic rigor and support are positively related to gains in student achievement. This is true regardless of student or school demographics. When either academic press or supports is weak, students learn less.

Academic Press

Academic press accentuates the rigor and accountability for student learning and achievement. It holds that students will achieve more when they clearly know what they are supposed to learn, when expectations for academic learning are high, and when they are held accountable for their performance. Press provides both direction for student work and incentives for students and teachers to achieve at high levels.

Many sources generate academic press. The school culture creates press when it sets expectations that every student can master a high-standards curriculum. Principals create press when they expect teachers to teach the curriculum and to help each student reach the required mastery levels. Teachers can create press by expecting each student to learn the class's objectives, by providing intellectually challenging and engaging work, by familiarizing students with the specific standards and criteria for work quality and quantity, and by the types and frequency of assignments and assessments they expect students to complete as evidence for accountability. Press also comes when school counselors include many demanding courses in students' educational programs.

Improving learning means urging all students to engage deeply in rigorous academic work. This push for higher standards typically results in more demanding content, understanding and applying concepts, problem solving, and developing students' facility with analysis, synthesis, evaluation, and creation. Likewise, it typically includes more homework, extended instructional time, more projects in which students can apply new learning in expanded products and performances, more difficult tests, and stricter requirements for grade promotion and graduation.

Teaching for intellectual rigor is not just for affluent suburban students. Teachers of low-income students may incorrectly believe that, because their students are so lacking in basic competencies, they should be teaching for memorization and transmission of basic facts and skills rather than teaching for concepts, generalizations, and connections. The truth is otherwise. Increasing the curriculum's personal meaning for students and dealing with ideas that matter and make sense to them—increasing its relevance—allow even low achievers to develop a deep understanding of the content and the ability to use it.

Research affirms that, where teachers become familiar with children's interests and life experiences, they can use interactive instruction to build on students' prior knowledge to engage them in higher-level thinking and comprehension. Students can learn to express their ideas orally, visually, and in writing. These students can engage in authentic intellectual work— the original application of knowledge and skills (rather than routine use of facts and procedures) using extensive understanding to create a product or performance that has meaning beyond school. This is the type of multifaceted intellectual work needed for success in life. Of particular note, students taught this way not only produce more intellectually complex work, but they also increase their scores on standardized tests.[14] Thus, teaching all students to interact with a cognitively demanding curriculum made meaningful and relevant to them can meet both learning and accountability demands.

Moreover, research links strong press for academic success with greater student effort, more time spent on academic tasks, and, ultimately, on higher student performance. In addition, academic success can strengthen student self-concept, a valued psycho-emotional school outcome. Evidence indicates that strong academic press is especially critical to student achievement in low-income schools. When levels of both academic press and social and academic supports for students are high, students learn and achieve more. But, when either academic press or supports is low, students learn less.[15]

SCHOOL CULTURE RE-BOOT 5.5
Academic Press and Student Achievement

High academic press can increase student achievement.

1. Read and discuss the characteristics of schools with high academic press for all students' achievement as identified below. Discuss other examples of what this might look like and add these to the list.

---

[14]Newmann, F. M., Bryk, A. S., & Nagaoka, J. K. (2001, January). *Authentic intellectual work and standardized tests: Conflict or coexistence?* Chicago: Improving Chicago's Schools. Retrieved October 22, 2012, from http://ccsr.uchicago.edu/publications/authentic-intel lectual-work-and-standardized-tests-conflict-or-coexistence

[15]Research linking academic press with student achievement can be found in the Research section of this chapter.

2. In pairs, discuss and assess the degree of your school's academic press for every student's achievement.

3. After the discussion, honestly assess your own classroom on these dimensions.

Ratings Key: 1–Unsatisfactory   3–Needs Some Improvement   5–Very Good

	Rating for School			Rating for Own Classroom		
High Academic Press and Student Achievement	*1*	*3*	*5*	*1*	*3*	*5*
The school sets, communicates, and enforces high achievement standards for every student.						
The school organizes the day to maximize every student's instructional and learning time.						
The school focuses on what is best for student learning when making important decisions.						
The school gives students clear responsibilities for raising their own achievement.						
Teachers expect students to do their best all the time.						
Teachers expect students to complete homework every night.						
Teachers encourage students to ask questions and do extra work when they don't understand something.						
The school provides teachers with sustained, high-quality professional development to improve instruction and press students toward more challenging work and higher-order thinking.						
The school's instructional goals are clearly articulated, and students and parents understand them.						
Students are assessed frequently, and results are used to inform instruction, gauge student progress, and hold teachers and students accountable.						
Additional example:						
Additional example:						
Additional example:						

(Continued)

(Continued)

4. As pairs report their school assessment, one member tallies points for the group as a whole for each characteristic. Discuss findings as a group:

- How well do we think teachers in this school provide academic press for each student's achievement?
- What examples (without names) can we offer to support this view?
- Which students in our school do not receive academic press?
- What is the comparison between each leadership team member's academic press and that for teachers overall? What does this mean for students?
- Which aspects of teachers' high expectations for every student's high achievement are presently strong?
- Which three aspects of teachers' expectations need improvement?
- What can members of this group do to begin improving teachers' high expectations for every student's achievement?

· The leadership team might want to conduct this activity with teachers so they can understand what academic press looks like and its effect on student achievement and assess its presence in their school and classrooms.

The leadership team might also want to give a version of this brief survey to students—in one of their classes or homerooms or to student leaders—to see how they perceive academic press at their school—and share findings with the leadership team.

Some suggest that strengthening the stakes attached to academic success or failure—such as tying grade-level promotion or retention to student performance on standardized tests—can increase academic press. This practice is not advisable. Increasing academic pressure without also increasing academic and social supports does not increase student achievement. When students face expectations that they believe are too difficult for them, weak-performing students may lose their motivation and give up. They may become alienated, disengaged, act out disruptively, and eventually drop out of school. Such potentially harmful outcomes are most likely in schools that enroll large proportions of low-achieving students. This is why schools, especially those with many low achievers, need both the academic press and accompanying high levels of academic and social supports to help them meet learning and achievement expectations.

Academic Supports

Academic supports are those practices teachers use to provide individualized opportunities for their students to strengthen and advance their learning. It means using instructional and assessment techniques that deliberately account for individual uniqueness, create more personal meaning for the content, and give students more occasions to give input into what and how they learn and how they express it. Finally, academic supports include giving struggling students more time and interactions with teachers to enlarge and reinforce their learning.

Connecting Students to Curriculum

Directly connecting the students to the curriculum—that is, increasing its relevance for them—is one way to increase students' academic support. To do this, teachers must know their students well as individuals and as learners. Using these student-centered insights, teachers can relate the content to each student's prior learning, experiences, and interests in ways that increase its meaning and relevance to the learner. Meaningful information is better remembered and available to use in new situations.

For instance, one English literature teacher motivated a reluctant student to link his own passions to the course goals. Through probing conversations, the teacher excited the high school football player, who focused only on winning a football scholarship and playing in the National Football League (NFL), with the chance to explore the medieval version of a football star—a knight—and how British literature addressed masculinity. With the teacher's encouragement, the student was able to reflect on his own ambition through the literature.

Assessing to Promote Learning

Accumulating evidence affirms that teachers' instructional interactions with children have the greatest value for students' performance when they are focused, direct, intentional, and characterized by feedback loops involving student performance.

First, students and teachers each use the ongoing, clear, and specific feedback to make sure students never veer too far away from the standards and expected learning outcomes. Students use the feedback to refine and improve their work. Over time, students develop the habit of reflecting seriously on their efforts, assessing their work products against standards of excellence, and mature their dispositions to continue learning after the class ends. Next, teachers can use the feedback to adjust their own instruction, to reteach essential information and skills, or provide extra guidance to identified students who need it.

Increasing Students' Choices

Teachers provide academic supports when they give students more occasions to have a say in their learning. Giving students a few options about routines or assignments can inspire strong cooperation and engagement. Teachers can let students select topics (often from a teacher-approved list) they wish to pursue within the unit. More capable students may be able to design their own projects within approved criteria. Students can have opportunities to express their preferences about sequence (which activity to do first or when the student can do the work), location (where in the classroom or school students can work on an activity), social preferences (with a partner, group, or working alone), or type of presentation to show their knowledge (oral, written, drawn, multimedia, or some combination). Having choices about their education gives students a greater investment in their own learning.

Engaging Resources

Technological tools and a common core curriculum make it easier to personalize learning. Increased customization of learning is what makes *virtual ed*—or education using technology to connect students with Internet resources or to receive online instruction—so popular. Online learning enables students to pursue special interests not offered on-site. It gives students a chance to learn and strengthen missed or tentatively grasped knowledge or skills, so they can catch up with classmates. While giving struggling students the time they need to learn at their own pace, online resources also extend opportunities for the most highly motivated and accomplished students to accelerate and deepen their learning—often anytime and anywhere. Websites offer a range of educational options including digital or adaptive lessons and exercises in various subjects; programs to help educators, students, and parents collaboratively build personal learning plans; and online science laboratory simulations.

Technology can help motivate reluctant learners. Students who lack confidence writing may stall or choke with paper and pencil but can often cruise in front of a laptop. Wanting to use these media motivates students to develop their academic skills to gain access. By embedding social web tools such as blogs and social bookmarks into the learning culture, both students and teachers can stay organized, focused, and advancing. At the same time, mature learners can use the objectives to explore topics of personal interest in greater depth.

More Time

Many struggling students need additional learning time and assistance. Frequently, students may not have the background experiences or vocabulary to make sense of what the teacher is teaching. They need more time to learn the terminology and ideas that underpin what they are learning before they can fully comprehend and apply it. When the students appear to not be grasping the lessons, teachers need to diagnose the weaknesses and make occasions to work with students to remedy these, so they can master the content and keep pace with peers.

For example, teachers may offer before- and after-school tutoring, Saturday mornings, and vacation catch-up sessions. Teachers may host study rooms after school on Monday through Thursday for students who have not completed their homework and for those needing extra help to get through the course successfully. Data from a variety of ongoing assessments can identify students who need extra help. Similarly, teachers may require students who earn grades below C in their course work to get extra help—perhaps retake tests until they earn a C or better. Certain students need extra time to complete tests or projects. Most pupils benefit from receiving one-on-one encouragement and coaching from a teacher who has confidence in their ability to master the learning objectives.

Social Supports

Learning is not always an easy process; it takes time, sustained attention, and energy. Discouragement and frustration are inevitable when learning new information and developing new skills. Even teachers face learning curves when trying to develop proficiency in unfamiliar approaches.

Social supports for academic learning refer to the personal relationships that students have with people who may help them achieve in school. Since the 1940s progressive education movement, social support has been recognized as an essential component of cognitive learning. Social supports create motivation for students to persist and achieve. They build students' confidence that they are capable of learning and attaining academic success. They also foster the psychological safety that allows students to value learning and achieving at school, take risks, admit errors, ask for help, and experience failure as they progress toward high levels of content mastery. Supports may come from parents encouraging their children to work hard in school; teachers providing individual attention, care, and help; and peers encouraging each other to study. Neighborhood members and community organizations may also aid, incentivize, and inspire students.

Support From Adults at School

Students' relationships with their teachers and other adults in schools can be especially valuable resources. Strong and affirming relationships with reliable teachers can create powerful incentives for students to keep attending school despite challenging expectations and occasionally vexing school experiences. Ties of caring and mutual respect boost students' self-assurance and strengthen their resilience and persistence to keep working and learning. Then, too, such relationships may serve as safety valves, providing young people with outlets to express their concerns and gain emotional support, encouragement, information, and guidance about how to best handle weighty personal or academic decisions.

In contrast, a variety of studies find that students who leave high school before graduation often point to a lack of social and academic support as one reason for doing so. Dropouts say they feel disconnected from teachers, even though they claim to have asked for help. Frequently, these former students complain that their teachers do not care about them, are not interested in how well they do in school, and are unwilling to help with problems. They admit that they do not get along with teachers or with other students. As a result, they were failing and did not like being at school. So, they left.

Support From Peers

Almost nothing is more important to most middle and high school students than having the esteem of their peers. If students are to achieve and behave well in school, positive and supportive peer norms can be an enormous help. Most students need to feel a sense of belonging with peers. If their peers expect to do well in school and work toward that end, their friends will likely do the same. If, in contrast, peers expect to do poorly in school and to seek dysfunctional avenues to escape from mainstream goals, their friends are also likely to do the same. Developing and using positive peer support for school achievement, therefore, is an essential dynamic in creating academic success in middle and high schools.

One of the landmark Coleman Report's findings was that, after family characteristics, the students with whom youngsters attended school were almost as important as family background in predicting academic success. Coleman found that African American students achieved better in schools that were predominantly middle class—with other students who typically expected to achieve well in school and live productive and satisfying lives—than they did in schools dominated by low-income students.[16]

When peers value achieving and acting appropriately in school, they reinforce a student-centered learning culture as "the way we do things around here." These student habits create powerful social control mechanisms that informally guide much of what students do every day in schools, freeing the faculty to concentrate on teaching rather than on policing or punishing. Enhanced effectiveness of instructional time results.

---

[16]Coleman, J. S., et al. (1966); Coleman, J. S. (1968). The concept of equality of educational opportunity. *Harvard Educational Review, 38,* 7–22.

In contrast, peer cultural norms can discourage students from learning or behaving well in school. John Ogbu, the late anthropologist, identified *oppositional culture theory*, which posited that African American students responded to institutionalized racism by believing that doing well in school is "acting white." According to this view, many minority students feel as if they have to choose between their minority identity and not learning (and keeping their peers happy) or learning and achieving well (and keeping their teachers and parents happy). As a consequence, these students enact a range of adaptive coping options—often disruptive to the learning environment or to their friendships—in attempts to placate their friends or their teachers.

Similarly, Stanford University Professor Claude Steele's *stereotype threat* theory argues that people tend to underperform when faced with situations that might confirm negative stereotypes about their social group. Here, highly capable students become so worried about performing poorly that they often end up making careless errors, they underachieve, or they stop caring about performing well. Rather than show their very real concern about failing, these pupils act coolly disinterested in school or its rules, become class clowns, study in secret, or avoid potentially threatening situations. Not caring about school sometimes becomes the group's norm.

Both personal experience and research data support the view that certain peer groups' norms actively discourage members from achieving well in school. Figure 5.1 illustrates findings from one study that show large differences in the relationships between academic achievement and peer popularity among whites, African Americans, and Latinos. At low grade point averages (GPAs), popularity within ethnic groups shows little difference. But, when a student achieves a 2.5 GPA (an even mix of Bs and Cs), clear differences start to appear. As the GPAs of African American students increase beyond this point, they tend to have fewer and fewer friends. An African American student with a 4.0 has, on average, 1.5 fewer friends of the same ethnicity than a white student with the same GPA. A Latino student with a 4.0 GPA is the least popular of all Latino students. In contrast, the higher the white students' grades, the more popular they are, especially in public schools.[17]

Geneva Gay, a multicultural scholar, observes that, if students feel that the school environment is alien and hostile toward them or does not affirm who they are (as many minority students believe), they will not be able to concentrate as thoroughly as they might on academic tasks. The stress and anxiety that accompany this lack of support and encouragement drains

[17]Fryer, R. G. (2006, Winter). "Acting white": The social price paid by the best and brightest minority students. *Education Next, 6*, 1. Stanford University, Hoover Institution.

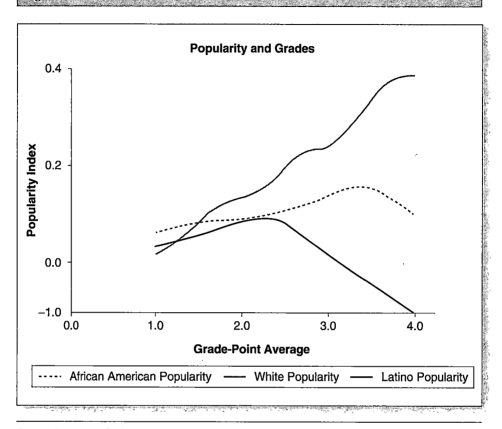

Figure 5.1 Peer Norms Affect Students' Achievement

Source: Fryer, R. G. (2006, Winter). "Acting white": The social price paid by the best and brightest minority students. *Education Next, 6*(1). Stanford University, Hoover Institution. Retrieved April 25, 2012, from http://educationnext.org/actingwhite/

their mental attention, energy, and efforts away from the academic tasks and toward protecting themselves from (psychological) attack. They become less willing to persist at academic tasks, less able to think clearly about the learning, and their schoolwork suffers.[18]

Yet, despite popular belief that schools cannot change peer norms, student-centered learning cultures can overcome them. In public, parochial, or charter schools, adults have created and sustained school cultures for academically disadvantaged young people where learning is cool and students encourage each other to work hard, achieve highly, and be nice. The Effective Schools Movement has 40 years of research documenting

[18]Gay, G. (1994). *A synthesis of scholarship in multicultural education.* Oak Brook, IL: North Central Regional Laboratory. Retrieved October 22, 2012, from http://www.ncrel.org/sdrs/areas/issues/educatrs/leadrshp/le0gay.htm

that school cultures that support all students learning to high level generate high student achievement.[19] Similarly, the Education Trust, a Washington, DC, research and advocacy organization, has extensive contemporary data confirming that teachers and administrators can create school learning cultures in low-income, high-minority neighborhoods in which peer norms work to increase learning and achievement.[20]

Building strong and caring relationships between educators and students and providing every student with the high expectations, academic press, academic and social supports, and positive peer norms are the factors that each child needs to succeed.

SCHOOL CULTURE RE-BOOT 5.6
Providing Academic and Social Supports

1. As a whole group, read and discuss the characteristics of schools with high levels of academic and social supports for all students' achievement as identified below. Discuss other examples of what this might look like and add these to the list.

2. Separate into pairs, and discuss and assess your school's academic and social supports.

3. After the discussion, honestly assess your own classroom on these dimensions.

Ratings Key: 1–Unsatisfactory   3–Needs Some Improvement   5–Very Good

Academic and Social Supports for Each Student's Achievement	Rating for School			Rating for Own Classroom		
	1	3	5	1	3	5
Teachers relate their subjects to students' personal interests and experiences.						
Most teachers provide one-on-one tutoring and after-school (or before-school) help to struggling students to help them keep up with the class.						

(Continued)

---

[19]Effective schools research supporting the idea that high-poverty schools can be high-performing schools can be found in the Research section of this chapter. The Education Trust resources can be retrieved from http://www.edtrust.org/dc/resources/publications.

[20]See, for example, Education Trust. (2012, June 26). *Building and sustaining talent: Creating conditions in high-poverty schools that support effective teaching and learning.* Washington, DC: Author. Retrieved October 23, 2012, from http://www.edtrust.org/sites/edtrust.org/files/Building_and_Sustaining_Talent.pdf

(Continued)

Academic and Social Supports for Each Student's Achievement	Rating for School			Rating for Own Classroom		
	1	3	5	1	3	5
Most teachers actively make their curriculum personally meaningful and relevant to every student.						
Most teachers make occasions to help students solve problems that interfere with their learning.						
School counselors work closely with teachers to help individual students succeed in their classes.						
Teachers make the time to get to really know their students as individuals.						
Teachers really listen and try to understand what students say and mean.						
Teachers really believe that each student can do well in school.						
Students believe their teachers have confidence in their ability to do well in school.						
Students encourage each other to perform well in school.						
Teachers use coaches, school staff, parents, and community members to help students with personal or academic problems.						
Additional example:						
Additional example:						
Additional example:						

4. Pairs report their school assessments, and one member tallies points for the group as a whole for each characteristic.

5. Discuss findings as a large group:

   - How well do you think teachers in this school provide academic and social supports for each student's achievement?
   - What examples (without names) can you offer to support this view?
   - How do the leadership team member's ratings compare with the overall teachers' ratings on academic and social supports? Why might they differ?

- How do you explain the differences between the classroom and school ratings?
- What does this mean for students?
- Which aspects of teachers' academic and social supports for student's high achievement are strong?
- Which three aspects of teachers' expectations need improvement?
- What can members of this group do to begin improving teachers' academic and social supports for every student's achievement?

The leadership team might want to conduct this activity with teachers in grade levels or departments to gain their perceptions about the school's academic and social supports for students' achievement and to heighten their awareness about how they can provide these supports to help their students learn and achieve.

The leadership team might also give a version of this brief survey to students—in one of their classes or homerooms or to student leaders—to see how they perceive academic and social supports at school—and discuss findings with the rest of the leadership team.

RELATIONSHIPS

Teaching and leadership are people professions. Relationships are essential means for accomplishing important professional goals. For students to succeed, they must be personally known at school and have strong bonds with the people there. While important interpersonal and professional boundaries exist, good teachers combine teaching's generalizable principles and subject-specific instruction with a genuine sensitivity to each student's uniqueness and humanness as a learner. In turn, when young people believe that their teachers, administrators, and coaches care about them and really want them to succeed, they will do virtually whatever is asked of them.

Relationships With Teachers

Of all the relations at school, students' affiliations with their teachers are the most important. Research confirms that effective teachers care about their students. They show concern in ways that students understand, see, and feel. These teachers bring out the best in students by affirming and encouraging them with respect, patience, trust, honesty, courage, listening, understanding, and knowing their students as persons and as learners. They establish rapport and credibility by emphasizing, modeling, and practicing evenhandedness and showing esteem. When students are having difficulties, these teachers work with them—rather than scold or ignore them. They tell students what they need to do right and get all the facts before speaking with students about what they did wrong. And, they treat students equitably and without favoritism.

Effective teachers show interest in their students both inside and outside the classroom. Attending student football games, plays, and choral concerts in which their pupils perform shows young people that their teachers genuinely value them. This increases students' feelings of belonging in their classrooms and their willingness to work hard for their teacher—even if they find the academic content less than stimulating.

The bonds teachers and students build together influence their engagement with classroom lessons. In sustained, personal, and authentic ways, teachers and other school staff get to know each student well, so they can tailor their instruction to best encourage and advance each student's learning and persistence despite setbacks. This human-to-human connection through private conversations, verbal or nonverbal encouragement, or specific help gradually persuades each student that school is not a faceless bureaucracy but a place where at least one person likes him or her and is working to help build success.

Researchers agree that the classroom's instructional and emotional aspects predict students' academic effort, perseverance, and achievement gains in reading, writing, and math. Young people in supportive relationships—with at least one adult who believes in and holds high expectations for them, models successful behaviors, and is consistently present in their lives—are able to flourish in school, while peers in similar circumstances but without this relational support do not. This is especially true for students most at risk for poor achievement.[21] Giving students a variety of affective and academic scaffolding helps them overcome barriers presented by poverty, low expectations, family instability, and other life situations. Likewise, investigators find that many boys are *relational learners*, who need to feel their teachers' warmth, mastery, and inspiration before opening themselves to invest in learning.

Strong and caring relationships with teachers help students achieve well at all grade levels. In the early grades, being in positive classroom climates with friendly, considerate teachers is linked to greater self-regulation, less disruptive behavior, and higher teacher-rated social competence among elementary and middle school students. Middle school teachers whose classrooms support increasing student autonomy and competence can build personal relationships in which students feel known, valued, and respected. Gains in middle grade achievement and reduced levels of

---

[21]For example, see Vargas, B., & Brizard, J-C. (2010, November 3). Beating the odds in urban schools. Commentary. *Education Week, 29*(10), 22–23; Reichert, M. C. (2010, November 17). Hopeful news regarding the crisis in U.S. education. Exploring the human element in teaching boys. *Education Week, 30*(13), 27.

disruptive behavior are evidence in classrooms in which expectations are clear, time is used well and productively, and teachers respond effectively to variations in students' motivation and focus. Similarly, strong, positive, and cooperative relationships with teachers increase high school students' likelihood of graduating.

A positive school culture that values teacher–student relationships also affects student behaviors in ways that keep them in school and learning. When a student acts disruptively, caring educators focus on what the errant student needs to get back on track rather than exact punishment with an out-of-school suspension. For example, schools that use *restorative practices*—disciplinary methods that show understanding of students' concerns that underlie their actions, provide consequences that have meaning for the student, help students see how their actions affect others, and problem solve with students, peers, and parents to help young people learn more effective ways of handling frustrations—work to resolve and prevent student misbehavior rather than penalize students by separating them from the classroom. In turn, students who believe that their teachers like and understand them are more willing to act appropriately and right any behavioral wrongs. The results are a calmer school environment and more children achieving well. [22]Although mutually respectful and trusting relationships with teachers generally benefit all students, those who often gain most are socially at-risk students, who enter high school with low educational expectations and a history of school-related problems.

Relationships With Other Educators

Students may also gain from relationships with other adults in school. Administrators, school counselors, teacher aides, coaches, secretaries, or custodial staff frequently offer students thoughtful listening, wise advice, and moral support. As school personnel attend to individual students, these adults come to understand each young person's concerns and values. Within professional but human boundaries, students, faculty, and staff feel safe to share their cultural perspectives, disappointments, and personal life experiences. Adults provide insight, encouragement, and new ways of understanding and responding to difficult situations. Adults can become advocates for their students with other educators, parents, college admissions officers, or community agencies. Well-achieving peers may serve as confidants and mentors to students as well.

One successful student told how his track coach encouraged him to do well in the classroom. This coach expected team members to graduate from

---

[22]See, for example, Shah, N. (2012, October 17). "Restorative practices" offer alternatives to suspension. *Education Week, 32*(8), 1, 14–15.

high school and go to college. This key relationship led the student to participate in long-term and meaningful ways with school activities, to set goals, and to meet friends with similar, positive aspirations. Over the summer, these optimistic influences continued as the coach connected the students to employment opportunities and the community recreation center.

In a like manner, a well-designed and run advisory program can deepen and expand relationships between students and adults at school. All professional staff members, including the principal, can advise a small group of 18 to 20 students and loop with the same students throughout their years in the school. An adjusted school schedule can provide advisory programs with regular occasions to meet daily or weekly. Advisors can regularly review each student's academic progress, encourage and advocate for the student as needed, and hold each young person accountable for staying on track. Advisory times can also give students and educators opportunities to share their views about events and issues important to them and to listen and learn from each other.

Building Students' Resilience

Strong relationships with teachers and other school adults can help young people foster their resilience to overcome difficult family circumstances, frustrating school experiences, and negative peer norms. *Resilience* can be defined as the process or capacity to have successful outcomes despite challenging or threatening circumstances. Research finds that children who experience chronic adversity fare better or recover more successfully when they have a positive, stable emotional relationship with a competent adult, are good learners and problem solvers, are likeable, and have areas of competence and perceived efficacy valued by self or society.

Teachers and other adults foster resilience when they mentor students, offer emotional support during hard times, act as the student's advocate when conflict arises in school or at home, or provide opportunities to pursue a special talent or interest. Likewise, teachers can identify, enlist, and help further develop their students' emotional, mental, spiritual, and relationship assets to support their school achievement.

Children who can access a variety of resources build resilience. Emotional resources such as stamina, persistence, and good decision making give children the ability to control their emotional responses, particularly to negative situations, without engaging in self-destructive behaviors. Mental resources include those abilities and skills such as reading, writing, and computing needed for daily life. Spiritual resources give children some belief in a divine purpose and guidance upon which they can rely for direction and support. Physical resources include good physical health and mobility or the capacity to use what abilities they have to influence and control their environments. Support systems include family, friends, and community people who are available in times of need. Relationships and role models are resources who nurture the child and who do not engage in self-harming behaviors. Finally, teachers may have to explicitly teach students knowledge of unspoken school and social rules—those verbal and nonverbal expectations, assumptions, and behaviors that in-group members continuously use to move easily through the system to meet their needs—and of which children living outside the mainstream may not be (but need to be) aware.

SCHOOL CULTURE RE-BOOT 5.7
Relationships and Student Achievement

Strong and caring relationships between students and adults in school can increase student achievement and boost their resilience.

1. Read and discuss the characteristics of schools that have strong and caring relationships between adults and all students as identified below. Discuss other examples of what this might look like, and add these to the list.

2. Separate into pairs, and discuss and assess how your school fares on these characteristics.

3. After the discussion, honestly assess your own classroom on these dimensions.

Ratings Key: 1–Unsatisfactory   3–Needs Some Improvement   5–Very Good

Strong and Caring Relationships Between Students and Adults in School	Rating for School			Rating for Own Classroom		
	1	*3*	*5*	*1*	*3*	*5*
Every student has at least one strong and caring relationship with an adult in this school.						
Each teacher and administrator in this school genuinely likes to be around the students.						
When students and teachers walk down the halls, you see and exchange lots of smiles.						
Teachers and staff actively mentor students who are struggling academically or personally.						

(Continued)

(Continued)

Strong and Caring Relationships Between Students and Adults in School	Rating for School			Rating for Own Classroom		
	1	3	5	1	3	5
The school has a program to systematically identify students needing mentoring and provides them with a suitable mentor and frequent opportunities to meet at school.						
Teachers greet each student daily by name.						
The school has an active and well-organized advisory program with a regular time each week (or day) for educators and staff to interact with a small number of students in personally meaningful ways.						
Teachers and school counselors regularly identify and use students' assets to help them solve problems and build resilience.						
Most teachers attend student concerts, plays, and sports events to watch their students perform.						
Additional example:						
Additional example:						
Additional example:						

4. Pairs report their school assessments and have one member tally points for the group as a whole for each characteristic.

5. Discuss findings as a group:
   - How well do you think teachers in this school provide strong and caring relationships for each student?
   - What examples (without names) can you offer to support this view?
   - How do you explain the difference between each leadership team member's profile on relationships and that for teachers overall? What does this mean for students?
   - Which areas of teachers' relationships with every student are widespread and active?
   - Which top three aspects of teachers' relationships with students need improvement?
   - What can members of this group do to begin improving teachers' and staffs' relationships with every student?

The leadership team might want to conduct this activity with teachers in grade levels or departments to gain their views about caring relationships between adults and students in the school and to heighten their awareness about the importance of these relationships to student learning and behavior.

The leadership team may also want to give a version of this brief survey to students— in one of their classes or homerooms or to student leaders—to see how they perceive relationships at school—and report findings to the leadership team.

Tradition, inertia, and a one-size-fits-all mentality (and, occasionally, budgets) stand in the way of establishing student-centered learning cultures. Although a budget may limit the number of computers with Internet access available for each classroom, it cannot stop teachers from implementing high expectations, finding ways to make the curriculum more meaningful and relevant for each student, providing helpful backstops to prevent students from failing, and developing genuine, caring relationships. Rather, teachers need the shared beliefs and actions necessary to encourage students' persistence, hard work, and resilience. These habits are not only essential to get through school but also to help students make their way in life. Only when teachers and administrators can re-boot their schools' cultures to value both the standards-driven curriculum as well as these student-centered approaches will each child benefit. Ensuring that every student succeeds is likely only when the school as a community becomes a student-centered learning culture.

RESEARCH

Brookover, W. B., & Lezotte, L. W. (1979). *Changes in school characteristics coincident with changes in student achievement.* East Lansing: Michigan State University, Institute for Research on Teaching.

Brophy, J., & Good, T. (1970). Teachers' communication of differential expectations for children's classroom performance: Some behavioral data. *Journal of Educational Psychology, 61,* 365–374.

Brophy, J. E., & Evertson, C. *Learning from teaching. A developmental perspective.* Boston: Allyn & Bacon.

Cuban, L. (1984). Transforming the frog into a prince: Effective schools research, policy, and practice at the district level. *Harvard Educational Review, 54,* 129–151.

Dusek, J. B., & O'Connell, E. J. (1973). Teacher expectancy effects on the achievement test performance of elementary school children. *Journal of Educational Psychology, 65,* 371–377.

Edmonds, R. (1979, October). Effective schools for the urban poor. *Educational Leadership, 37*(15), 15–24.

Edmonds, R. R., & Fredericksen, J. R. (1978). *Search for effective schools: The identification and analysis of city schools that are instructionally effective for poor children.* Cambridge, MA: Harvard University, Center for Urban Studies.

Education Trust. (2005, November). *Gaining traction, gaining ground. How some high schools accelerate learning for struggling students.* Washington, DC: Author.

Ferguson, R. R. (2003). Teachers' perceptions and expectations in the black-white test score gap. *Urban Education 38*(4), 460–507.

Grogger, J. (1997). Local violence and educational attainment. *The Journal of Human Resources 32*(4), 659–692.

Heck, R. H. (2000). Examining the impact of school quality on school outcomes and improvement: A value-added approach. *Educational Administration Quarterly, 36*(4), 513–552.

Heck, R. H. (2005). Examining school achievement over time: A multilevel, multi-group approach. In W. K. Hoy & C. G. Miskal (Eds.), *Contemporary issues in educational policy and school outcomes* (pp. 1–28). Greenwich, CT: Information Age.

Hoy, W. K., & Hannun, J. (1997). Middle school climate: An empirical assessment of organizational health and student achievement. *Educational Administration Quarterly 33*(3), 290–311.

Goddard, R. D., Sweetland, S. R., & Hoy, W. K. (2000). Academic emphasis of urban elementary schools and student achievement: A multi-level analysis. *Educational Administration Quarterly, 36*(5), 683–702.

Lee, V. E., Smith, J. B., Perry, T. E., & Smylie, M. A. (1999, October). *Social support, academic press, and student achievement: A view from the middle grades in Chicago.* Chicago: Improving Chicago Schools. Retrieved April 13, 2012, from http://ccsr.uchicago.edu/publications/p0e01.pdf

Levine, D. U. (1990). Update on effective schools: Findings and implications for research and practice. *The Journal of Negro Education, 59*(4), 577–584.

Lezotte, L., & Snyder, K. M. (2011). *What effective schools do: Re-envisioning the correlates.* Bloomington, IN: Solution Tree.

Mayer, D. P., Hoy, W. K., & Hannun, J. (1997). Middle school climate: An empirical assessment of organizational health and student achievement. *Educational Administration Quarterly, 33*(3), 290–311.

McDonald, R., & Elias, P. (1976). The effects of teaching performance on pupil learning (Vol. I, final report). In *Beginning teacher evaluation study, phase 2, 1974–1976.* Princeton, NJ: Educational Testing Service.

Mullens, J. E., Moore, M. T., & Ralph, J. (2000). *Monitoring school quality: An indicator's report.* Washington, DC: U.S. Department of Education, National Center for Education Statistics.

O'Connell, E., Dusek, J., & Wheeler, R. (1974). A follow-up study of teacher expectancy effects. *Journal of Educational Psychology, 66,* 325–328.

Rist, R. (1970). Students' social class and teacher expectations: The self-fulfilling prophesy in ghetto education. *Harvard Educational Review, 40,* 411–451.

Rotter, M., Maughan, B., Mortimore, P., Ouston, J., & Smith, A. (1979). *Fifteen thousand hours: Secondary schools and their effects of children.* Cambridge, MA: Harvard University Press.

Scheerens, J., & Bosker, R. J. (1997). *The foundations of educational effectiveness.* New York: Elsevier.

Promoting and Creating Strong Parent–Community Ties

FOCUS QUESTIONS

- What are the positive outcomes to students of family involvement in their education?
- What are the conditions that families use to support their children's education?
- What challenges do school leaders face in working with parents in culturally diverse communities, and how can these be overcome?
- How can educators develop and display cultural competence?
- What ways can schools involve families with their children's education?
- How can school partnerships with the community benefit student learning?

E ducators often assert that their greatest job satisfactions come from the strong rapport they develop with students and teachers. Their attitudes about working collaboratively with parents and community members are mixed, however. While educators publically tout school–parent engagement, many privately prefer that parents participate only to the extent that teachers and principals feel comfortable. If parents seem "over-involved" or critical, they are perceived as a nuisance or a threat. And, even when educators do view school–home collaborations as a key to increasing children's school success, they often lack the insights into how to make cooperative relations with families and communities a reality.

If they are to be effective for all children, schools need to make deliberate and constructive connections with their families and communities. Schools cannot shut their doors and leave the outside world's troubles at the curb. Schools are porous and permeable institutions; what happens in families and communities affects how students learn in schools. Increasing poverty rates create hungry and tired children who cannot concentrate. Changing demographics place teachers in classrooms with children who have unfamiliar backgrounds and unclear learning needs. Economic conditions are forcing schools to do without many needed resources. At the same time, schools are losing their monopoly on educating, as high percentages of young people have personal computers and Internet access for information gathering and social networking—without teachers' supervision—further dissolving the line between school and the larger community.

Joyce Epstein, a Johns Hopkins professor and an expert in school–family relationships, observes, "The way schools care about children is reflected in the way schools care about the children's families. If educators view children simply as *students,* they are likely to see the family as separate from the school. If educators view students as *children,* they are likely to see both the family and the community as partners with the school in children's education and development."[1]

To make schools places in which all children can be successful, school leaders must create a culture of achievement that fosters authentic partnerships focused on student learning among teachers, parents, and the community. In a culture re-boot, leaders may have to help teachers and parents realize that each side has much to gain from the other about how to best inspire each child to learn what the school teaches. To help all parties realize their mutual goal—a quality education and a successful future for each child—educators, parents, and community members need to build trusting relationships anchored in clear, two-way communication and dedicated to promoting positive student outcomes. This chapter explains how to make this happen.

FAMILY INVOLVEMENT AND STUDENT OUTCOMES

While teaching quality is the most important in-school factor affecting student achievement, family and neighborhood influences matter more. Steven Brill, a Yale journalism professor and author of *Class Warfare: Inside the Fight to Fix America's Schools,* argues that the steady research

---

[1]Epstein, J. L. (1995, May). School/family/community partnerships: Caring for the children we share. *Phi Delta Kappan, 76*(9), 701–712.

consensus is that, at most, teaching accounts for about 15 percent of student achievement outcomes, while socioeconomic factors account for about 60 percent.[2] While not all would agree with these numbers, it is abundantly certain that out-of-school factors, such as generational poverty, family income, parents' education, and health care, usually count more toward student success than all in-school factors. So, when school, parents, and community work together to focus on increasing student learning, they more than even the odds.

Developing a student-centered learning culture means being able to accommodate children's varied background experiences, interests, and learning styles in ways that advance their learning. Because school–parent–community ties have direct effects on students' motivation and school participation, they have an indirect influence on the teachers' instructional effectiveness.

Family Involvement and Student Achievement

The link between student achievement and parent involvement is well established. More than 40 years of research show that family involvement is a powerful influence on student achievement. When schools work together with families to promote student learning, children tend to succeed not just in school but in life. These students attain the following results:[3]

- Earn higher grades and test scores, and enroll in higher-level programs
- Attend school regularly and do more homework
- Merit promotion to next grade, pass their classes, and earn more course credits
- Show higher math and improved reading proficiency
- Receive fewer placements in special education
- Have better social skills, show improved behavior, and adapt well to school
- Receive fewer disciplinary actions
- Have higher graduation rates
- Have greater enrollment in postsecondary education

---

[2]Brill, S. (2011). *Class warfare: Inside the fight to fix American education.* New York: Simon & Schuster as cited in Goldstein, D. (2011, August 29–September 5). Can teachers alone overcome poverty? Steven Bill thinks so. *The Nation.* Retrieved May 5, 2012, from http://www.thenation.com/article/162695/can-teachers-alone-overcome-poverty-steven-brill-thinks-so

[3]Research studies confirming the relationship between parent involvement and student achievement can be found in the References section of this chapter.

Just as important, research shows that what a family does is more important to student success than what a family is or earns. Parental involvement is the most reliable predictor of academic achievement whether the child is in preschool or upper grades, whether the family is financially struggling or affluent, and whether the parents finished high school or earned graduate degrees. Regardless of family income or background, children succeed in school—in ways identified above—when their families are able to accomplish the following three conditions:

- Create a home environment that encourages learning (and parents are loving, supportive, and use adequate discipline)
- Express high (but not unrealistic) expectations for their children's achievement and future careers
- Become involved in their children's education in school and in the community

In fact, parent expectations and involvement at home exert the most influence over student achievement, while parents' attendance at school events has the least.

Research shows that, when schools support families in these three areas, children from low-income families and varied cultural backgrounds earn the school grades and test scores that approach those attained by students from middle-class families. They are more likely to take advantage of a full range of educational opportunities after graduating from high school. Even when only one or two of these conditions are in place, children do measurably better in school.

Family, Community, and Cultural Assets

Schools cannot provide children with all the help they need to learn. It is well established that people who have *social capital*—that is, strong and durable networks of relationships with other people—are healthier, happier, and live longer. Investigators find that *family social capital*—such as parents checking homework and stressing the importance of academic achievement—counts more than *school social capital*—such as teacher morale and student involvement in school activities—in influencing students' academic success.[4] Children with social capital have multiple supportive relationships with adults and institutions that nurture their development, and the adults in their lives know and work with each other. Social capital is frequently identified with children's and adolescents' resilience—their

---

[4]Molnar, M. (2012, October 17). Study: Parents influential in academic success. Blogs of the week. *Education Week*, 32(8), 10.

ability to cope with both small and large disruptions in their lives. As Chapter 5 noted, the greater the child's resilience and the more people involved in the child's support system, the greater the likelihood of success. Schools and their communities, therefore, must be connected in many ways and spaces if their children's safety nets are to remain strong.

Social capital, resilience, and civic capacity (the interests, knowledge, and skills required to participate competently as citizens in a democracy) all focus on assuming that every community has assets that can be used to support children and youth. Unlike the *deficit model*, which looks at non-traditional families, economic decline, or the presence of immigrant groups with different traditions as creating cumulative obstacles to community well-being and school success, the cultural *asset model* looks for the positive features in all children's cultures.

For many educators who see families and communities as forces over which they have little or no sway, the cultural asset model represents a major shift in thinking. Building social capital for children means having educators enter into partnerships with parents, caregivers, community leaders, and local agencies—and effectively address their trust and responsibility issues—to generate more resources for children and their families. Studies find that social cohesiveness outside the school supports shared learning objectives and helps generate political support for the schools.

Benefits of Collaboration for Schools, Families, and Communities

Schools that are integral and positive parts of their community see higher academic achievement, fewer discipline problems, higher teacher morale, higher teacher ratings by parents, better reputations in the community, and improved use of resources. Benefits of collaboration also include the following:

• **Supporting learning at home**—school–home collaborations may encourage parents to play a direct role in working with their children on educational activities. Teachers may ask parents to read books with their children. They may send newsletters home previewing what children will be doing in class and what parents can do at home to better support this learning, and they may suggest how to create home routines to support homework and reinforce study habits. Teachers may also want to ask parents what the school can do to help them support learning at home. Teachers and school counselors can show parents how they can participate in making decisions essential to their children's well-being and future plans. These activities can help parents better understand their children's development and be more effective parents.

- **Resolving issues that limit parent involvement**—collaborating with parents can identify and remedy concerns that interfere with their involvement in their children's learning. These include helping provide child care and transportation to reduce parents' barriers to coming to school, providing language translation during student enrollment and school–family events, making encouraging phone calls or sending e-mails with frequent and balanced news (offering positives about the child as well as concerns).

- **Increase supports for their children**—teachers working with parents have higher confidence in the parents and higher expectations for the children. In turn, parents develop more confidence about helping their children learn at home, identify the people and resources in school to aid their children, and understand more about themselves as parents. In addition, when parents become involved in their children's education, they often enroll in continuing education courses to advance their own learning.

- **Increase teacher–parent trust**—teachers depend on parents as essential partners in student learning to get students to school every day on time, encourage and oversee schoolwork activities at home, and share problem solving around student behavior. In turn, parents see teachers' genuine caring for their children and their follow-through on practices that advance students' success.

- **Increase community support for their children**—schools can give parents contact information about school and community resources to help them solve problems related to their children and their own adult education (such as literacy, job skills, or citizenship preparation). Community health, recreation, social service agencies, and the police department are especially beneficial to low-income children and their families who may need a range of supplemental services to remedy problems that interfere with learning—from getting free dental checkups and treatment to getting mental health services for dealing with neglect or abuse.[5]

- **Providing positive and relatable role models**—youth service organizations including the Boy and Girl Scouts, Boys and Girls Clubs, church groups, and the YMCA offer programs of positive peer pressure and examples of successful coping and advancing in difficult environments. These increase the likelihood that children become and stay engaged in school.

Simply put, school–home–community collaborations generate benefits for all participants and especially for children.

---

[5]Many of these services are arranged through local agreements between the school district and other public agencies and private institutions rather than directly through the school itself.

CHALLENGES OF WORKING WITH PARENTS IN CULTURALLY DIVERSE COMMUNITIES

Race, ethnicity, and social class are often undercurrents in schools where educators have difficulties developing trusting and mutually respectful relationships with parents and communities. Different languages, interaction styles, social norms, and educational beliefs, as well as teachers' comfort levels with parents, often create obstacles to working well together. Successful relationships that bridge cultures and languages typically require serious effort to create and sustain. Additionally, educators need to learn their families' *funds of knowledge* and *cultural assets*—ways of knowing, learning, and acting—in order to see children's and families' strengths rather than deficits.

The same sensitivity and intentionality required to re-boot the school's culture for in-houses changes must also be used to connect the school with parents and community members. The more the school's culture creates a welcoming climate to parents, builds trust and mutual respect, and acknowledges the community's values and aspirations, the stronger the level of parent and community involvement can become.

Today's Families and School Involvement

Because today's families and homes come in a wide range of configurations—children raised by two parents, single parents, same-gender parents, grandparents or other surrogates, older children, foster homes, home caretakers, and nannies, to name a few—schools seeking to build constructive school–home partnerships by narrowly defining *parent* may be screening out those very persons they need to engage as allies in increasing students' achievement and aspirations.

Families also vary in other ways that affect their relationships with schools. Work schedules, caretaker's economic or health status, immigrant status, number of children in the home, whether English is spoken at home, extended families, military families, families where parents are in prison, and those who are homeless all complicate families' relations with their children's schools. Likewise, caregivers differ in their attitudes about school based on their own experiences as students and their current encounters with school personnel. How well their child is doing at school plays a role, too.

Yet, more parents are increasing their children's school readiness at home. Research shows that today's parents—especially low-income parents—are more engaged with their young children than they were a decade ago and in ways that can boost children's academic achievement. Several indicators on the U.S. Census Bureau's 2009 survey show American children are spending more time with their parents, reading, playing, and eating dinner together than they were in 1998. What is more, parents are speaking to their children using a larger vocabulary and more complex syntax and structure, more like that a teacher might use and that helps children learn to read. This is certainly a positive trend and likely reflects the widespread efforts in the early to mid-2000s to make parents aware of how important their involvement in general—and reading with children in particular—is to their school success.[6]

In short, making assumptions about today's families is an uncertain business. Familiar generalizations may not accurately describe the variety of home lives from which our children come and the emphasis families place on learning in school. For educators, these issues are less moral than practical ones.

Barriers to Parent or Caretaker Involvement

To develop successful relations with parents, administrators and teachers may have to first overcome a host of interacting factors: institutional, impersonal, and personal (as well as negative attitudes, lack of skills or means, and practical limits). Table 6.1 illustrates these obstacles and how they relate.

Institutional Barriers

Institutional barriers include a school culture that is indifferent or hostile toward parent involvement, negative attitudes by school administrators and staff, insufficient personnel assigned to planning and engaging in parent participation activities, and limits in available resources (typically money, space, and time) devoted to parent and community relations. The school may lack a policy committed to advancing school–home collaboration, and school leaders may lack interest or feel uncomfortable increasing their interactions with parents. Or, if the school has a school–home policy, school leaders may halfheartedly set up a formal home involvement program but not target the necessary resources to upgrade teachers' and staffs' skills for working effectively with parents who are different than they are.

Impersonal Barriers

Impersonal obstacles to home–school collaboration occur as well. The rapid influx of immigrant families may overtake the school personnel's

---

[6]Sparks, S. D. (2011, August 24). Census points to positive trends in parent involvement. *Education Week, 31*(1), 10.

Table 6.1 General Barriers to Parent–School Involvement

	Negative Attitudes	Lack of Skills, Means	Practical Limits
Institutional	School culture, school administration, and teachers are hostile toward increasing home involvement.	Not enough staff is assigned to planning and implementing ways to enhance involvement: only a token effort is present to provide for different languages.	School administration gives low priority to allocating space, time, and money resources to increase involvement with families.
Impersonal	School administration is indifferent to increasing home involvement.	Rapid increase of immigrant families overwhelms the school's ability to provide relevant home involvement activities.	Schools lack resources; most homes have concerns related to work schedules, child care, and transportation.
Personal	Specific teachers and parents believe home involvement is not worth the effort or feel uncomfortable with such involvement.	Specific teachers and parents lack relevant languages and interpersonal skills that could facilitate increased school–family involvement.	Specific teachers and parents are too busy or lack resources to support increased school–family involvement.

Source: Adapted from Center for Mental Health in Schools at UCLA. (2011, December). *Enhancing home involvement to address barriers to learning: A collaborative process.* Los Angeles, CA: Author, p. 7. Retrieved May 10, 2012, from http://smhp.psych.ucla.edu/pdfdocs/homeinv.pdf

capacities to gather essential assets—especially teachers qualified to teach English-language learners, appropriate classrooms, and instructional materials—to keep up. Issues including inconvenient work schedules, child care, language, and transportation may prevent both school and families from making and sustaining necessary ties to build constructive working relationships.

Personal Barriers

Certain key school administrators or teachers may not have the necessary attitudes, skills, or temperaments for working with parents because developing these requires time, effort, and the willingness to overcome complex racial, cultural, and possible language differences. Absent a perspective that views family diversity as a potential asset and without persuasive information about the importance of home involvement to make both teachers and students more successful, administrators and teachers may lack the interest to become involved with children's families.

SCHOOL CULTURE RE-BOOT 6.1
Assessing Barriers to School–Home Collaboration

Successful school–parent collaboration starts with assessing one's own personal and school's attitudes, emotions, and actions about working with parents.

1. Using Table 6.1, individually reflect on the institutional, impersonal, and personal barriers to parent involvement as they may appear in your own (or colleagues') negative attitudes, lack of skills, and practical limits. What may you or your fellow teachers and administrators be thinking or doing to either advance or undermine building collaborative relationships with parents?

2. After working alone, form groups of four to discuss your findings.

   • What are the institutional, impersonal, and individual barriers you are finding that limit relationship building with parents?
   • What can you as individual teachers and administrators do to remove these barriers?
   • What can you do as a school organization?

3. Recombine as a whole group to discuss your findings. What conclusions can the group draw about its own involvement with parents to support student learning, and what recommendations for improvement seem appropriate?

School leaders may want to conduct this activity with teachers to assess their beliefs and practices in working with parents and heighten their awareness of the benefits to be gained by school–parent cooperation. School leaders may also want to survey key parents to gather their views on this issue to identify where additional reflection and revised approaches would be helpful.

How Parents View School–Home Collaboration

Middle-class and affluent families tend to be highly invested in their children's education and actively seek avenues to influence their children's schooling. They want to ensure that their children have the best teachers, the highest-status courses, and all the skill-building and leadership-developing activities that their children can shoehorn into their schedules. As successful former students themselves, these parents believe they know what quality education should look like and how teachers and principals should provide it. Their respected economic and social standings in the community give them the confidence to see school personnel, at best, as expert peers, and at worst, as hired help.

Working with low-income and minority parents brings different challenges. These parents often face psychological as well as demographic obstacles to working with their children's schools. Although extensive research shows that these parents generally have great respect for education and high ambitions for their offspring's school success, they may lack confidence in their own academic abilities. Many have had few years of formal schooling and do not see themselves as capable of helping their children's education. Additionally, low-income parents may experience principals and teachers as intimidating, reflecting their own humiliating and painful experiences as pupils—and anticipating more of the same. Finally, many low-income parents are working several jobs and simply do not have the time or flexibility to attend school conferences.

With so many social hurdles between schools and families reflecting variations in educational background, economic well-being, skin color, ethnicity, culture, and language, it is understandable why some parents are acutely sensitive to whether teachers genuinely respect and care about their children. This is especially true if the only communications these parents receive from the school tend to be impersonal newsletters, informational flyers, and upsetting phone calls about their children's failures or misbehaviors. Actual face-to-face or affirming interactions are rare. No wonder that these parents may be too busy or otherwise unable to attend school events.

Trust in School–Parent Relationships

Relationships run on trust. This is even truer for principals and teachers working with parents because parents do not share educators' professional norms. Nor have parents been inducted into the same school and district assumptions, expectations, and procedures. What principals and teachers accept as givens—such as "teachers knows best how children should learn"—parents find open to question. But, regardless of one's title or formal power in the school community, all parties depend on others to achieve their desired outcomes and feel their efforts are making a difference. Each person in the relationship holds certain expectations about their own and others' obligations. These often unvoiced understandings form the basis for judging the actual social exchanges that occur. Because educators' professional (and, perhaps, personal) backgrounds, assumptions, and expectations may markedly differ from those of their students' parents, principals and teachers must be especially conscious of what they say and how they act if they are to develop trustful relationships with them.

Why Trust Between Educators and Parents Is Important

A focus on building trusting, collaborative relationships among teachers, families, and community members is one of the key practices of higher-performing schools—especially those serving children in diverse neighborhoods. Trust between parents, teachers, and principals provides three essential resources for the school:

• **Commitment**—broad teacher and parent buy-in on school reculturing and improvement efforts occur more readily with strong relational trust. All parties are confident they are working toward a shared and valued goal: helping their children succeed.

• **Effort**—school improvement asks parents who are already working hard to earn a living and raise families to take on more responsibilities for helping their children learn and connecting with teachers to facilitate school achievement. Relational trust creates an incentive for taking on more tasks.

• **Reduced vulnerability**—trust allows parents to feel safe that their children will learn with particular teachers and accept teachers' suggestions about what the child should do to be a successful student and ways parents can help.

Improving parent–teacher trust is both an important goal and positive outcome of successful school–home programs. Teachers depend on parents as essential partners in student learning to get students to school on time, support schoolwork activities at home, and share problem solving around students' academic or behavior concerns. Similarly, teachers' and parents' social ties can be a significant cache for school improvement initiatives concerning school safety, remedying absences and tardiness, and ensuring regular homework completion.

Developing Cultural Competence

To work effectively with children and parents whose backgrounds differ from their own, teachers and school leaders must develop *cultural competence*—the ability to interact well with people of dissimilar traditions. This capacity requires respect, empathy, knowledge of self and others, skill, and care. Individuals must look inward as well as outward. Because educators can control nothing but themselves, only when they examine their own beliefs and assumptions (and prejudices and stereotypes) can they reach out to children and families in ways that leave everyone within an encounter feeling respected and strengthened.

Building one's cultural competence consists of the following:

- Becoming aware of one's own cultural worldview
- Understanding one's attitudes toward cultural differences
- Gaining knowledge about varied cultural practices and perspectives
- Learning and refining one's cross cultural skills

Becoming culturally competent requires a commitment to learn and grow, professional development time dedicated to examining one's own beliefs and assumptions about families and communities, sharing views and experiences with colleagues, reflecting on what one is learning and how it fits with what that person has always believed, and practicing new attitudes and skills. Becoming culturally competent may mean ending many educators' comfortable assumptions that they are the "experts" in every discussion about student learning. Instead, educators must be willing to learn from children and families who they are, the nature of their assets, their aspirations, and how they learn best.

Family involvement in children's education is especially important for students whose cultures place a high value on parents and extended family. Parents have firsthand knowledge about their children and opinions about teaching and learning. They need occasions to express their ideas and ambitions for their children to their teachers. In turn, when teachers increase their understanding about students' home and community norms, values, and expectations, they gain insights about the children's capacities and available strengths that help them learn. This is especially true in urban schools where teachers and students may not share the same life experiences and world views. Because a basic foundation for designing instruction depends on linking the new content to students' prior knowledge, interests, and skills, having a deep understanding of students' backgrounds gives teachers the insights and resources they need to make academic knowledge relevant and personally meaningful to each student. At the same time, this process increases school–home trust.

Suggestions for strengthening principals' and teachers' cultural competence to work with a wide array of parents include these actions:

- **Recognize that all parents want their children to do well in school.** Regardless of income, education level, or cultural background, all parents have high expectations for their children's education and life options. Assume that all families can help improve their children's school performance and will respond positively to information and support about how to do this.

- **Be welcoming.** Be sincerely pleased that parents are coming to work with you to boost their children's success. Make sure every staff member is courteous and respectful and gives prompt attention to parents and community members when they arrive. Listen to their concerns. Use everyday language rather than professional jargon. Be confident that they will have the desire, skills, and knowledge needed to help their children.

- **Be respectful.** Educators must be able to treat all others—professors, colleagues, students, and parents—as worthy and important individuals. Educators must not only talk; they must listen to what their students and parents tell them about their dreams for their children and how to best motivate their children's learning.

- **Be willing to learn.** Principals and teachers must learn to know their students as individuals. Through their actions, words, and decisions, educators need to create a culture of respect that shows a profound sensitivity and appreciation of other persons' core beliefs and values, situations, needs, traditions, and goals for their children—and the role parents want to take to support their child's school success. Find the strengths, and build from there.

- **Link engagement efforts to student learning.** Keep the focus on ways to improve student achievement throughout school improvement and family–school events. Help families understand what their children are learning and what their child needs to learn. Also, explain how parents can plan the child's academic program and prepare for college or postsecondary education and a career. And then, help them do it.

- **Give parents a say (and options).** Families appreciate having choices about how they support their children's academic and social learning. Ask families about expectations for their children's education, the ways they encourage their children's education at home, and how they share their cultural traditions. Parents might prefer to visit their child's classroom when it is convenient for them rather than at a formally scheduled meeting—or have the chance to meet with teachers and principals at a time and place accessible for parents (such as at a housing or recreation center or place of worship) rather than at school.

- **Communicate personally.** Phone parents at home to provide good news about their children or information about available school programs. Extending a personal invitation to a school event lets the parents know that someone at the school cares about their children and values the parents' involvement (as compared with slipping a newsletter or flyer into the children's backpacks). This is especially useful when the caller speaks in the parent's language.

- **Be professional, but be real**. Apart from their titles and formal roles, school leaders and teachers need to present themselves to parents and the community as genuine, caring people. Providing occasions for parents and school personnel to talk, share anecdotes about their children, laugh together, and show authentic interest can build enduring relationships. Human contacts such as these create strong ties and increase credibility.

- **Develop capacity.** Increase the opportunities for professional development for teachers, administrators, aides, and clerical and custodial staff on the advantages of school, family, and community connections, how the faculty and staff can foster trusting and respectful relationships with parents, and how to be culturally competent. To make this growth happen, teachers and school leaders must create safe spaces and multiple occasions to look inward, learn, and practice (and assess the effectiveness of) evolving perspectives and ways of interacting with others.

- **Recognize and celebrate people and their contributions**. People and organizations need occasions to value their efforts and accomplishments if they are to keep growing and contributing. Schools can bring parents into celebrations of their children's successes and publically acknowledge the parents' roles in their children's progress. These occasions reinforce school's and parents' mutual commitment to their children's learning and maturation.

- **Build strong ties between school and community organizations.** Connecting to community groups can expand resources available to both staff and families. Organizations such as the Boys and Girls Clubs, the YMCA, and religious organizations can offer programs that encourage reading, writing, studying, and tutoring—linked to the school's curriculum— during evenings, weekends, and summer. Involve them in school improvement teams. Be willing to let community groups help set the agenda for change—and work with the school to leverage their political and grassroots influence to improve school quality and safety.

Becoming culturally competent is a personal journey, not merely a professional one. It requires the desire to grow and many opportunities to learn and practice. Being self-reflective and a good listener are essential first steps. At the end of the day, educators need to be genuine, thoughtful, sensitive, and intentional about inviting parents into collaborative relationships.

For almost 400 years, public schools have served as powerful agencies to socialize ethnic and racial communities to American norms. Educating children of parents from varied cultures, they have helped develop a common heritage and loyalty to this country. Building cultural competence continues this tradition. Respecting and using families' cultural assets and values to promote children's school success helps them learn the high-level knowledge and skills needed to become competent, self-sufficient citizens of a democratic republic in a globalized world. Respecting family culture fits well within American tradtion, which accepts diversity as a benefit. As it reads on the seal of the United States and is visible on most U.S. currency—*E Pluribus Unum*—out of many, one.

SCHOOL CULTURE RE-BOOT 6.2
Developing Cultural Competence

Educators who develop cultural competence to work effectively with parents who come from different backgrounds than themselves gain partners for advancing student learning and achievement.

1. Working in threes, have teachers read and discuss the cultural competence indicators below.

   • What does each cultural competence indicator look like in action?
   • How do you now routinely use—or not yet use—each indicator in relationships with parents? (Give examples on table below.)
   • In what ways does each teacher believe that the indicator can improve teacher–parent collaboration for children's school success?
   • Which indicators might be easy or uncomfortable for each teacher to learn?
   • Which cultural competence indicators should be a topic for further study—and which indicators are your top three priorities for further study and practice?

Cultural Competence Indicators	Examples of Cultural Competence as Practiced in Our School	Priorities for Study, Recommendations, and Practice
Recognize that all parents want their children to do well in school.		
Be welcoming.		
Be willing to learn (from students and parents).		
Be respectful.		
Link engagement efforts to student learning.		
Give parents a say (and options).		

Cultural Competence Indicators	Examples of Cultural Competence as Practiced in Our School	Priorities for Study, Recommendations, and Practice
Communicate personally.		
Be professional, but be real.		
Develop capacity.		
Recognize and celebrate people and their contributions.		
Build strong connections between school and community.		

2. After the teacher triad discussions, reassemble the whole group and discuss triad findings. Identify those cultural competence indicators that are presently in widespread use among your administrators, faculty, and staff and give examples. Which cultural competence indicators are less evident and should be top priorities for further study, practice, and use?

School leaders may want to have each department or grade level repeat this activity with a school leadership person serving as a facilitator. It also might be used as a discussion starter with parent leaders or to survey parents representing diverse cultural backgrounds. Data from these meetings can be used to identify and plan for professional development in building cultural competence.

WAYS TO INVOLVE FAMILIES WITH SCHOOLS

Emphasizing students apart from their family or community contexts ignores countless relevant factors that affect their learning. Children live in families; families live in neighborhoods. Schools are located in communities. Everyone shares goals related to educating and socializing the young. Promoting students' well-being, academic progress, and resilience obliges all stakeholders to combine their knowledge of children—generally and specifically—in ways that benefit each child. Charting this path moves educators beyond the time-honored one-size-fits-all school–parent events and toward those that meet more individual needs.

Personalizing Parent Involvement

Schools tend to invest their efforts on parents who want to work with teachers and who regularly attend school meetings. Although these parents' involvement encourages their children's achievement, they represent only a small percent of families. Ironically, schools target fewer efforts toward involving families of youngsters who are faring poorly in school. When teachers invite these parents to meetings to discuss the child's difficulties—such as lagging academic progress, poor attendance, or behavior problems—parents too often leave the schools feeling frustrated, angry, and guilty—and their child does not improve. Parents' lack of enthusiasm for returning for more unpleasantness seems understandable. Neither teachers' finger wagging nor parent education classes are realistic options to improve these school–home relationships.

Despite the past 15 years of federal policy calling for enhancing parent involvement, research indicates only promising rather than proven parent involvement practices. Findings make it clear, however, that efforts to involve reluctant parents and primary caretakers—many of whom have one or more children who are not doing well at school—require more personalized interventions. Just as students vary in their individual motives and abilities to invest their attentions and energies at school, so do parents and other caretakers.

Wise educators use their understanding of intrinsic motivation when designing ways to collaborate with families. Appreciating the incentives that inspire people to act in certain ways means recognizing how critical it is to avoid teacher–parent conferences that aim mainly at "fixing problems," limiting options, or making family members feel disrespected, controlled, or coerced. Although educators may not intend these effects, they may be the parents' realities nonetheless.

Research suggests that constructive involvement is related to positive outcomes and is higher when conditions are supportive and authentic, while providing opportunities for choice and offering enough structure to accomplish the intended purpose. In contrast, not wanting involvement is associated with threats to feelings of competence, self-determination, and relatedness to valued others. Therefore, sustaining engagement with parents and caregivers and reengaging individuals who feel no affinity for schools requires an atmosphere that minimizes conditions and practices that negatively affect parents' intrinsic motivation and maximizes those that positively impact their motivation.

Roles for School–Parent Collaboration

Having an array of options helps educators tap parents' actual interests and talents in ways that personalize their involvement. To this end, Joyce Epstein, a Johns Hopkins Professor and Director of the University's Center on School, Family, and Community Partnerships, has developed a framework of parent involvement to help educators construct varied and comprehensive school and family partnerships. These include parenting, communications, volunteering, learning at home, decision making, and collaborating with the community. Each type of involvement allows for an array of practices. Table 6.2 identifies and defines these roles and gives examples of them in action.

As students move from elementary to secondary schools, most families reduce their involvement with teachers. Similarly, many educators make less effort to keep families involved as their children grow and mature.

Table 6.2 Epstein's Framework for Parent–School Collaboration

Types	Definitions	Sample Practices
Type 1: Parenting	Help all families establish supportive home environments for children.	Express high but attainable expectations for students' education. Suggest home conditions that support learning at each grade level. Conduct neighborhood meetings to help parents understand schools and schools understand families.
Type 2: Communicating	Establish effective two-way exchanges about school programs and children's progress.	Ask parents or caregivers how and where they would like to work with the school to help their child learn and achieve. Hold parent- or school-initiated contacts about academic performance, students' academic programs, and postsecondary plans. Provide language translators as needed. Send weekly or monthly folders of students' work home for review and comments. Provide regular schedule of useful notices. Make phone calls rather than send fliers.
Type 3: Volunteering	Recruit and organize parent help and support for school and student learning activities.	Participate in schools and classroom volunteer programs to help teachers, administrators, students, or other parents. Provide a parent room for meetings and resources for families.

(Continued)

Table 6.2 (Continued)

Types	Definitions	Sample Practices
Type 4: Learning at home	Provide information and ideas to families about how to help students at home with homework and other curriculum-related materials, decisions, and planning.	Provide information for families on skills required for students in all subjects at each grade, information on homework policies and ways to monitor schoolwork at home, and a regular schedule of homework that requires students to discuss with families what they are learning in class.
Type 5: Decision making	Include parents in school decisions and parent organizations. Develop parents from all backgrounds to serve as representatives and leaders in school committees.	Encourage active parent groups, advisory councils, and committees for parent leadership and participation. Enlist interested parents in independent advocacy groups to lobby and work for school improvement.
Type 6: Collaborating with the community	Identify and use resources and services from the community (such as museums, businesses, and so on) to strengthen school programs, family practices, and student learning and development.	Provide information for students and families on community health, cultural, recreational, social support and other programs or services as well as information on community activities linked to learning skills and talents. Create opportunities for students, families, and schools to serve the community.

Source: Adapted from Epstein, J. L., Sanders, M.G., Simon, B. S., Salinas, K. C., Jansorn, N. R., & Van Voorhis, F. L. (2002). *School, family, and community partnerships: Your handbook for action* (2nd ed.). Thousand Oaks, CA: Corwin.

Nonetheless, parents still have important guiding and decision-making roles to play as their children develop. Teachers and administrators must make special attempts to invite parents at appropriate times into their children's education careers, provide effective two-way communication, and encourage ongoing family engagement with schools as children grow older.

SCHOOL CULTURE RE-BOOT 6.3
School–Home Collaboration Survey

The following statements are true for schools with strong ties with parents. Some statements are more relevant to elementary than secondary levels. First, conduct this survey among the leadership team to collect and discuss their views. Then, survey the faculty and staff as well as students and parents to assess the frequency and visibility of each behavior listed below. Comparing answers from various respondents can provide an interesting perspective on school–home collaborations and suggest areas for improvement as well as for celebration.

1. On the questions below, indicate the level of frequency with which teachers in this school regularly practice the following behaviors:

School–Parent Collaboration Behaviors	Rare–Often–Daily
1. Teachers send home folders of student work weekly or monthly for parent review and comment.	
2. Parents and teachers hold formal conferences at least once a year.	
3. Teachers regularly call parents to discuss their children's progress and problems.	
4. Teachers schedule regular, interactive homework that requires students to demonstrate and discuss what they are learning with a family member.	
5. Teachers understand and relate positively to students of diverse backgrounds.	
6. Teachers feel comfortable understanding and discussing parents' concerns about their children's academic, social, and behavioral progress.	
7. Teachers call on parents to use their talents and interests in school to help students learn.	
8. Teachers use their awareness of families' perspectives when developing policy and making decisions.	
9. Teachers and administrators continually look for ways to involve parents, students, and the community in school decision making.	
10. Schools provide clear information in the parents' preferred language (or through translators) about ways parents can help students learn at home with homework, other curricular-related activities, program decisions, and planning at each grade level.	

(Continued)

(Continued)

School–Parent Collaboration Behaviors	Rare–Often–Daily
11. The school offers parents various options for involvement, including helping students in school, at home, and joining educators in leadership and decision-making roles.	
12. The school provides clear and understandable information to parents about the curriculum, assessments, and achievement levels and report cards.	
13. Bilingual or multilingual employees work in locations to meet and greet parents.	
14. Family support programs help families with health, nutrition, and other services.	
15. Parent volunteers from various student demographics work visibly in the school.	
16. Students better understand and follow school rules and policies because they have discussed these with their parents.	
17. The school schedules its events at different times during the day and evening so that all families can attend some throughout the year.	
18. The school provides a community resource directory for parents and students with information on community services, programs, and agencies.	
19. Parent–teacher conferences focus on factors directly related to student achievement and performance on learning outcomes.	
20. Parents of lower-achieving students are given extra support by the school to encourage their involvement in parent–school activities.	
21. The teachers and administrators involve parents in selecting, evaluating, and revising school activities.	
22. The school regularly invites feedback from parents who attend school-sponsored events and programs.	
23. Parents monitor and assist their child in completing homework assignments.	
24. Parents and teachers work together to encourage students to do school-related work at home.	
25. The school asks for input from parents regarding their preferences for meeting topics, dates, times, and locations.	

2. After reviewing survey findings, identify which school–parent collaboration activities are most frequently practiced in this school.

- How does the school know if these collaboration activities are improving relationships with parents and increasing student achievement?
- Which practices should the school increase in frequency?
- What—if any—professional development do our teachers need in order to carry out these new collaboration activities? Who inside or outside the school is capable of providing this training?

WORKING WITH THE COMMUNITY

People with school-aged children comprise only about one third of the population. Even if all these parents were supportive, they could not provide the widespread public backing that schools need. As a result, high-performing schools—especially those in high-poverty neighborhoods—build positive and productive relationships with the broader community. *Community* refers to the neighborhood or places around the school, the local residents who may or may not have children in the school, and neighborhood groups.

School leaders need links with community members, district leaders, policy makers, and others to develop a network of shared interests, foster wider understanding, and nurture trust that people need to work constructively toward common goals. These extensive connections allow school leaders "to both *scan* the environment—to learn about issues, concerns, and new developments outside the school—and *seed* the environment—to put insiders and advocates into positions of power and influence on the outside."[7] Particularly in a time of declining resources and increasing demand for public services, schools need partners who leverage the strengths of multiple organizations to improve student outcomes.

Purposes of School–Community Partnerships

Partnerships between schools and communities can take a variety of forms and emphases. Activities may occur inside the school, in the community, or a combination of the two. The partnerships' focus may be strictly educational, such as increasing student learning or, more broadly, improving schools. Or, the partnership may aim at providing a full range of social and health services essential to support student learning and family and

---

[7]Hatch, T. (2009, October). The outside-inside connection. *Educational Leadership, 67*(2), 18.

community well-being. Students' needs determine the type and nature of community partnerships that will work best.

Examples of school–community partnerships are plentiful:

- **Provide occasions to educate and recruit community members.** Schools can use the obligatory orientation meetings, open houses, conversations over coffee, and information nights to ensure that everyone understands the school's basic goals, philosophy, and work—and to invite (recruit) parents and other stakeholders for varied roles and responsibilities within the school. For instance, establishing a community relations committee consisting of teachers, parents, and local business representatives tasked with bringing attention to any emerging issues about the school and district can provide an early heads-up about local or district changes that will impact teaching and learning—and provide crucial public support for the principal when needed.

- **Provide incentives to support students' success.** Working with neighborhood organizations, government agencies, churches, community groups, and businesses can garner incentives to encourage student success. When one of the authors was a high school principal, he used business partners to incentivize student improvement in achievement, attendance, and attitude. He networked with local bankers to create a Triple-A Club. All students who earned all As or Bs, had perfect attendance (no unexcused absences), and no office discipline referrals for a marking period were invited to a Bankers' Breakfast. Bankers paid for the meal. In addition, each attendee was entered into a drawing for a U.S. Treasury Savings Bond (a $1,000, four $500, and ten $100 bonds at each breakfast), also complements of the bankers. Although the first Bankers' Breakfast was sparsely attended, within two years, 60 to 70 percent of the students in the high school were Triple-A Club members and breakfast honorees. Likewise, grades, attendance, behavior, and graduation rates were all up; the Triple-A program helped re-boot the school's culture.

- **Provide opportunities for career development and relevant instruction.** Businesses and local industry might be willing to provide job shadowing and internships for students as part of their career exploration as well as sponsor professional development for teachers. Companies may be willing to hire teachers in content areas aligned with the business to work with the firm's experts during the summers to help teachers create more high-interest and relevant links for students between classroom content and real-world applications. Likewise, colleges can partner with schools to prevent the need for academic remediation, such as allowing first-generation high school students to take an occasional course or seminar on a college campus to familiarize them with what university work involves. College faculty and high school teachers can collaborate on ways to match instructional methods and intellectual rigor across both institutions to ease students' transitions.

• **Gain support for collective action**. Religious institutions provide a base of existing relationships among congregation members who can be galvanized to support collective action infused with a moral purpose— adding a powerful catalyst for change. This feature is especially noteworthy in urban African American communities, which historically have very high rates of religious participation and where many churches have been actively involved in providing services and advancing community development and political action.

• **Access essential health, social, and protective services**. Partnerships with community health, recreation, social service agencies, the military services, and the police department are essential to ensure students' academic success. Many children need a range of supplemental services to address problems that interfere with learning. These may be as simple as getting eyeglasses or tutoring or as complex as dealing with a chronic illness or living apart from a deployed parent. Police and mental health officials can help school administrators develop policies and procedures to prevent cyberbullying and fake social networking profiles—forms of harassment via the Internet that can substantially disrupt a student's education.

• **Extend learning beyond the classroom**. Teachers will be more successful to the extent that they blend professional expertise with community-based knowledge and practices. Maintaining permeable school boundaries allows the schools to incorporate educational experiences that their communities value. Community leaders can help teachers get to know their neighborhoods, resources, and histories well, so they can identify educational opportunities within them.

Positive Outcomes From School–Community Partnerships

More important than the individual events, community collaborations seek to envelop youngsters in a wide-ranging culture of achievement, repeating the point with a series of activities in varied locales throughout the year. The message to children is this: "We, the larger community, believe in you and your ability, which—with extra effort—will help you achieve and succeed not just in school but in life."

Over time, regular contacts between school and community persons can become long-term relationships with allies who understand the school, provide access to resources, and serve as public advocates in times of crisis. Public and parent voices sometimes speak more loudly than educators. For example, although a principal may be unable to persuade the district office to get rid of the school's rodent problem for a year, the school's parent group, upon learning of this health concern, can motivate the superintendent and school board to send maintenance crews to fix the problem by the weekend. Readers probably can recall similar examples from their own experiences.

Finding the Balance

While collaborative relationships with outside agencies, organizations, and influential people create a strength-in-numbers dynamic that puts schools in a stronger position to deal with changing external environments, finding the right balance between cultivating external networks and maintaining organizational flexibility is important. Relationships have reciprocal expectations. While schools working with community partners may gain crucial assets, personnel, and expertise, school leaders need to monitor the partners' expectations in return so as not to overextend school personnel or sidetrack the school from achieving its goals. It is essential that school leaders negotiate with external allies to shape their demands in ways that will truly benefit the schools—or decide which partnerships expect too much in exchange and limit their participation.

Specifically, school–community collaborations are strengthened when they share these things:

- **Clear ground rules**—this will enable principals and teachers to be sure they are using their time to address goals they genuinely value.
- **A common vision**—partners need to agree on the same goals and expectations.
- **Formal relationships**—establishing formal relationships and collaborative structures will accomplish more than scheduling ad hoc get-togethers.
- **Open dialogue**—open and honest discussions about challenges and solutions should encourage frank, respectful, and constructive participation by all parties.
- **Data**—provide clear information so all stakeholders can understand where things stand and hold each other accountable for making measurable progress.
- **Central office involvement**—having a central office administrator as a contact person demonstrates the district's commitment to sustaining and developing the community partnership.

- **Access to financial assets**—partners need to find ways to capitalize on their financial assets and funding streams to support programs and activities aligned with their common vision.

Sometimes, challenges inside the school are connected to and complicated by events outside the school. Schools face many external demands and pressures. But, with the relations, support, and expertise that come from interacting with a range of people, organizations, and institutions in the community, schools can develop the goals, staff, or productive work environment they need to help each child achieve well.

Collaboration Around Student Attendance

Chronic student absence is a key issue around which to engage community involvement. *Chronic absenteeism*—or missing 10 percent or more of school days for any reason—is a well-recognized early warning sign of academic risk and school dropout. New research suggests that as many as 7.5 million students—one in 10 American students—miss a month of school each year.[8] Political and educational leaders now recognize that reducing students' chronic absences starting in the early grades is a clear-cut, doable collaborative action to improve schools and community health.

The figures are alarming. Nationwide, nearly 10 percent of kindergartners and first graders are chronically absent. They tend to continue their poor attendance habits. By third grade, children who missed too much of kindergarten and first grade are falling behind in reading. By sixth grade, chronic absence becomes an early-warning sign that students will drop out of high school.[9] Regardless of a student's socioeconomic background, being chronically absent, especially in the early grades when children are learning the basic academic skills that lead to becoming proficient readers, undermines their school success. For children of poverty who are less likely to have the resources to make up lost classroom time, school absences are particularly damaging.

This harm occurs even for absences "excused" for illness or when parents keep them at home for a particular reason. Missing school days because of unreliable transportation, inadequate access to health care, and disruptions from family relocations or homelessness also jeopardize

---

[8]Sparks, S. (2012, May 23). Attendance. The importance of being in school: A report on absenteeism in the nation's public schools. *Education Week, 31*(32), 5.

[9]Bruner, C., Discher, A., & Chang, H. (2011, November). *Chronic elementary absenteeism: A problem hidden in plain sight.* Des Moines, IA: Attendance Works and Child & Family Policy Center, p. 2. Retrieved May 14, 2012, from http://www.edweek.org/media/chronicabsence-15chang.pdf

students' learning and achievement. An absence is an absence, and a lost month or more of school throughout the year seriously compromises a child's chances to make academic progress.

In addition, absences affect classmates who are present. When students who missed lessons return, teachers tend to slow their instruction to accommodate those who missed the lesson the first time it was taught. A study of New York City fourth graders found that even students with good attendance rates had lower standardized test scores than their peers when they attended schools where nearly 10 percent of students missed class every day.[10] What is more, in districts where the state bases its funding on attendance, chronic absence costs the schools money.

Causes of chronic absenteeism lie with schools and with students. Schools with 20 percent of students chronically absent must address systemic issues—such as ineffective instructional practices, negative school climates, unsuccessful discipline methods, disorderly classrooms—as well as individual student concerns. Family and community challenges include lack of access to health care, missed buses, broken cars, high levels of violence, or unaffordable housing. Parents may be keeping kindergartners and first graders at home because they do not understand that academic expectations have increased in these grades since parents were students. Older students are more selective about which classes they miss, choosing to attend classes that they find interesting or where they feel the teacher cares about them. Only when educators and parents know the extent and nature of the absentee problem can they take appropriate steps to correct it.

The community is in a good position to help schools address issues related to students' absences. For example, in New York City, where asthma is the primary health issue causing students to miss school, the health department has developed an asthma ambassador program in 24 pilot schools. Each school has a trained staff member—often a physical education teacher, parent, or community volunteer—who helps students get health appointments at clinics close to the school and often walk the children to appointments (and back) rather than have the parent keep the child home.

Similarly, in a Washington, DC, neighborhood where fights and bullying on the way to school were frightening some children into staying home, safe passage volunteers now walk with students to school. In Baltimore, instead of suspending students for truancy and minor infractions—and forcing them to miss additional instructional time—schools now assign

---

[10]Musser, M. P. (2011, May). *Taking attendance seriously. How school absences undermine student and school performance in New York City.* New York: The Campaign for Fiscal Equity, Inc. Retrieved May 15, 2012, from http://www.attendanceworks.org/wordpress/wp-content/uploads/2010/04/CFE_Attendance_FINAL.pdf

in-school detention, mentoring, and anger-management or conflict-resolution sessions.

All schools benefit from analyzing their absences to determine patterns of absenteeism, identify students who are chronically out, and design interventions. When teachers and principals know who these children are, educators are better able to work with them, their parents, and the community to individualize strategies to get them to attend school daily to continue their learning.

Strategies to address chronic absenteeism are many. For example, schools can hold focus groups for students habitually late (and their parents) to discuss problems that prevent regular attendance. Schools can reinforce good attendance with posters highlighting the reality that completing high school and postsecondary education pays off big-time by opening up more jobs and careers, more opportunities to find interesting and meaningful work, plus thousands of extra dollars in wages over one's working life. Business partners might want to purchase alarm clocks for the school office to loan to students who have difficulty getting up in time. The office may want to keep spare gym uniforms, a washer and dryer for students who don't have them at home, and partner with a local barber to offer free haircuts and grooming on certain days to students who need and want it. Through these and many other means, schools can work with the surrounding neighborhoods to end students' excuses for not coming to school, educate their parents about the importance of daily school attendance, and motivate young people to take advantage of the real and long-term benefits of learning in school each day.

SCHOOL CULTURE RE-BOOT 6.4
Assessing Your Attendance Issues

Learning and school success is related to students' daily attendance in class.

1. Ask all teachers to identify their students who have missed five or more school days per marking period (usually three months)—and, depending on the time of year, identify students who have missed 10 or more days by February 1. Have teachers create a grid with student name, number of days absent to date (regardless of whether excused or unexcused), and grade earned in the class.

2. Meeting in small groups first, and next as a faculty, discuss:

   - Who has students who have missed five or more days in a marking period or ten days by February 1?

(Continued)

(Continued)

- What is the relationship between their number of absences and their measured achievement (classwork, course grades, and standardized tests)?
- What are the known causes of their many absences?
- Is there a meaningful difference in student learning between having an excused or unexcused absence? Explain.
- How might the instructional practices or class management be affecting these particular students' attendance?
- How do repeated absences affect your teaching and planning?
- How do repeated absences affect other students' learning?
- What interventions has the teacher made with each identified student and at least one of the student's parents or caregivers to remedy this situation?
- What can teachers do to increase these students' attendance and achievement? When do you want them to begin doing it?
- What can the school counselors do to increase these students' attendance and achievement? When do you want them to begin doing it?
- What can the school administrators do to increase these students' attendance and achievement? When do you want them to begin doing it?
- What can the school do with parents—especially the parents of these chronically absent children—to remedy this situation?
- What can the school do with the community to remedy this situation?
- Who are the community contact persons you might want to involve in this initiative?
- Does your school give the impression that it is more interested in enforcing attendance regulations than helping solve attendance issues? What evidence makes you draw this conclusion?

WHERE DO WE GO FROM HERE?

By now, principals and teacher leaders reading this book are probably asking themselves, "How am I going to put this all together and make culture re-boot work in our school?" With so much to do and such complex tasks involving both ideas and people, it would be natural to feel both excited and a bit overwhelmed.

The next chapter will help you. Chapter 7, Developing a Plan of Action, offers a structured and sequential, easy-to-follow road map to culture re-boot. It provides a realistic five-year calendar and planning guide to help school leaders move from identifying members to serve on the leadership re-boot team to enacting widespread sustained and improved professional practice. It identifies the issues to address before the first full year of active culture re-boot, suggests how to fit culture re-boot within the existing school teams, and proposes the key activities that should occur—and when—during the first few years of the re-boot process. Of course, principals and teams are free to revise and adapt the planning document as they see fit to meet the needs of their faculty and school. But, with this clear road map as a starting place, school leaders can confidently collaborate with faculty, staff, students, and parents to re-boot their school culture and improve student outcomes.

Because schools in a democratic society educate the majority of each generation's voters, taxpayers, jurors, neighbors, and leaders, school outcomes affect everyone. Accordingly, everyone has reason to stay involved in the public conversation about school quality. The interdependence between educators, parents, and the larger community makes the collaborative efforts to take on and sustain this difficult work of improving schools necessary. No one involved in the endeavor to create high-quality schools can succeed without the others.

If schools are to develop mutually supportive relationships with their parents, families, and communities, they must first develop a culture and climate that welcomes parents and community members with, "Come on in! Let's get to know each other. We are in this together." And, because every school community has its own values, interests, traditions, and ambitions, educators need to evaluate and refine their efforts within their own settings.

In the words of a Native Alaskan educator, "In order to teach you, I must know you."[11]

RESEARCH

Epstein, J. L. (1991). Effects of students' achievement of teacher practices of parent involvement. In S. B. Silvern (Ed.), *Advances in teaching/language research (Vol. 5). Literacy through family, community, and school interaction* (pp. 261–276). Greenwich, CT: JAI Press.

Epstein, J. L. (2005, September). *Developing and sustaining research-based programs of school, family, and community partnerships. Summary of 5 years of NNPS research.* Johns Hopkins University, National Network of Partnership Schools (NNPS). Retrieved May 3, 2012, from http://www.csos.jhu.edu/P2000/pdf/Research %20Summary.pdf

Epstein, J. L., & Dauber, S. L. (1991). School programs and teacher practices of parent involvement in inner city elementary and middle schools. *Elementary School Journal, 91*(3), 289–305.

Epstein, J. L., Sanders, M. G., Simon, B. S., Salinas, K. C., Jansorn, N. R., & Van Voorhis, F. L. (2002). *School, family, and community partnerships: Your handbook for action* (2nd ed.). Thousand Oaks, CA: Corwin.

---

[11]Cited in Delpit, L. (1995). *Other people's children. Cultural conflict in the classroom.* New York: W. W. Norton, p. 183.

Henderson, A. T., & Berla, N. (Eds.). (1994). *A new generation of evidence: The family is critical in student achievement.* Washington, DC: National Committee for Citizens in Education. Retrieved May 14, 2012, from http://eric.ed.gov/ERIC Docs/data/ericdocs2sql/content_storage_01/0000019b/80/13/66/e0.pdf

Henderson, A. T., & Mapp, K. L. (2002). A new wave of evidence. The impact of school, family and community connections on student achievement, annual synthesis 2002 (Eric Document No. ED 474521). Austin, TX: Center of Family and Community Connections with Schools, Southwest Educational Development Laboratory. Retrieved May 14, 2012, from http://www.sedl.org/con nections/resources/evidence.pdf

Jeynes, W. H. (2007). A meta-analysis of the relation of parental involvement to urban elementary school student academic achievement. *Urban Education, 42*(1), 82–110.

Muller, C. (1993). Parent involvement and academic achievement: An analysis of family resources available to the child. In B. Schneider & J. S. Coleman (Eds.), *Parents, their children, and schools* (pp. 77–113). Boulder, CO: Westview Press.

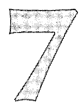

Developing a
Plan for Action

FOCUS QUESTIONS

- What is a realistic time frame for planning a school culture re-boot from generating ideas to sustaining improved practice?
- What issues should principals and school leaders address prior to the first full year of school culture re-boot?
- How does school culture re-boot fit within existing school teams?
- What key activities of school culture re-boot should occur during the first full year?
- What key activities of school culture re-boot should occur during the second and later years?

A fter exploring the varied parts of school culture re-boot, it is logical to ask, "Where do we go from here?"

Because school improvement processes are context-driven, systemic, multifaceted, and ongoing, no single path is best for all schools. How development starts and moves forward will largely depend on the school's base capacity; the leadership's particular skills, interests, and concerns; and the community's characteristics. Culture is organic to its community. If culture changes, everything changes.

Ample evidence exists that effective school leaders, supported by motivated and highly qualified teams of teachers and school counselors, are capable for transforming failing schools and making them successful within three to five years. To sustain them operating at high levels takes a few years longer. Schools that are neither failing nor functioning at full capacity—like most schools in need of culture re-boot—can reasonably look to this time horizon, too. No matter how charismatic, highly qualified, or energetic the principals and teachers may be, improving school practices and student outcomes is urgent and difficult work requiring focused attention, considerable effort, and sufficient time.

Accordingly, making generalizations about how schools can advance a culture re-boot is fraught but essential. School leaders and their teams should weigh and discuss the recommended guidelines below and decide how to adjust them, so they work for their specific school.

PLANNING OVERVIEW

School culture re-booting must fit within educators' already overfilled schedules. An essential leadership challenge is to build and keep the re-boot momentum and related changes going while also managing the school's operations day to day.

Culture re-boot is not a separate committee: It is the school improvement team, possibly with revised membership, which uses an enhanced way of thinking about and acting upon school improvement. Integrating school culture re-boot viewpoints and actions within a reformulated school improvement team offers an efficient and effective way to guide school improvement to successful outcomes.

Most likely, the school's strategic (or school improvement) plan already contains a variety of objectives and strategies focused on increasing student learning and achievement. It probably includes (but perhaps expressed in other terms) developing teachers' instructional and leadership capacities, creating academic press and academic and social supports for all students, making the school a more collaborative and professional work environment, providing effective professional development targeted to school goals, and promoting strong school–parent–community ties. This makes culture re-boot a natural fit. If any of these objectives are not currently in your school's plan, a year with the leadership team actively reading and engaging in *Culture Re-Boot* will prompt their inclusion. Developing the strategic plan and related action steps with input from teachers and teacher leaders—as is done in culture re-boot—benefits a collaborative culture, keeps the plan grounded in reality, and increases teacher buy-in and commitment to making it succeed.

Planning for culture re-boot needs short-, medium-, and long-term objectives punctuated by small wins and celebrations that publicly appreciate individuals and reinforce group gains. The following outline identifies issues for school leaders to consider as they implement school culture re-boot and offers a proposed timeline for putting the plan into action. School leadership teams are invited to integrate this outline with their present school improvement plan and calendar and revise as needed.

PRIOR TO YEAR 1

The Principal Considers Culture Re-Boot and Gains the Superintendent's Support

Culture re-boot works best from the ground up, that is, when principals and their teacher leaders decide they want to adopt this approach to improve their school. Because they will have to do the intellectual, emotional, and physical work, their genuine commitment is essential if they are to invest the needed time and energy to make re-boot happen. Imposing this enormous assignment on principals and teachers from the outside (that is, from the central office) may gain compliance (and, possibly, resentment) but not commitment, and the efforts will falter.

At the same time, schools exist within districts that supply the personnel, policies, and resources that make schools run. Superintendents are accountable to the school board and the community for the schools' practices and outcomes. After speaking informally with several teacher leaders in the school and gaining their enthusiastic endorsement for culture re-boot, wise and strategic-thinking principals will want to share their ideas and tentative plans for culture re-boot with the superintendent to gain central office backing before moving too far ahead.

School district superintendents need to know what their schools are doing if they are to champion their goals and activities in-house and in the community. As former principals themselves, many superintendents may have helpful suggestions to aid the principal in gaining teachers' and parents' backing for the re-boot process and upcoming changes. As advocates for improved teaching and learning, superintendents may secure the necessary resources—such as pay for substitutes to allow teachers to engage in school-time professional development; allow the district's data person to work with the school team to identify, collect, and analyze student outcomes; or purchase videorecording equipment for the professional learning communities (PLCs) to help teachers see themselves in action—to help the school successfully re-boot. The superintendent might even invite the school to become a pilot site (with all accompanying fanfare and matériel) for culture re-boot in the district. In short, gaining the superintendent's blessing is an essential early step in culture re-boot.

The Principal and Key School Leaders Read *Culture Re-Boot*

Culture re-boot is an intensely cognitive and affective experience. Becoming familiar with the book's ideas and experiential activities before leading others in shared learning about their school and themselves gives school leaders a firsthand feel for the intellectual, emotional, and interpersonal challenges the book brings to its readers. Frequently, assistant principals, school counselors, or other professionals on staff have the personal and professional skills necessary to help colleagues through the re-boot process. With *Culture Re-Boot* as a common reading, principals and these key individuals can meet in the months immediately prior to Year 1 to discuss their personal and professional responses to the book's content and process, identify potential leadership team members, consider how to establish a cooperative and reflective work culture within the leadership team, and prepare themselves for the year ahead.

The Principal Selects Team Members for Leading Culture Re-Boot

Members of the culture re-boot leadership team should include teacher leaders (such as department chairpersons or grade-level coordinators), assistant principals, and school counselors. Additional members may include the school media center director (who has a schoolwide view), at least one teacher who is an informal leader but does not head a department, and one or two additional persons (perhaps the parent–teacher organization president or other parent leader), a student leader (where appropriate) who can reflect widespread peer views, and a staff person who has an exceptionally high awareness of parent and community concerns.

- This group may include the same individuals as in the school improvement team, principal's cabinet, or school leadership team— plus a few additional members invited for their unique professional skills or perspectives to help the team work more effectively.
- A 12- to 15-person leadership team is a workable number: small enough for everyone to have a say and large enough to allow flexible subgroupings for activities in which every member will be actively engaged.
- Each member must commit to attending each complete meeting and remain on the team for at least the first year.
- The principal should personally invite these individuals to join the culture re-boot team (by whatever name it is called) before the end of the current school year. This will give members the chance to review the *Culture Re-Boot* book read about change, school culture, and school improvement during the summer. Seeing the culture re-boot activities

ahead of time will make them more, rather than less, effective when conducted during the first year because team members will have had time to think about the questions and construct thoughtful answers.

Decide How to Incorporate the Culture Re-Boot Team Into the School's Leadership and Improvement Structure

Many professional groups with varied purposes operate within every school. The principal should decide whether culture re-boot should exist as an overarching purpose and framework within an existing (but with a slightly expanded or repopulated) school leadership or improvement team or whether it should be a separate group entirely. Practically speaking, it makes more sense to refocus an existing leadership group and add a few key new members than to create an entirely new group, which will likely duplicate much of the work another team is already doing. Typically over-extended, educators will resent having additional responsibilities placed on them when one committee will do. The authors refer to the re-boot group as the *leadership team*, but each school can craft its own moniker (such as steering committee, principal's cabinet, or other name).

Gather Baseline Student Attendance, Behavior, and Achievement Data

Student performance data are among the benchmarks for whether culture re-boot strategies are working as intended. As such, basic student performance indicators for appraisal need to be identified and built into the schedule up front. Although comparing student cohorts is not an accurate means to assess improvements in students' achievement, attendance, and behavior, schools can collect and meaningfully use these data in a variety of valid ways.

Before beginning Year 1 of school culture re-boot, decide what baseline data you want to collect—and what is available—for your student population and what would be most meaningful. This requires making many decisions.

- In which subjects does the leadership team want to monitor achievement? Are English language arts and mathematics the only disciplines worth assessing, or do all core subjects deserve attention, at least to begin the process?
- Does the leadership team want standardized test scores grouped by teacher and course, or are average scores for key courses enough information? Does the team want to collect achievement data for individual students or for student groups or both? Should the data

be disaggregated into student subgroups or provide gross averages? Are these data available through the central office or at the school site? If they are not available, what alternate means can provide evidence of students' academic growth?

- Does the school want to collect student attendance data? If so, what information about the absences will be most helpful to the leadership team? In what format should it be organized to make it most useful? Are these data available through the central office or at the school site?

- Does the team want to collect information on students' disciplinary referrals, and if so, does it want student names, frequency of referrals, types of infractions, locations where incidents occur, and referring teachers—or simply the student names, grade levels, and the type of infractions? Is there a format most useful for collecting and analyzing these data? Are these data available through the central office or at the school site?

- What additional data does the leadership team need? Are these available through the central office or at the school site?

- Do the data sought already exist, or must they be generated? Who would have to generate them? What can be collected so as not to burden teachers or staff?

- How can the school district make data collection more manageable and useful?

A central office person responsible for data collection and analysis may help suggest useful data, identify options, and help develop or adapt existing software to help organize and manipulate these data.

- Depending on the types of data the team wants, the software must be able to track individual students across the grade levels in your school by gender and race or ethnicity, by teacher and course title, and by annual grade-level proficiency in English language arts and mathematics (at a minimum; science, social studies, languages, arts, and health and physical education are important, too), attendance, and types and numbers of disciplinary referrals. The software must be able to disaggregate data along student demographic categories to ensure that every child is benefitting from enhanced instructional practices. If these software data resources are not available through your school district, what data can you obtain?

- Compile current year baseline data on, for example, students' achievement, attendance, and behavior as individuals and as groups. For each student, collect classroom (course title and teacher) details, demographic information, and grade levels.

- It may be possible to partner with a local university's educational leadership or curriculum and instruction doctoral programs to make collecting, assessing, and interpreting student (group) performance data from culture re-boot a class, thesis, or doctoral project. This would be a win-win collaboration.

Identify Healthy Organizational Cultures for Potential Site Visits

Identify local schools and organizations with similar demographics to your school, which have wholesome and successful cultures and positive student outcomes. Contact a knowledgeable person who can explain the culture and its impact on employee work satisfaction, productivity, and student achievement; discuss a workable format for making a site visit happen (whom to contact, best time frame during day or year for visits, topics to include in the site visit, and other concerns); and secure district permission for leadership team members to visit the organizations during the coming year.

Think Professional Development

- One or two effective teachers may produce phenomenal learning in their classrooms, but only when all the teachers use the same effective practices (as appropriate to their disciplines and students' maturity) can they reach every child in every classroom. Therefore, changing educators' beliefs, attitudes, and practices will require frequent opportunities for adult learning, and professional development will have to be woven deeply throughout the re-boot process. Faculty and staff will need to familiarize themselves with the concept of school culture if they are to make sense of and fully engage in the re-boot events.
- Teachers and administrators will have to learn new ways to view, understand, and work with each other and with students, parents, and the community.
- Much of the initial learning will occur as school leaders conduct re-boot activities (provided in each *Culture Re-Boot* chapter) in the leadership team and in their respective departments, areas, or grade levels.
- Although each re-boot activity helps teachers understand an essential dimension of their school culture, re-boots can be so engaging that teams may not be able to complete all chapter re-boots during the meeting. Leaders may want to identify the most important ones to complete during the meeting and assign the less essential ones as "homework" (for teachers to complete in pairs or trios during "working lunches" or after school) or make them optional.

- Once teachers understand the expectations for their improved instructional skills, academic press and supports for every student, and collaborative leadership, they will be able to make excellent suggestions about what they need to learn, and the priority order, to take them where the school is going.
- Although teachers in grade levels or departments will participate in one culture re-boot activity each month during Year 1, many may enjoy the engagement process so much that they want to do all the re-boots for each chapter. If this is the case, the leadership team may want to provide additional, optional re-boot activities before or after school for interested faculty and staff. Team members could rotate leadership responsibilities for this extra activity.
- If planned ahead, the district's human resources office may be willing to grant continuing education credits for teachers leading and completing a sequence of culture re-boot activities and showing the resulting products generated during their experiences.

Plan to Communicate Clearly and Often With the Team, the Faculty, and the School Community

Having school leaders meet regularly to discuss school culture and improvement will generate a lot of buzz among teachers. To prevent their natural interest from spinning into rumors and gossip, plan with leadership team members to report on meeting topics and insights (protecting the confidentiality of who said what) to their respective groups at least once a month. Having teachers within departments or grade levels participate in culture re-boot activities during the same month as the leadership team provides a relevant and meaningful way to express what is happening. Re-boot updates in the weekly faculty memo or newsletter will also help keep all informed. The more relevant and personally meaningful information teachers have about culture re-boot, the more momentum re-boot—and its accompanying attitude and behavior changes—will gain. Sending congratulatory e-mails, notes, newsletter features, and small gifts to teachers who have contributed positively to the school culture and student performance also communicate well.

YEAR 1

Orient the Leadership Team

At the September meeting, the principal should introduce all members, speak with them about their leadership roles and responsibilities in the school, tell what culture re-boot is about and what members will be doing during (and in between) their meetings, stress the importance of their work for student learning, and highlight the positive differences they will make in students' and colleagues' lives. The superintendent should be invited to welcome team members and to publicly recognize their leadership on behalf of an enhanced school culture and increased learning for all students. When the meeting is over, each member of the leadership team should be able to answer these questions: Why I am here, and how I will help myself, my colleagues, and our entire school community make our students successful?

Read and Discuss *Culture Re-Boot* as a Team

Leadership team members read *Culture Re-Boot*, one chapter each month. Members preread each chapter before the leadership meeting (prereading Chapter 1 for October's meeting and so on) to make the limited time, discussions, and exercises more personally meaningful. This will permit the team to complete the book in April—leaving May, June, and summer to prepare the plan for Year 2. A more complete month-by-month description of leadership team meeting agendas follow below.

Select Change Process Guides

School culture re-boot requires organizational learning. To make this happen, it is important to continually weave Chapter 1's three conceptual models of change throughout group discussions each month. Although each team member should be encouraged to actively apply these insights, *change process guides* become dependable observers who listen carefully to the discussions, regularly remind the team where they are in the change process, and identify what additional factors they need to consider before taking the next steps or finalizing any plans. Three leadership team members may be invited to take on this role, each person responsible for a different model but free to invoke any of the three when they believe it is appropriate. Change process guides should be insightful, flexible thinkers who can attend carefully to process and content at the same time. A school counselor or a graduate student in school leadership currently working on staff as a teacher may be excellent candidates for this role.

Conceptual models and helpful change process guides' questions include the following:

- **The 3-step change model**—at this moment, is the leadership team dealing with unfreezing, movement, or refreezing? What are the special considerations your plan must include—or potential obstacles to overcome—given your school's stage in the change process?

- **Single- and double-loop learning model**—in thinking about solutions to school problems, is the team looking at the symptoms (highly visible but relatively superficial indicators) or at the governing variables (underlying values and assumptions) in the school culture that can lead to real and sustained change? How do we move from looking at symptoms to looking at and addressing the real causes?
- **Multiple frames model**—has the team considered the structural, human resource, political, and symbolic frames as you design your plans? Which frames need to be thought through and appropriately addressed before the team moves forward?

Meet Once Monthly

Leadership meetings should last three consecutive hours once a month to permit the full exploration of each chapter and thoughtful participation in the chapter's experiential learning re-boot activities.[1] The goal is to make the reading and activities personally meaningful and highly relevant to the school context. Rushing through chapters without deeply exploring ideas, how they relate to the particular school, and the authentic meaning they have for each team member will not generate a culture re-boot. Deep understanding is key to organizational learning.

Although re-boot activities note approximate times for completion, they are highly engaging, and members may want to extend them. Because time is limited, however, consider asking one member to serve as a timekeeper and signal to the group when it is time for them to bring the activity to closure. If the team does not complete all chapter re-boot activities during their meeting, members can conduct them in small groups at their convenience during the month. To keep the re-boot momentum going, it is important to fully complete one chapter each month.

Conduct Culture Re-Boot Activities
With Faculty and Selected Parents and Students

Participating in culture re-boot activities facilitates organizational learning. The re-boot activities in each chapter make the topic relevant to a particular school and generate personal meaning for participants. Leadership team leaders can facilitate (or cofacilitate) one or two activities from each chapter within their own faculty groups or at a schoolwide

---

[1]If the team cannot meet once monthly for three hours, schedule two meetings each month, each for 1.5 to 2 hours.

faculty meeting during the same month that the leaders take them. Conducting these re-boot activities within teacher groups increases faculty awareness of school culture, deepens their understanding how their beliefs drive their practices, develops a set of common ideas about every student's worth and achievement, creates the rationale for teachers' expanding their own skills and effectiveness, and considers their essential roles in school improvement. It also provides valuable feedback about teachers' views to the leadership team. School leaders may want to involve selected students (when appropriate) and parents, separately, in similar or adapted re-boot activities to orient them to the school's goals and to get their views on these issues to use as input for planning.

Begin Small-Scale Changes

As the team reads the chapters, re-boot activities help members identify ways they can make immediate changes in their beliefs and practices. Several members may decide they like a certain idea and want to act on it at once. They should be encouraged to discuss these ideas with the leadership team and try them out, refining and revising as needed. Informed risk taking with improved practices is a good thing. Members will continue to update the team on how these practices are working and receive feedback to help them polish their efforts and improve outcomes. Eventually, grade levels or classrooms in which teachers are successfully using these new approaches may evolve into *demonstration classrooms*, which colleagues can visit to see an improved approach to increasing student learning in action.

Set Up Study Groups

Teachers' study groups may be called by different names: study groups, professional learning communities (PLCs), or task forces, to name a few. The leadership team—with teacher input—should decide which title to use.

Professional Learning Communities and Study Group Memberships

Before the school year ends, the leadership team will identify PLCs and study groups that teachers will join. PLC members should share a common core curriculum and grade level. Study group members are teachers, counselors, and administrators representing varied grade levels; they will address school improvement in needed school climate domains. Each PLC or study group should meet at least once monthly for two hours.

PLCs in high-performing schools use an attitude of inquiry, develop shared instructional norms, collaboratively examine instructional practices (and professional practices overall), and assume collective responsibility for student learning. Study groups' and PLCs' topics should directly connect to school culture re-boot and school improvement topics, such as these:

- **Developing teachers' instructional capacities**—each core academic department should have its own PLC groups of teachers who teach the same curriculum focused on improving instructional capacity and increasing student learning. Vertical articulation should follow later.
- **Establishing a student-centered learning culture**—along with building instructional capacity and increasing student learning, PLCs should consider ways they can establish the academic press and supports needed to develop a student-centered learning culture in their classrooms and throughout the school. The study groups can also work to identify and develop schoolwide programs to strengthen the student-centered learning culture.
- **Developing teachers' leadership capacities**—the PLCs and study groups should provide occasions for members to take on leadership roles in instruction and in schoolwide leadership.
- **Promoting and creating strong parent–community ties**—study groups' topics are of interest to parents and the community and parent–teacher organization members, and a community leader may be willing to work with relevant study groups to find programs to help all children succeed in the school.
- **Study groups address schoolwide issues**—a study group's membership reflects a cross section of the school and community with counselors, administrators, students, and parents working together to find schoolwide programs to benefit students. Study topics might include the following: how teachers may form caring relationships with challenging students; discipline programs that improve both student behavior and increase their achievement (and keep students in school); how to prevent student bullying and suicide; how blended learning opportunities may allow for more personalized education; and which social-emotional learning programs can enhance student behaviors and achievement in school. The school's and students' needs should determine each study group's focus.

Guidelines

The leadership team will ensure that every teacher and instructional support staff is assigned to an appropriate PLC or study group. Each PLC and study group will begin by reviewing and discussing the professional literature's conclusions about designing successful professional development.

- Effective professional development that positively affects student learning must be job embedded, classroom based, ongoing, coherent, intense, and include 30 to 100 hours over six months to a year.[2]
- Teachers should look for proven approaches to effective instruction and coherent, content-rich curriculum, not attractive but unproven innovations.
- By a given deadline (such as the end of first semester, Year 2), each PLC and study group will be expected to identify best practices in their assigned area, support these with professional journal articles to share with other teachers and the principal, prioritize adult learning needs, and identify the best formats and resources to make this learning meaningful to teachers and sustainable.
- They give their recommendations to the leadership team in time to plan a professional development schedule for the remainder of Year 2 and a tentative schedule for Years 3, 4, and 5. The same topic should be a professional development focus for more than one school year, including updates, refreshers, orienting new faculty members, and continuous improvement.
- The leadership team reviews and recommends revisions to plans.
- Teams begin enacting their reviewed and revised plans.

Meeting Frequency

Group members will select meeting dates, times, and locations. If the PLCs are to evolve into meaningful teams that assess the quality of student work and develop shared practices, assessments, and rubrics, they will want to meet at least twice each month for at least one hour per meeting. Study groups focus on an agenda such as promoting and creating strong parent–community ties or finding an appropriate student discipline model, and will meet monthly, unless the school decides otherwise.

---

[2]See, for example, Darling-Hammond, L., & Richardson, N. (2009, February). Teaching learning: What matters? *Educational Leadership, 66*(5), 46–53; and Guskey. T. R., & Yoon, K. S. (2009, March). What works in professional development? *Phi Delta Kappan, 90*(7), 496–500.

Survey Teachers

As a needs assessment, leadership teams might wish to survey their faculty to see how teachers perceive their school.[3] This may be done to accompany many chapters through a formal instrument (found in the Resources sections of Chapters 1 through 4) or via the re-boot activities. Do teachers feel the psychological safety and support needed for them to try out unfamiliar techniques and grow? Are most teachers ready for shared responsibility for student learning, or do they need to first build trust, expertise, and collective accountability? What do teachers think they need to learn and practice in order to hold high expectations for every student, teach every student to high levels, and provide additional supports for struggling learners? What do they need to work more effectively with parents? What help do they want from their colleagues, so they may expand their professional capacities? Findings will help leaders plan the next steps.

Plan and Conduct Whole-School Culture-Building Activities

Plan for at least one whole-school culture-building activity for students and teachers for the current school year and at least two (tentatively) for the coming school year. Include the school's touchstone (developed during Year 1), which identifies and reinforces the school's cultural symbols and cherished values as a motivator of student learning and respect for selves and others. Identify the individuals who will cochair the planning for these events, determine available resources (money and other), and set a date for when the recommendations are due to the leadership team for review and approval. Revise the plan as needed, take actions to make the event occur, and hold the event. Debrief afterward to see what has been accomplished, what has been learned, and how to improve the event the next time it occurs.

Celebrate Year 1's Successes

Make an occasion for the leadership team to commemorate what they have learned about their school and their expanded beliefs about student learning and achievement, relational trust, teacher leadership, academic press and supports, creating strong parent and community ties, their school as a learning organization, and future goals. Include parents, advisory group members, and students in the event. Consider creating a small

---

[3]Survey faculty using assessments provided in the Resources sections in Chapters 1 through 4 or from other sources.

folder or touchstone memento to give to each leadership team member, each teacher and staff member, every new teacher to the school, every student, and every family as a visible and tangible reminder of "This is who we are" and "This is the way we do things around here." If possible, provide small refreshments. Be sure to invite your district superintendent and other central office folks who helped you during the year.

Collect This Year's Student Performance Data and Review Progress Toward Goals

Collect data on individuals and student groups on grade-level proficiency in English language arts and mathematics (at a minimum), attendance, and behavior. Be able to connect individual students' results with their teachers, if that is what the leadership team decided. Separate data demographically to ensure that students in every subgroup are making gains. Make initial comparisons (eyeball and statistical) with baseline data to see if any changes appear. Remember to share progress data with your superintendent.

Consider Other Activities

What other activity does the leadership team believe it needs to accomplish during Year 1?

YEAR 2

School Leadership Team Meets Monthly

The team continues expanding and refining the culture-building practices developed during Year 1 to increase student achievement and make the school's cultural values relevant, meaningful, inspiring, and visible. The team also receives monthly feedback from the study group leaders (who are also leadership team members) on their progress.

Provide Leadership Opportunities

Create opportunities for interested and capable teachers to take on formal and informal leadership roles in the school. These may include the following: serve on a school improvement team, chair a school committee, provide expertise to a study group, organize and edit the culture re-boot minutes or newsletter, interpret student performance data, or pilot a new instructional or student support approach. The principals and teacher

leaders can mentor and coach colleagues trying on leadership responsibilities to help them grow in the roles. Certain experienced teacher leaders
or administrators interested in their own professional renewal may welcome the chance to mentor a younger or less-experienced colleague.

Study Groups Meet Twice a Month

The PLCs and study groups will continue to meet monthly for at least
two hours (meetings may occur twice monthly for one hour each, during the
day if possible, before or after school if necessary). After studying about
instructional improvement during Year 1 and making recommendations to
the principal about their learning priorities, Year 2 professional development brings minds-on and hand-on learning the attitudes and behaviors,
which help teachers recognize and promote high-quality student work.
Members reconfirm (or revise) what instructional techniques they want to
learn; the priority order in which they want to learn them; and how they can
help each other practice, refine, and master these approaches, gather or
develop the necessary resources, and begin to put their learning into action
in their classrooms and during PLC meetings. Groups may wish to invite a
teacher-friendly central office supervisor or university professor with expertise and high-quality resources (possibly including professional journal
articles and training videos or CDs) in the area under study to participate as
a short-term group member for resources, expertise, feedback, and support.

Design and Conduct Ongoing Professional Development

The leadership team will receive monthly updates from PLCs and study
groups about their recent activities, future plans, and outcomes for teacher
and student learning. To present clear expectations, the team may want to
develop a brief (half page at most, online is easiest), common template by
which teams can report their activities and outcomes. While professional
development in Year 1 consisted mainly of teachers participating in monthly
culture re-boot activities, professional development in Year 2 will be focused
more directly on increasing instructional and leadership capacities.

Demonstration Classrooms

PLC members are encouraged to try out certain instruction and student
support approaches they feel comfortable learning and using in their classrooms. Members of their PLC will assist with planning, observations, coaching, and feedback. When the demonstration classroom teachers are
reasonably comfortable with their practice and student outcomes, colleagues

outside their PLC will be welcome to observe the practice in action in the classroom as a work in progress.

Monitor, Assess, Refine

Review the new practices and activities begun by leadership team members to determine what is working well, what to keep, what and how to refine (if needed), and what to expand to a larger group for professional development and classroom practice. Identify which instructional, student support, and leadership approaches are working well enough to name them a *demonstration classroom*, which welcomes other teachers to visit and observe the new practice in action.

Plan and Conduct Whole-School Culture-Building Activities That Might Become Annual Events

Plan and conduct at least two culture-building events for students and teachers during the current school year, which may become annual events. Include the school's touchstone (developed during Year 1), which identifies and reinforces the school's cultural symbols and values. Identify the individuals who will cochair the planning for these activities; set a date for when recommendations are due to the leadership team for review and approval; identify available resources; target audiences, invitation format, and content; revise and enhance the plan as needed; conduct the events; and debrief afterward.

Collect This Year's Student Performance Data

Collect data on student groups on grade-level proficiency in English language arts and mathematics (and any other subjects the leadership team decides), attendance, and behavior. Be able to identify the data by teacher. Be sure to disaggregate data to ensure that students in each subgroup are making gains. If they are not, investigate the reasons and revise practices to improve future outcomes. Make initial comparisons (eyeball and statistical) with baseline and Year 1 data to see if any changes appear. Communicate findings to the leadership team, teachers, the superintendent, students, parents, and the community.

Celebrate Year 2's Successes

Commemorate the year's efforts and accomplishments. Include students, the advisory group, and parents. Recognize individual and group achievements, leadership, learning, and triumphs.

Consider Other Activities

What additional activities does the leadership team want to accomplish during Year 2?

YEARS 3 TO 5

Monitor and Advance Progress

The leadership team continues to meet monthly to monitor progress from PLCs, study groups, and student outcomes and suggest new strategies to accomplish culture building, organizational learning, trust building, instructional leadership, student-centered learning, and parent–community collaboration programs or practices. Revise those practices that do not appear to be working as desired, and add new elements to the school's overall program for student learning and achievement. PLCs will continue to meet regularly and increase their scope to enact varied ways to measure and promote high-quality learning and work from students and teachers.

Provide Leadership Opportunities

Continue to provide school leadership opportunities for able and interested teachers. Monitor, coach, and provide positive and constructive feedback to help build and refine their skills.

Continue to Collect Student Performance Data

Continue to collect and assess student attendance, behavior, and achievement data. Compare individuals with themselves to assess growth, and compare student groups on percent of students showing grade-level proficiencies in English language arts and math (and other disciplines) and improvements in attendance and behaviors from baseline data to the present. Be sure to disaggregate data to ensure that students in each demographic are improving. If they are not, investigate the reasons, and revise practices to improve future outcomes. Celebrate successes, and refocus attention and interventions in areas still needing improvement. Share these findings with your superintendent.

Study Group Reassignments

Change study group topics to better address school needs. Likewise, allow teachers and other staff to change their study group assignments to better fit with their professional goals and interests.

Celebrate Successes

Be sure to include those from earlier celebrations in addition to new members.

MONTHLY YEAR 1 CALENDAR FOR SCHOOL CULTURE RE-BOOT

The following calendar provides an agenda of topics and activities for the leadership team during Year 1.

SEPTEMBER

Meet With and Orient the Leadership Team

These teachers, students, parents, and community members are individuals whom the principal has invited last spring to participate in this year's school culture re-boot. The superintendent may wish to attend this meeting as a public gesture of district support and to salute the leadership team members in their important undertaking. At this meeting, the principal introduces all the team members, orients the group to their purpose, and provides an overview of the year's agenda. Leadership team members are assigned to read Chapter 1 of *Culture Re-Boot* individually and be prepared to participate in discussion about it during October's meeting.

Begin to Understand the Organizational Learning Process

Help the leadership team understand the organizational learning process that will occur inside this group.

- The readings and discussions will be highly meaningful as well as cognitively and emotionally rigorous and uncomfortable at times.
- The goal is for members to understand the dynamics of school culture that underpin school improvement in relevant and personally meaningful ways. In turn, their understanding promotes and sustains changes in teachers' assumptions, attitudes, beliefs, and behaviors, which benefit student learning and achievement.
- Trust building, each member's active participation, and clear, honest speaking and listening from each member are expected.
- Confidentiality is important. Group members are encouraged to discuss meeting topics and conduct re-boot activities with others not inside the leadership group—*but not to identify specific members' views*

or statements. Members need to feel safe to openly express their thoughts and ideas only to those sitting with them at that time, and listeners need to respect and protect this safety.

- All the ends lead to improved outcomes for students. Benefits in effectiveness, collegiality, and working conditions for teachers are fortunate by-products.

Schedule Visits to Schools and Organizations With Healthy, Strong Cultures

The principal or other school leader arranges for interested leadership team members (and possibly key parents and students) to visit schools or organizations that have strong and healthy cultures to learn more about how to develop and sustain a positive school culture.

Assign Members to Have Completed Reading Chapter 1 of Culture Re-Boot *Before October Meeting*

This expectation—come to meetings having already read and thought about the next chapter—will be a constant for every leadership team meeting this year. It allows members to make the most meaningful use of their limited time together.

OCTOBER

Chapter 1: School Culture and Change as Learning

Preread individually at home, and come to the meeting prepared to discuss key ideas and participate in re-boot activities.

- Give leadership team members in-group experiences that generate personal meaning about their assumptions, beliefs, and practices in support of student learning. Start becoming a learning organization.
- Identify, understand, and discuss how your school communicates its culture and values to teachers, students, parents, and the community (see School Culture Re-Boot 1.1).
- Identify the positive components of your school's culture.
- Assess yourself, your leadership team, and your faculty as a learning organization (see School Culture Re-Boot 1.2).
- Learn the mental models as conceptual tools for understanding and leading school culture re-boot:
  - o Understand and use the three-step change model (see School Culture Re-Boot 1.3).

- o Understand and use single- and double-loop learning (see School Culture Re-Boot 1.4).
- o Understand and use multiple frames in school improvement (see School Culture Re-Boot 1.5).

- Develop a profile of your school's culture (see School Culture Re-Boot 1.6). Assess the strength of each culture element, examples of where the element is present in your school, and whether the leadership is satisfied with the element or wants to strengthen it.
- Identify how aspects of your school's culture have evolved over time by having the entire faculty and staff think about the school's cultural roots and how the school's culture influences their daily work (see School Culture Re-Boot 1.7).

Select activities from Chapter 1 to use as professional development with your faculty to generate awareness of school culture and to get their perceptions about how the school's culture expresses its assumptions and values. Decide how to organize teachers for re-boot activities (in academic departments, by grade levels, or in some other arrangement). Leadership team members will facilitate (or cofacilitate) the activities and discussions and set the dates, times, and locations for these activities.

Optional: Select activities from Chapter 1 to use with students or parents as focus groups to generate feedback about their perceptions on school culture.

NOVEMBER

Chapter 2: School Leadership as Culture Building

Preread Chapter 2 individually prior to meeting. Discuss and participate in culture re-boot activities during a leadership team meeting. Look deeply at your school culture to understand how its symbols and values are expressed.

- Identify how your school's cultural symbols advance and reinforce the school's core values (see School Culture Re-Boot 2.1). Identify which symbols are working well and which need to be rethought and refined.
- Analyze past school culture surveys (if available) for insights into your school culture.
- Develop symbols, graphics, key words, and images that can support a school vision (see School Culture Re-Boot 2.2).
- Compile and synthesize the data, and identify patterns, strengths, and weaknesses in your school's culture.

Create a school touchstone using leadership team and stakeholder feedback that expresses how things are done at a school, its culture, and the core academic and ethical qualities that a school community seeks to develop in its members (see School Culture Re-Boot 2.3).

Select activities from Chapter 2 to use as professional development with your faculty and to generate awareness of school culture, and secure feedback from student and parent groups about how they perceive the school's culture expresses its assumptions and values. Decide how to conduct these activities, which leadership team members will be present to facilitate the activity and discussion, and the dates, times, and locations for these activities.

Optional: Identify the values your leaders, teachers, students, and parents desire in your school's culture, and reinforce these with schoolwide activities. The leadership team may want to create a small subgroup to plan and organize these activities.

Optional: Use a school culture survey or activities from this chapter to gain input from students, parents, and staff. Consider conducting interviews or focus groups with these stakeholders to better understand their perspectives on your school's culture—and perhaps recruit several to work with your study groups or the leadership team.

Optional: Ask students, staff, and parents to respond, perhaps on posters, to the following questions: "What do I want to keep?" "What do I want to change about the ways we do things around this school?"

DECEMBER

Chapter 3: School Culture, Ethical Behavior, and Relational Trust

Preread Chapter 3 individually prior to meeting. Discuss and participate in culture re-boot activities during a leadership team meeting.

- Consider the ways and extent to which your school is fulfilling the moral dimensions of acculturating, providing knowledge access, providing nurturing pedagogy, and enacting responsible stewardship (see School Culture Re-Boot 3.1).
- Reflect on incidents of insensitivity and broken trust in your school, how you or another repaired it, and what you learned from the experience (see School Culture Re-Boot 3.2).
- Consider examples of behaviors that build—or discourage—relational trust, assess your school's culture for evidence of trust-promoting

behaviors, and identify areas in which more trust is needed (see School Culture Re-Boot 3.3).

- Generate feedback for each leadership team member on how well he or she is communicating the varied facets of trust—namely, benevolence, reliability, competence, honesty, openness, integrity, and sharing control or promoting teamwork—to others and to strengthen trust among team members (see School Culture Re-Boot 3.4).

Circulate the draft of the touchstone to all school stakeholders for their feedback. Select activities from Chapter 3 to use as professional development with your faculty and to generate awareness of school culture and gain their feedback.

Optional: Use selected activities from Chapter 3 with student and parent groups to gain their perceptions about the school's culture and how it expresses its assumptions and values. Decide how to conduct these activities and which leadership team members will be present to facilitate the activity and discussion, and the dates, times, and locations for these activities.

Optional: Consider surveying the faculty about their perceptions of their trust in their colleagues, in the principal, and in the school's students and parents. Use this feedback to design and implement plans to improve relational trust in your school (See Chapter 3 Resources: The Omnibus T-Scale).

Optional: Consider surveying your teachers and administrators about the extent to which they perceive their principal and colleagues as supportive, directive, collegial, intimate, or disengaged (See Chapter 3 Resources: The Organizational Climate Description Questionnaires).

Optional: Consider surveying the faculty about the school's organizational health (including characteristics of collegial leadership, resource influence, teacher affiliation, and academic influence). Use the feedback to design and implement plans to improve your school climate on these dimensions. (See Chapter 3 Resources: Organizational Health Inventory.)

JANUARY

Chapter 4: Developing Professional Capacity and Shared Influence

Preread Chapter 4 individually prior to meeting. Discuss and participate in culture-re-boot activities during a leadership team meeting.

- Discuss instructional capacity and the contemporary factors that increase expectations for effective teaching.

- Identify and describe the school culture factors that affect the development of professional capacity.
- Identify the knowledge and skills that today's students need to be successful 21st-century employees and citizens, review the Common Core State Standards, and discuss how these affect teachers' professional capacity.
- Identify the 10 Interstate New Teacher Assessment and Support Consortium (InTASC) Standards, and assess the school's capacity for 21st-century teaching (see School Culture Re-Boot 4.1).
- Discuss the features and practices of effective professional learning communities (PLCs).
- Discuss the school culture factors that support professional learning communities.
- Identify areas for instructional improvements (see School Culture Re-Boot 4.2).
- Identify potential teacher leaders in your school, the areas of teacher leadership where they might make meaningful contributions, and their readiness factors (see School Culture Re-Boot 4.3).
- Detailed discussions about the variance between results of "my classroom" and "my school" may be uncomfortable for teachers. Consider inviting a school counselor to lead this discussion. In addition to effectively responding to the possible affect generated, teachers may be more willing to speak openly with the counselor facilitating the group.

Select activities from Chapter 4 to use as professional development with your faculty and to generate awareness of school culture, and secure feedback from student and parent groups about their perceptions about how the school's culture expresses its assumptions and values. Decide how to conduct these activities, which leadership team members will be present to facilitate the activity and discussion, and the dates, times, and locations for these activities.

Continue work on the school touchstone:

- Reword and finalize your touchstone.
- Make your touchstone widely and prominently visible. Print the touchstone on student ID cards, have student groups and art classes use the touchstone to create classroom posters, and read it as part of morning announcements.
- Analyze how all school programs (including those during and after school) and other school aspects relate to the touchstone; consider strengthening those that support the touchstone's values and altering (or ending) those that do not.
- Commit to making the touchstone values as the school's guiding principles.

Chapter 5: Establishing a Student-Centered Learning Culture

Preread Chapter 5 individually prior to meeting. Discuss and participate in culture re-boot activities during a leadership team meeting.

- Discuss the demographic, economic, social, and fairness needs to educate every child to high levels.
- Discuss the differences between the attitudes and behaviors of administrators and teachers working in school cultures that favor "I taught this" as compared with "They learned this."
- Discuss the meaning of a *student-centered learning environment* and what this would look like if practiced in your school. What are real-world examples of the following factors: developing high teacher expectations for each student, creating a safe and orderly learning environment, providing academic press and academic and social supports, fostering helpful and respectful relationships, and affording supportive peer norms? How well does your school provide these factors—and by what evidence can you support this view?
- Assess the degree to which your school provides teachers and students with a safe and orderly learning environment (see School Culture Re-Boot 5.1).
- Discuss the research findings on the relationship between teacher expectations and student achievement, identify what these might look and sound like in an actual school, and name the benefits to students when teachers hold these beliefs (see School Culture Re-Boot 5.2).
- Discuss the seven principles that inform teachers' beliefs when they want to help all children learn to high levels and what they would look like if practiced in your school (see School Culture Re-Boot 5.3). Also rate your school on the extent to which high expectations practices are evident (see School Culture Re-Boot 5.4).
- Discuss what academic press looks like, and assess the degree to which it is present in your school (see School Culture Re-Boot 5.5).
- Discuss what academic and social supports look like, and assess the degree to which they are present in your school (see School Culture Re-Boot 5.6).
- Discuss what strong and caring relationships between teachers and students, which benefit student learning, look like, and assess the degree to which they are present in your school (see School Culture Re-Boot 5.7).

- Discuss how peer norms can either encourage or discourage students' learning and achievement and how the school can increase peer norms that support academic excellence.

Select activities from Chapter 5 to use as professional development with your faculty to generate awareness of school culture and gain their feedback.

Optional: Conduct a re-boot activity from this chapter with student and parent groups separately to gain their perceptions about how the school's culture expresses its assumptions and values. Decide how to conduct these activities, which leadership team members will be present to facilitate the activity and discussion, and the dates, times, and locations for these activities.

MARCH

Chapter 6: Promoting and Creating Strong Parent–Community Ties

Preread Chapter 6 individually prior to meeting. Discuss and participate in culture re-boot activities during a leadership team meeting.

- Discuss the meaning of Joyce Epstein's statement, "The way schools care about children is reflected in the way schools care about the children's families. If educators view children simply as *students*, they are likely to see the family as separate from the school. If educators view students as *children*, they are likely to see both the family and the community as partners with the school in children's education and development." How does it reflect the way teachers look at students and parents in this school?
- Discuss the positive student outcomes from parents' involvement in their education.
- Discuss the meaning of the research finding: What a family does is more important to student success than what a family is or earns. To what extent do teachers in this school agree or disagree with this finding—and why?
- Discuss the benefits to schools of having strong school–family ties.
- Identify and discuss the varied barriers to school and family involvement, and assess your school—and yourself—on the degree to which you are overcoming these barriers (see School Culture Re-Boot 6.1).
- Explain what *cultural competence* means, describe the attitudes and behaviors that positively convey it to students and parents, and provide evidence of these practices in your school. Also, recommend which cultural competence factors deserve additional study, recommendations, and practice (see School Culture Re-Boot 6.2).

- Describe the variety of roles available for school–parent engagement, and discuss how these may be used to personalize and motivate parent involvement with the school.
- Assess your school on the frequency of certain school–home collaboration activities by surveying the leadership team, faculty and staff, and parents and students (see School Culture Re-Boot 6.3).
- Identify and discuss the variety of ways that schools can work with community partners to encourage and support student learning and achievement.
- Assess your school's student attendance status, and identify ways your administrators, teachers, and staff could work with specific community partners to improve overall student attendance and reduce chronic absences (see School Culture Re-Boot 6.4).
- Explore the possibility of forming a Triple-A Club in your school.

Select activities from Chapter 6 to use as professional development with your faculty to generate awareness of school culture and secure their feedback.

Optional: Conduct an activity from this chapter with student and parent groups separately to get their perceptions about how the school's culture expresses its assumptions and values. Decide how to conduct these activities, which leadership team members will be present to facilitate the activity and discussion, and the dates, times, and locations for these activities.

APRIL THROUGH MAY

Chapter 7: Developing a Plan for Action

Preread Chapter 7 individually prior to meeting. Make study group or PLC assignments and develop timelines for recommendations, professional development topics, and dates for the following year.

- Review the overview, prior planning, and suggested calendars in Chapter 7, and decide which you would like to follow in the coming year, which you would like to amend to better suit school needs, and what you would like to add.

Plan and conduct a celebration during the last weeks of school for the leadership team to recognize what they have learned and done during this year that will make them more successful teachers, colleagues, and leaders. Include parents, community members, and students (where appropriate). This celebration would be an excellent opportunity to invite the entire faculty and the superintendent to review what the leadership team—and the faculty, through their own professional development activities about school culture—have learned this year and their plans for the future (including the start of study groups next year).

Identify and set up PLCs and tentative teacher study groups for Year 2. Identify the study groups to be established, identify which teacher leader or teacher will head each group, and design a means to communicate this expectation and its larger purpose to all teachers. Design a means for every teacher, if so desired, to select membership on one additional study group. Teachers are not expected to participate in more than one PLC or study group.

Create a schedule of study and re-boot activities for the following year. Identify any additional committee members from faculty, students, parents, and the community you want to invite to work with the leadership team or with the study groups.

YEARS 2, 3, 4, AND 5

See Planning Overview above. Continue to assess, define what's working well and what needs improvement, study the issues, make recommendations, provide relevant and ongoing professional development, implement the strategy, assess, and continue the process.

Culture re-boot is a long-term, whole-school commitment. It takes many years of targeted study, frank professional conversations and collaboration, significant amounts of adult learning, and revised classroom practices for a school to become a highly effective community of teachers who can advance each student's learning in every classroom. Strong principal leadership establishes the climate for collective leading, learning, and responsibility. In turn, teachers create a safe, healthy, supportive learning environment for every child and colleague. In these ways, everyone's learning moves forward.

Building a culture focused on student achievement usually begins with an individual or small group of leaders committed to the goal of successfully teaching every child. Experience verifies that a school can overcome powerful obstacles to student learning. As Michael Fullan, international expert on school leadership and change, observes, "High-trust cultures make the extraordinary possible, energizing people and giving them the wherewithal to be successful under enormously demanding conditions—and the confidence that staying the course will pay off."[4]

School re-boot is a process that will pay off with high returns for students and teachers—as well as for our communities, our states, and our national future. And in the process, culture re-boot gives principals the opportunities to truly become transformational leaders.

---

[4]Fullan, M. (2005). *Leadership and sustainability.* Thousand Oaks, CA: Corwin, p. 73.

Index

Pages followed by f, t, or n indicate figures, tables, and notes.

CORWIN

A SAGE Company

The Corwin logo—a raven striding across an open book—represents the union of courage and learning. Corwin is committed to improving education for all learners by publishing books and other professional development resources for those serving the field of PreK–12 education. By providing practical, hands-on materials, Corwin continues to carry out the promise of its motto: **"Helping Educators Do Their Work Better."**